Conscious Finance

Uncover Your Hidden Money Beliefs
and Transform
the Role of Money in Your Life

Rick Kahler, CFP®
Kathleen Fox

Advance Praise for *Conscious Finance*

Money has been around a long time but we still know very little about how deeply and profoundly it affects our lives. Our histories, our experiences, our deepest fears and our most cherished goals are inextricably tied to our relationship with money. Rick Kahler and Kathleen Fox have performed a seminal service to the world of personal finance with this breakthrough work which has taken that which was hidden and brought it into the light of CONSCIOUS FINANCE. They'll help you discover the truth about money in your life, and that truth will set you free.

Mitch Anthony
Author, *The New RetireMentality*
Founder, The Institute for Financial Life Planning

Conscious Finance gently dissolves the curtain we keep around our money beliefs, emotions, and behavior, shedding new light on the part of us that forms the powerful undercurrents directing our financial and life choices. This book is an important addition to the new body of knowledge called Interior Finance. It will become a textbook for those seeking expertise in Interior Finance. But for most readers it will first be received as a great relief to finally understand this unseen side of money, and then be used as a trusted guide to a vital, well balanced relationship with their money.

Susan K. Bradley, CFP®
Author, *Sudden Money*
Founder, The Sudden Money Institute®
and Women, Meaning, & Money®

Rick and Kathleen will show you how to finally take charge of your financial decisions!

J. Grady Cash, CFP®
Author and Retirement Futurist

As a financial planning professional, I am disappointed in many of the self-help books on personal finance that stress the quantitative steps necessary to accumulate wealth and ignore the more important interior issues. Rick and Kathleen have written a wonderful book that helps readers to not only improve their finances, but to improve their lives.

Roy Diliberto, CFP®
Chairman, RTD Financial Advisors, Inc.

Conscious Finance dares to go where very few books in the financial or psychological professions have wanted to explore. It helps the reader look at core money issues in a way that is gentle and supportive. I would recommend this book to anyone who is struggling to understand their frustrations around money.

Dave Jetson, MS, LPC
Jetson Counseling

What a delight to read a book written by gutsy, down-to-earth people, in plain English, not rife with psycho-babble. A book that, quite literally, EVERYONE! should read.

Nancy Langdon Jones, CFP®
Author, *So You Want to Be a Financial Planner*

Rick Kahler has been a leader in the Life Planning movement, the most dynamic movement in the financial services industry, one whose mission is to humanize our relationship to money. In writing Conscious Finance, Rick and Kathleen have made a most significant contribution to that movement.

George Kinder
Author, *The Seven Stages of Money Maturity*
Founder, The Kinder Institute of Life Planning

Rick and Kathleen get to the heart of the etiology and maintenance of dysfunctional money beliefs and behaviors and offer essential knowledge and practical tools for recovery. Conscious Finance is perfect for those who want to take control of their financial futures, both inside and out!

Bradley T. Klontz, PsyD, CSAC
Clinical Psychologist, Researcher and Author

What do you get when an accomplished author and one of the top financial planners in the United States begin talking with each other? *Conscious Finance* is one of those rare opportunities to hear two very personal stories we can all relate to, told with an honest down-to-earth ease that gently leads the reader into that most rarified place, exploring our personal relationship with money.

Ted Klontz, MA, MAC
Executive Director, Onsite Workshops

Money—it's one of the most powerful and most misunderstood forces in the world. This book helps you to put it in the proper perspective, take the mystery out of its power, and help you to begin to make financial decisions in concert with your life's true goals and objectives as well as your deepest values and motivations.

Steven S. Shagrin, JD, CFP®, CRPC®, CRC®, CELP
President, Planning For Life
Past President, International Society for Retirement & Life Planning

Conscious Finance is a blessing—articulate, clear, and enlightening. It offers help to deal with difficult issues that interfere with financial well-being. The best intentional combination of personal interior and exterior finance that I have seen.

Richard Wagner, CFP®, WorthLiving, LLC

Contents

Acknowledgements

As with any contribution to the world, this book was not born in a vacuum. We could not have written it without the support and contributions of a number of people.

We want to thank those who unselfishly gave their input by reading and commenting on early manuscripts: Carol Anderson, Julie Cummings, Nancy Langdon Jones, Susan Kendall, Laurie Shaffer, Steven Shagrin, Deanna Sharpe, Curt Weil, Mary Kay Wright, Mary Zimmerman, and Margie Zugich. We especially want to recognize Marcia Welch-Kahler, Dave Jetson, and Rich Colman, who pulled no punches, respecting us enough to tell us what they really thought of a concept or idea.

Mitch Anthony and Bob Veres were generous with publishing information and encouragement.

Our thanks to Julie Schad for all her help with the graphics and in setting up the website. Carolyn Linn's editing skills and directness helped make this a stronger book—as well as saving many trees that might otherwise have died for our verbosity.

We are grateful for the ongoing support, encouragement, and wisdom of the Saturday morning group, with special thanks to Jerry for putting up with so many planning sessions over coffee and bagels.

RK

Rick: There would be no *Conscious Finance* without the encouragement and guidance of my co-author, Kathleen Fox. It was her "thinking out of the box" that freed me to embark on this project. Not only is she an accomplished writer, a person of impeccable integrity, and a loyal friend, she swings a mean red pen.

I want to thank my biggest cheerleader, my wife Marcia. Whenever the project hit a snag, she would encourage me to keep going. She affirmed my writing when I saw nothing but a jumble of inarticulate words. She was also my biggest critic, who was never afraid to tell me what I had just written was indeed unintelligible garble! She shared me for evenings and weekends with my computer. She is the "wind beneath my wings," steadfastly encouraging and supporting me to reach for the golden ring and live my passion.

George Kinder's seminal book, *The Seven Stages Of Money Maturity,* and his workshop by the same name brought it all together for me. His book was the first to unite the emotions of money with the knowledge of money. Many of the concepts presented here are based upon his book and his workshops. His genius was brought home to me time and time again during the writing of this book. I am deeply appreciative of his thorough training, passion for the financial planning profession, and most importantly his friendship. Much aloha, George.

I want to especially thank Dick Wagner. His contributions to the financial planning profession are legendary; however, without his contributions to my understanding of interior and exterior finance, this book would have never been written. In many regards this book is a portrait of his passion for financial planning, and it was my pleasure to have been one of the artists.

Ted Klontz is one of the most insightful, creative, wise, and caring human beings I've ever met. Even though he joined me late in my "money journey," his contributions to my process, this book—and to deepening and broadening the concept of interior finance—are monumental.

Brad Klontz, Psy.D., provided significant academic contributions to the development of the principles and concepts in this book. His passion for financial integration work is second to none.

I am indebted to my fellow Pioneers: David Brand, Elisa Buie, Rich Colman, Elizabeth Jetton, Troy Jones, Gayle Knight-Colman, Michael Smith, Dick Wagner, and Marcee Yager. Their passion for life and the interior journey has nurtured, energized and supported me in a way I will never forget.

The fellow responsible for me even becoming a financial planner was my friend, mentor, and former business partner, George Chell. George is truly one of the pioneers of financial planning. He not only introduced me to the fledgling field of financial planning in 1979, but he also was my first introduction to "the program" long before I ever understood "the program."

I am grateful to all my friends and associates in the Nazrudin Project who gave me valuable input and who served as a sounding board for my experiences and ideas.

Thanks to my office manager, JoVayne Cappa, who has so competently served me for eight years. She has kept a steady hand on my financial planning practice, allowing me the time to research, test, and teach the concepts in this book.

The influence and support of my coach, Tracy Beckes, has been foundational in helping me decide how "outrageously" I want to live the second half of my "one wild and precious life."

My deep gratitude to Pete Sweitzer, Laura Longville, and everyone associated with Onsite Workshops, who have given so generously and lovingly of their insight, wisdom, and support.

My children, London and Davin, added to this book by reminding me of lessons long forgotten and providing me with some wonderful insights into my own relationship with money.

Kathleen: One of the blessings of this project has been the fact that two years of collaboration on an ever-evolving book has only deepened the friendship Rick and I share. His integrity, humor, and passionate commitment to the concepts in this book made working together a pleasure. Because of that, I may even forgive him eventually for the wicked enjoyment he displayed at seeing me on the receiving end of another editor's red pen.

I am grateful to the friends in the program who have shared their experience, strength, and hope with me for so long and who supported me through the darkest time of my life.

My deep gratitude to Alvis for believing I could do this and for helping strengthen my belief in myself.

For my children, thank you all for the lessons you have taught me and for the opportunity to be a part of your lives as you make your way in the world.

Introduction

Managing money wisely sounds simple enough. You just figure out how much you earn and how much you can spend, write out your budget, decide how much you need to put away for retirement, make an investment plan, and follow both the budget and the plan faithfully. The result: a life free of fear, anxiety, guilt, or worry around money. Unfortunately, it isn't that easy. If it were, all of us would have done it successfully years ago.

If you have picked up this book, it is likely that you are not completely satisfied with the financial aspects of your life. You may be struggling with overwhelming debt, worried because you are not saving for retirement, uncomfortable at the thought of spending money, feeling guilty about having money, or just dissatisfied generally with the way you manage your money.

Take a moment to think about some of the difficulties you may have when it comes to money. See if any of the following fit for you:

- Do you feel you have more debt than you can ever repay? Or are you consumed with anxiety about your finances, even when your balance sheet would tell you that you have enough?
- Do you think money isn't important? Or does money dominate your thoughts?
- Do you seem unable to save enough money? Or is it painful for you to spend any?
- Do you believe that because you work hard, you will be taken care of? Or do you micro-manage and plan your future to the point of compulsivity?
- Are you unable to follow a budget? Or do you have to follow one with painful rigidity?
- Do you dither for weeks over major purchases? Or do you buy big-ticket items on impulse and then fret because you may have made a mistake?
- Do you feel more of an obligation to take care of others than to take care of yourself? Or are you unable to give to others without feeling angry, taken advantage of, and manipulated?

- Do you and your spouse fight about money? Or are you unable to discuss it?
- Do you believe you aren't capable of learning about investing? Or has learning more and more about investing not brought you the financial ease and freedom you were hoping for?
- Do you see being wealthy as somehow shameful, so you find yourself making decisions that keep you poor, in debt and unable to retire? Or does having wealth seem to separate you from others?

Your behaviors around money may include overspending, chronic debt, hoarding, giving too much to your children, being unable to follow a spending or saving plan, avoiding money decisions, or obsessing about financial security or accumulating wealth. These may generate feelings of shame, guilt, anger, and fear that keep you from enjoying a balanced relationship with money.

Whatever your particular monetary difficulties may be, they are not likely to be caused simply by a lack of financial knowledge. Instead, your self-destructive or ineffective behavior around money may be rooted in your deepest beliefs—beliefs that you don't even know you have.

Many of our financial decisions are governed, not by logic and facts, but by our emotions and beliefs about money.

These guide our choices even though we aren't consciously aware of most of them. Only by becoming aware of these hidden beliefs can we begin to change our financial behaviors and begin to make more conscious and balanced financial decisions. Doing this requires that we learn to blend both the technical knowledge about money (exterior finance) and the emotions and beliefs related to money (interior finance).

Without any doubt, money is entangled with many of the problems in our lives. Our unconscious choices around money are sources of significant conflict, chaos, and pain. For that reason, it might seem logical that both financial planners and therapists would address their clients' emotional issues related to money. But surprisingly, this is not the case in either field.

*Working with both the interior and exterior aspects of money
requires skills that neither financial planners
nor therapists are currently taught.*

While traditional financial planners do a wonderful job of collecting the cognitive or exterior financial data, they are woefully under-trained and inexperienced at gathering a client's interior or emotional data. Nor do many of them, oriented by both training and inclination toward the exterior, see any need to do so. At the opposite end of the scale, therapists have the skills to help clients do deep interior work to heal even such painful areas as addiction and family trauma. Yet they are not taught to consider money as a possible component of such emotional issues. Neither are they generally comfortable with exterior money tools. In fact, many therapists—drawn to a helping profession where making money is seen as somehow not quite acceptable—have their own financial difficulties, and they are uncomfortable even talking about their clients' pain around money.

If you are to change the behaviors around money that do not serve you well, you most likely will have to go it alone. That is precisely why we wrote this book. It describes a process we call financial integration that provides the tools you need in order to overcome your hidden beliefs about money and learn to make your financial decisions consciously and authentically. Through this process, we have been able to change or modify many of our own unconscious money behaviors. We're also helping others do the same, with exciting results, so we know these tools can work for you.

We touch briefly on strategies for solving your immediate money problems, such as getting out of debt, following through with a retirement savings plan, or managing your day-to-day spending. We also direct you to other resources you will find useful. But providing comprehensive strategies is not our primary purpose. Instead, our goal is to help you learn to heal the underlying issues that create your money problems and keep you repeating them. We want to help you move out of the cycle of financial unconsciousness that keeps you from making good financial choices and living the life you really want. You can learn instead how to make those choices knowledgeably, clearly, authentically, and consciously. You can build a relationship with money in which it is a trusted and valuable servant rather than your master or your enemy.

Is this book going to show you shortcuts to financial success? Not in the typical way you may think about financial shortcuts. It won't teach you a new way to time the stock market or give you an idea that will make you rich overnight. But we will show you how to find your own path to financial and personal success, which may end up being shorter than the path you are currently following. Will it teach you how to get rich? Well, it may, depending on your definition of rich. If having a lot of material resources is your goal in life, you can find all kinds of books written on just accumulating, investing, and managing money. While we will teach you the basics of accumulating and managing money, and even a few new strategies you probably have never been exposed to, our purpose goes much deeper.

What this book will do is
- Help you gain more control over your financial life
- Teach you how to become more comfortable around making money decisions
- Help you use the knowledge and information that you've gathered about money to actually make some progress toward your goals
- Teach you something about money that goes beyond the knowledge needed to accumulate a lot of material resources
- Help you understand why you've made some of the money decisions you have
- Help you actually change behaviors around money you've tried unsuccessfully to change in the past
- Help you become authentically clear about what you want in life and put a plan in place to get it, using money in a healthy and balanced way as one of your tools

If you choose to accept and practice what we offer,
you will be able to make your financial decisions more wisely,
because you will make them consciously instead of unconsciously.

You will find your behaviors around money becoming more integrated with your values and aspirations. You will learn how to stop making destructive money decisions and start making smart money decisions that will nurture you and support your life's aspirations and goals.

Maybe that will help you get all the money you'll need to live a joyful and prosperous life. Or maybe it will help you discover that having an abundance of money isn't really important to you. Perhaps it will help you discover that having money is an important component of wealth, but that it isn't your goal. Or it may help you discover that, for the first time in your life, you can feel at peace earning and having a lot of money. Maybe you will discover you already have enough money or even that it is really okay for you to have enough. What matters is that you will learn to make the financial choices that are in integrity with who you are and what is important to you.

Since much of *Conscious Finance* is about emotions and self-discovery—an unexpected perspective for a book about money—at first glance it may seem idealistic or quixotic. This information, however, is neither theoretical nor extreme. Financial integration is a practical, functional way to use money productively and comfortably in your everyday life. We know it works, because we have seen the results in our own lives and those of others.

This book is divided into three sections. Part I deals with the interior aspects of money, Part II with the exterior aspects of money, and Part III with the ongoing practice of financial integration. Chances are you will be much more at ease with either the interior or the exterior, and if this is the case you may be tempted to read the part that is more comfortable for you and skip through the other. Please don't give in to that temptation.

Keep in mind that, whichever part of this book you want to skip, that is the information you probably need the most.

Throughout the book, we illustrate the process of financial integration with examples from our own lives. From time to time we also include the stories of others. While all of the stories are true, personal details have been changed to protect the anonymity of those involved.

We refer in several places to specific resources, including programs, people, books, and websites. Rather than providing a detailed bibliography or list of resources at the end of the book, we have chosen to put that information on our website. Because lists of addresses and resources become outdated so quickly, this will help us give you the most current information on an ongoing basis. To find those updated resources, go to **www.consciousfinance.com**.

Just one more thing. Since personal growth means honesty, it's time for a confession here. In researching this book, we've read dozens of books on the psychology of money. That's in addition to dozens of other books on personal growth and recovery we've read over the years. Many of those books are wonderful sources of wisdom and change. Many of them include exercises and hands-on activities. Here's our confession: both of us almost never do the exercises. We have shelves full of books without a single pencil mark on the write-in pages.

Yet, hypocritical as it may seem, we've included exercises in several of our chapters. We hope you'll do as we say, not as we do, and actually follow through with the activities we suggest. The reason we urge you to do the exercises is simple. You can't read your way to financial balance. (We know—we've both tried it and failed.) It is true that exterior knowledge alone can help us change some of our unconscious beliefs and behaviors. For the deepest and most painful ones, however, knowledge is not enough. Because those beliefs were learned at an emotional level, changing them must also be done at an emotional level.

We know this is true, because it's what we have done and are doing ourselves. We both have participated in cognitive seminars as well as emotionally focused workshops, groups, and therapy. We have done and are still doing the painful, life-changing work required for deep emotional healing.

We both have learned, sometimes the hard way, that the key to growth and change is more than just increased knowledge or awareness.

The key to becoming financially integrated is *doing something different that will actually change our thoughts and behaviors.* The way to begin *doing something different* requires activity as well as information. So please, if you really want to benefit from this book, do the exercises. They are important. We promise they'll be useful. And yes, we've done them ourselves.

About the Authors

Rick has been in business since he got out of high school, at age 19 becoming the youngest real estate broker ever in the state of South Dakota. He went on to become the first Certified Financial Planner (CFP®) in South Dakota and eventually to earn a Master's Degree in Personal Financial Planning. He is also a State Certified General Appraiser and holds a South Dakota Real Estate Broker's License. He has a fee-only financial planning practice, a financial coaching firm, business interests in real estate, a real estate brokerage firm, a commercial appraisal business, and a mortgage origination company.

Between 1998 and 2003, he served as a member and then chairman of the South Dakota Investment Council, responsible for managing a multi-billion-dollar portfolio for the state retirement system as well as several other state trusts. He has served nationally in several leadership capacities with the Financial Planning Association and has been a featured speaker and workshop facilitator on various financial topics nationally and internationally. He has been featured or quoted in *The Wall Street Journal, Money Magazine, Journal of Financial Planning, Counselor Magazine*, and *USA Today*. He is a member of two national financial-planning think tanks, the Nazrudin Project and the Pioneers, both comprised of the brightest and most accomplished planners in the nation.

In the late 1990s Rick became an instructor of the "Seven Stages of Money Maturity®" seminar created by George Kinder, CFP®. He subsequently formed a partnership with psychotherapist Ted Klontz, of Onsite Workshops in Tennessee, to create the Financial Integration Workshop, the first program in the nation to combine cognitive money information and experiential therapy techniques. He and Ted also offer individual financial counseling through their consulting firm, Financial Awakenings.

Kathleen has been a writer and editor since 1989 and has edited numerous self-help books. For three years, she wrote a column on stepfamilies for *The Dallas Morning News,* and she is the author of *Making the Best of Second Best: A Guide to Positive Stepparenting.* Her other professional experience includes working as a legal secretary, building computers and providing technical support, and serving as executive director of a company that offered workshops and treatment for co-dependency.

Our approaches to money are poles apart. For example, both of us are firm believers in the KISS principle. There's just one slight difference. Kathleen thinks KISS stands for "Keep It Simple, Stupid." Her eyes glaze over after 30 seconds' worth of details about amortization and capitalization and diversification. She stops breathing at the merest thought of financial risk, and she'd really prefer to let Rick handle all the details of managing her money so she wouldn't have to think about it. She'd rather read an unabridged dictionary than the financial pages. On the other hand, given the slightest encouragement, she'd be delighted to subject you to a lecture on the difference between "its" and "it's" or why using "impact" as a verb should make you shudder.

Rick, however, thinks KISS stands for "Keeping It Simple IS Stupid." His eyes light up at the prospect of putting together the "perfect portfolio." He can disappear for hours into the world of technical information about investing: co-variances, standard deviations, r-squareds, alphas, and betas. He gets excited about protecting your assets by setting up trusts, which own corporations, which own other trusts, which own goodness knows what else. Rick could tell you more than you'd ever even imagine wanting to know about tax strategies, real estate, asset protection, and investing.

Maybe that's why Rick is the financial planner and Kathleen is the client.

Despite our different perspectives, however, we have both found great success in using the tools of financial integration. We believe you can do the same.

Part I

Interior Finance

1

Your Relationship With Money

"I just don't want to be controlled by money."

This is how Kent, a self-employed furniture restorer and woodworker, explains the financial chaos that fills his life. He routinely pays his bills two or three months late. He sometimes neglects to collect payments from his clients. His personal and business expenses are so enmeshed that sorting them out is a task better suited to a magician than a CPA—which may explain why Kent hasn't filed income tax returns for the past three years.

Kent has to pay full retail prices for his wood and supplies because his credit history is so poor that he can't establish contractor accounts at local stores. Despite the sometimes hazardous nature of his work, he has no health insurance because he can't afford it. Predictable expenses, such as Christmas gifts for his kids or the annual licensing fees for his truck, seem to take him by surprise year after year, becoming emergencies that require creative last-minute juggling. All this financial finagling and fussing take up significant amounts of his time and energy. Ironically, Kent's refusal to deal with finances has exactly the opposite result from what he wants. Money, or the lack of it, does control his life.

Kent, like many others, is controlled by money because he makes his financial decisions unconsciously. Instead of being his tool and servant, the money that he tries so hard not to think about is his master. His relationship with money is upside-down.

Do not value money for any more nor any less than its worth;
it is a good servant but a bad master.
Alexandre Dumas, Camille, *1852*

This quote is often cited to describe someone who is obsessed with making or having a great deal of money. Yet you will notice that Dumas cautions against valuing money too little as well as too much. By trying to ignore money or pretend it is not at all important, you make it your master just as you do by believing it to be the most important thing in life.

We need to learn to give money its balanced and appropriate place in our lives. This does not mean we should minimize its significance. Quite the opposite is true; we need to recognize money for the role it plays in our lives and our society. Dick Wagner, a leading financial planner and theorist, says, "Money is the most powerful and pervasive secular force on the planet." Lynn Twist, author of *The Soul of Money,* says, "Money is not an option, it is a requirement." Because money is such an important factor in our society, it is imperative to learn to use it consciously. Then you can honor and employ money as the important and valuable tool it is, instead of misusing it to try to meet needs in your life that it cannot fill.

The goal of *Conscious Finance* is to help you establish a healthy, balanced relationship with money. In such a relationship, money is not regarded as a goal or an end in itself. Neither is it scorned as something not quite "nice" or incompatible with integrity and altruism. Instead, it is appreciated for what it can add to your life, and as a result it is maintained and managed in the same way as any other valuable tool.

You may have never thought of money as something you have a relationship with. Yet you do. Your relationship with money has to do with the way you think about it, behave around it, and feel about it. Yes, you have feelings about money, lots of them, whether you are aware of them or not. You have thousands of thoughts about money, too. In fact, people think more about money than about anything else, including sex. And all of those thoughts and beliefs, most of which are unconscious, drive your behaviors around money. That aspect of your relationship with money is called interior finance.

Interior and Exterior Finance

The idea of integralism and interior and exterior was first introduced to us through the work of Ken Wilber. He suggests that everything has an interior and exterior component, and there is an "I" and "we" component to each. For those of you familiar with Wilber's work, we mostly deal with the "I" components, or as he describes them, the upper left and the upper right quadrants. If you are not aware of his work and want to learn more, his book *A Theory Of Everything* is perhaps the best place to start. However, a knowledge of Wilber's theories is not essential to understanding financial integration.

To some degree, we're using the terms "interior" and "exterior" quite literally. Much of the exterior component of your relationship with money is your environment—the people around you, your financial circumstances, the society you live in, and events and situations in your life. Dick Wagner says exterior finance is "financial information you can see and touch, that you can put in front of your face and see." It is the mechanics of money, such as your checkbook balance, the return on your IRA account, or your will. Exterior finance also includes the banking system, stock exchanges, and laws dealing with finance. Conversely, interior finance is comprised of what cannot be seen. It includes your emotions, beliefs, and values about money, as well as the way you process messages about money that come to you from the world around you. It also encompasses community and social values, beliefs, and agreements. Wagner defines interior finance as "those aspects of our individual and social relationships with money, including the fact that money even exists."

Another way to put it would be that exterior finance is the cognitive, left-brained, logical aspect of money and interior finance is the emotional, intuitive, right-brained portion. Financial integration, this book's goal for you, is a melding of the two.

At first glance, the combination of interior attributes like beliefs and feelings with exterior attributes like investments and budgets may appear incongruous. After all, to most of us money decisions seem to be left-brained, logical operations. Making wise choices around money ought to require spreadsheets rather than sentiment, equations rather than emotions.

Unfortunately, it's not that simple.

Whether we realize it or not—and most of us do not—our financial decisions are based at least as much on emotion as they are on logic.

We tend to assume money choices are made based on numbers, bottom lines, budgets, and other left-brain factors. In fact, all of our decisions, including those about finances, involve our emotions. We certainly need the cognitive information. But after we've gathered the information, strategized, crunched the numbers and made the lists, in most cases we still make the final decision based on how we feel. As long as that emotional component remains hidden, we don't realize how deeply it affects our behavior around money.

Hidden Beliefs About Money

All of us develop beliefs about money based on messages we receive in childhood. These messages usually come from our exterior environment—from parents, siblings, teachers, and society in general. Some of them are told to us directly, perhaps by parents saying such things as, "Money that you didn't work for is not worth having." Even more messages come indirectly from our observations of those around us, particularly our parents. If we see them spending impulsively, saving fearfully, or using money to manipulate and control one another, we learn to behave in those same ways around money.

As children, we take in this direct and indirect information and process it with our immature skills, internalizing the messages into conclusions about "the way things are." Based on those conclusions, we develop our own sets of unconscious beliefs and thoughts that shape our behavior. These beliefs are not necessarily wrong, but most often they are incomplete or partially true. We follow them unconsciously, never questioning or examining them, because we don't even realize they exist.

When you make financial decisions unconsciously, based on your unexamined beliefs, you will eventually run into trouble. You might have the most complete and accurate information you can possibly get about managing your money or making financial choices. But if you have unconscious beliefs around money that are destructive or limiting, it may not matter how much cognitive information you have. Those hidden beliefs are still going to sneak over from the right side of your brain and sabotage your decisions, resulting in illogical or destructive financial behavior. When this behavior is repeated again and again, it becomes a cycle of financial unconsciousness.

The first step toward financial integration is learning to identify your own hidden beliefs about money and bring them into your conscious awareness.

Once you know what your beliefs are, you can begin to change them in order to develop a healthier relationship with money. Then you can start to use money in a balanced way as a tool to help you accomplish what is most important to you and have what you want in your life.

When you begin to understand the issues and beliefs that underlie your financial difficulties, you are likely to uncover painful emotions or memories that seem at first to have little to do with money. In part this is because it is impossible to separate money issues from other aspects of your life. The interior isn't divided into tidy little compartments labeled relationships, work, money, and so on. Your hidden beliefs, emotions, and painful unfinished business from the past affect all aspects of your life, including money.

For that reason, this book touches on areas such as addictions, workaholism, and relationship difficulties that aren't specifically "money problems." When you begin changing one area of your life, you will affect much more than just that one facet of your behavior. You might think of your interior emotions, pain, and hidden beliefs as the central core of a private room. That painful center results in self-destructive behaviors that may take a variety of forms: relationship difficulties, chemical addictions, compulsions, eating disorders, sexual addiction, workaholism, and destructive money choices. Regardless of the form the behavior may take, however, the pain behind it is the same. Money concerns are just one of the doorways through which you can access and ultimately heal that inner pain.

Applying the principles of financial integration can do much more than help you make better financial decisions. It can help you begin to live life in general at deeper and richer levels. Through this process, you can uncover more of your authentic goals and dreams and learn to align your behaviors with your deepest values. Financial integration is not an end in itself, but a tool to enrich your life in many areas. Like any other tool, this one will require practice and effort if you are to use it skillfully.

Financial Integration

One essential part of that practice is learning to become comfortable with both the interior and exterior components of money. It takes both to change your beliefs and behaviors around money.

*You cannot make healthy financial choices consistently
if you use only exterior or only interior skills.*

Most of us approach financial integration from one side or the other. If you tend to be left-brained and logical, you are likely to be comfortable with or already know much of the exterior information in Part II. Chances are you will find it less easy to make sense of Part I. If you are more right-brained and intuitive, the opposite may be true. You might already be familiar with identifying emotions or have done a considerable amount of introspection, but you'll be inclined to skip over the exterior material. Since the whole idea is to become able to blend the two, the section you have the most resistance to is the one you need to read most carefully. In order to change, you will need to be willing to move out of your comfort zone.

You can do it, too, no matter which direction you start from. We both have. Fifteen years ago, Rick wouldn't have even imagined doing anything feeling-related around finances. He was strictly on the left-brain, spreadsheet, mechanical side of money. Kathleen could do feelings with the best of them, but would have groaned at the very idea of having to learn what "asset class diversification" might mean. Over the years, we've both learned that we're capable of using both the interior and exterior tools. The combination helps us make more of our financial decisions consciously. We don't always do it perfectly, but we're getting better at it, and the process is changing the way we deal with money.

𝓡𝓚

Rick: As you can see from the introduction, I am a busy guy. And yes, I know a lot about finance and business. At an earlier time in my life, I would have told you those exterior aspects of myself and thought I had shared everything that was important to know.

But now my greatest assets and joy in life are my relationships with my family, which includes my wife, Marcia; daughter, London; and son, Davin. Having started a family somewhat late in life, we are still involved with Thomas the Train, Veggie Tales, lost teeth, and allowances while many of our peers are dealing with graduations and grandchildren. Which is not necessarily a bad thing; it certainly gives us access to a lot of good advice.

My awareness that financial decisions have an emotional component developed gradually. Since my entire career has dealt with numbers and money, up until perhaps fifteen years ago I would have scoffed at the very idea that I might have painful behaviors around money that were negatively affecting my life. I knew how to earn it, how to save it, and how to manage and invest it—what more was there? By the average person's exterior financial measures, I was considered a financial success. And, not surprisingly, I was a workaholic.

Then my first wife filed for divorce. The pain of this experience pushed me to begin attending 12-step meetings and to start counseling to deal with my workaholism and other issues. Over the next few years I began to realize that I actually had a lot of unconscious beliefs and feelings around money. Very slowly, I began to employ various tools to help me begin to feel and learn from those feelings. I learned that there was much wisdom to be gained by listening to them, rather than ignoring them.

Kathleen: Most of my financial skills have come from that demanding instructor, Experience. The primary lesson it taught me about money was, "Don't spend it except on essentials." I knew how to balance the checkbook, pay the bills, and do the taxes, but it would never have occurred to me that I needed to learn anything about investing or planning for the future. It was tough enough trying to cope with the present—stretching the current month's paycheck to cover the current month's expenses.

When my two children were young, I started working for a company offering workshops and treatment for co-dependency. That job may have quite literally saved my life because it introduced me to 12-step programs and therapy. Not long afterward, I was divorced after 16 years of marriage to a man who was an alcoholic. This was a time of self-discovery and personal growth, but also a period of financial struggle. I was almost the sole provider for my children, and I remember all too well shopping for clothes at rummages sales and buying generic macaroni and cheese.

A few years later I married a man with three children. In addition to the emotional challenges that go with building a stepfamily, we faced financial difficulties for several years. At first we couldn't even afford to buy a house, so we lived for several years in a rented one that was too small for our blended family. I managed a busy and often chaotic household while my husband, Wayne, worked hard to build a successful construction business. We gradually worked our way out of debt until we were able to buy the kids' clothes at the mall instead of second-hand stores and to have some financial breathing room. Eventually we became financially comfortable and finally totally debt-free.

We were just beginning to get used to the idea of having enough and to realize that we might actually think about spending some money once in a while. Our house was paid for, the kids were almost all out on their own and doing okay, and we would have been able to travel or do nearly anything we wanted to do.

Then, at age 49, Wayne was killed in an accident. He was a pilot with his own small plane, and he and one of his company's superintendents died in a plane crash as they were flying to look at a prospective job.

All of a sudden my life was turned upside down and shaken to pieces. I was thrust into a whole new set of challenges in the need to deal with the pain and loss, to grieve, and to go on and rebuild my life. Among those challenges were financial ones. Thankfully, I was not left in poverty or faced with overwhelming debt. For me, the toughest part of all the financial decisions was the emotional side. At first, even accepting life insurance and Worker's Compensation payments felt horrible—as if by doing so I were somehow saying that Wayne's death didn't matter. I worried about making financial decisions that were fair to all the kids. I wanted to do everything wisely and responsibly. In settling the estate, I tried to make decisions that Wayne would have approved of, even though he had not made a will to guide those decisions. All at once, I was in charge of managing a significant amount of money, and it didn't feel like mine to manage.

In the midst of all these challenges, I attended one of Rick's workshops. The understanding it provided was a valuable tool as I made my way through the financial complications that had suddenly become my sole responsibility.

Now I am working to get used to the idea that I have a degree of financial and personal independence I have never known before. My role with the kids—two adult children, three adult stepchildren, and four grandchildren—is shifting to one of support and encouragement (trying not to give advice unless asked) rather than one of active parenting. I am free to do almost anything I wish, including work that I love instead of work I have to do. What I find is that such freedom is one of the most frightening things I have ever faced in my life. The financial integration work I am continuing to do is a crucial piece of my ongoing journey toward a balanced and healthy life.

∽∾

2

Why This Matters:
The Rewards of Financial Consciousness

It's one thing to talk theoretically about the interior and exterior aspects of money, hidden beliefs, and unconscious behavior around money. But that isn't why we've written this book. There is nothing at all theoretical about living with the results of unconscious money decisions. You already know this if you have ever struggled with ongoing financial chaos, overwhelming debt, chronic fear about money, feeling taken advantage of financially, or feeling shame and guilt around how much or how little money you have. We have seen those painful consequences in others, and we have experienced some of them ourselves.

The following two examples from our own lives illustrate the importance of becoming able to make financial decisions consciously. As we were writing this book, both of us bought and moved to different houses. For various reasons, neither of us bought our "dream house." Yet one of us is happy with the purchase, while the other is not. We're including the stories of those transactions here because they show clearly the different results that come from making financial decisions consciously rather than unconsciously.

❧

Kathleen: As I write this, I'm sitting in the recliner in one corner of my home office. It's about nine o'clock on a June morning, still pleasantly cool, with a breeze stirring the curtains at the open window beside my chair.

I like this office. I like the walk-in closet in my bedroom. I like the patio that runs along the east side of the building and faces the pleasant back yard. Those are almost the only things about my house that I do like. Otherwise, I don't much care for the driveway, the garage, the living room, the kitchen, or the basement.

Since I don't especially like this house, the obvious question is why I am living in it. Did I inherit it? Do I have to stay here because I can't afford to live anywhere else? Am I compromising to suit someone else's taste or needs?

None of the above. This is a house I bought several months ago, under no outside pressure because of time, money, or limited options. I picked it out myself. No one conned or bullied or persuaded me into choosing it. I simply made a choice that I now wish I had not made. In buying this house, I made an important financial and lifestyle decision that wasn't the right one for me. I did so because I was operating unconsciously, following deeply held beliefs I didn't even realize I had.

Why did I make this decision the way I did? Nine years ago, Wayne and I bought a house. David, our real estate agent, showed us house after house, trying to help us find the one we wanted. When we finally did find the right house, it was for sale by owner. After all his work, David didn't make a penny on our transaction.

When the last kid left home, Wayne and I decided to sell the house and get something smaller. We agreed, without even discussing it, that we would list our house with David. After all, we owed him one.

Before we had taken any action in this direction, Wayne was killed. Among all of the decisions I had to make during the next few months, it was clear to me that I still wanted to sell our house.

So when I decided to put it on the market, of course I called David. His first question to me was, "Are you sure you're ready to do this now?" He took great pains to assure me that there was plenty of time to find a smaller house and I didn't have to make any decisions in a hurry. I thought I paid attention to everything he said. Actually, though, I didn't take in a word.

This was partially due to unconscious factor number one: *guilt*. Because I had taken up so much of David's time nine years earlier, I believed I owed it to him to buy a house from him now. That part was fair enough. However, in addition, I believed I had to find something quickly in order to make up for all his wasted effort back then. Without consciously realizing it, I was determined to be the perfect, no-hassle, easy-to-work-with real estate client.

David recommended finding a replacement house before I put mine on the market, and he started showing me houses. By the time we had looked at six or seven, I was becoming anxious. In my mind, I should have found a house by that time.

This was unconscious factor number two: *my dislike of shopping.* "Shop till you drop" for me means, on a good day, an hour and a half at the mall. I don't like crowds, weighing options, looking for stuff, or comparing prices. Above all, I don't like making decisions that involve spending money. I don't find shopping entertaining or fun; I just want to buy what I need as inexpensively as possible and get it over with.

A couple of weeks later, David called me one morning, full of enthusiasm. A great house had just come on the market; it was a good deal, a real bargain.

When we went to look at the house, the first thing I noticed was that the driveway sloped up steeply. My immediate gut reaction was, "I don't want this house because of that driveway." When we went inside, I found other things about it that I didn't like. The east windows were shaded by the patio, meaning I wouldn't get the morning sunshine that is important to me. The lower level was quite unabashedly a plain old basement; I hate basements. The garage was attached, but had no access directly into the house, which was the reason I wanted an attached garage.

All this time, David was saying things like, "This is a great value. What a well-kept house. This would make a great rental property." He was right, too. The house was in excellent shape, in a nice neighborhood, with a beautiful back yard. The price was appropriate. The size was what I needed. The only thing wrong with it was that I simply didn't like it very much.

Along came unconscious factor number three: *my need to please,* even at the cost of disregarding my own better judgment. I was too reluctant to disagree, especially with someone I saw as an expert. I didn't want to say, "David, this house may be a great buy, but it isn't what I want."

David also told me he was sure this house wouldn't be on the market for more than a few days. Its combination of price, condition, location, and size meant it would be snapped up in a hurry. If I wanted it, I needed to make an offer right away. I'm confident that he wasn't saying this to pressure me. Besides being a person of integrity, David is too competent a sales professional to stoop to the tacky sales technique of, "You have to decide right now."

He didn't have to; I did it for him.

This was unconscious factor number four: my fear-based belief that *I had to settle* for what was available because there probably wouldn't be enough to go around. The reflexive message in my head sounded something like this: "Sure, this house isn't quite what you want. But it's okay. It's good enough. If you don't buy it, you'll probably regret it. There's not likely to be anything better out there, anyway."

So we went back to David's office, and I made an offer. It was accepted. My buyer's remorse kicked in almost immediately. I hoped the home inspector would find something to let me out of the deal. He didn't. I hoped the sellers would change their minds. They didn't. Inexorably, the process continued through until closing. I signed the papers. I bought the house. I moved in—sort of.

Several months later, I still haven't made this place feel like my home. My stuff is all here, unpacked and put away. I have painted, put in carpet, and planted tomatoes. But I have never really taken possession. Yes, this is an okay house, a good-enough house, a place I can stay for now. But it isn't my house. It isn't my home, and emotionally it never will be.

The Impact of Hidden Beliefs

I understand much more clearly now why I bought the house. The four unconscious factors influencing my decision were: my guilt over taking up David's time, my dislike of shopping, my need to please, and my belief that I had to settle for what was available. When I look at them now, I can see clearly how those were part of my hidden beliefs about money.

"Don't ask for anything; if you're good enough, you will get your turn after everyone else has had theirs." This belief has led me to repeatedly ignore and postpone my own needs, and it has also given me an exaggerated need to be absolutely fair. Because we had not bought our earlier house from David, in my mind we had not treated him fairly, and my resulting feelings of guilt compelled me to buy a house as quickly as I could so I wasn't wasting any more of his time. My need to please and my unwillingness to disagree with an "expert" were also part of that belief. After all, I was being offered "my turn" and had better take it, rather than being "bad" by asking for something else instead.

"It is wrong to want anything, especially if it will cost money." With a belief like that operating in my unconscious mind, of course I would hate shopping. If I couldn't even face the prospect of an afternoon at the mall, it makes perfect sense that the idea of spending weeks looking at houses would be overwhelming.

"Don't spend anything, because there might not be enough to go around." The other side of this belief, of course, is, "If you do have to

buy something, you'd better settle for whatever you can get and take it before it's gone." This house genuinely was a good value—which didn't mean it was the right house for me. I didn't have the confidence to let it go by because unconsciously I was too afraid that, if I didn't buy it, another one might not be available.

As a consequence of acting according to these hidden beliefs, I am living in a house I don't like. I'm still here because I promised my friends I wouldn't subject myself to the stress of moving again for at least a year. (I choose to believe that they extracted this promise out of concern for me, without any consideration of the fact that I own an upright piano made from solid oak.) I tell myself that if this house would make such a great rental property, I can keep it as an investment and find another house to live in. I know this house wasn't "The Big Mistake." The worst that has happened is that I own a nice house in a good neighborhood, worth what I paid for it. That is hardly a justification for self-flagellation and terminal regret.

Even so, every time I pull into the steep driveway, I am reminded that I made a mistake. I settled for something that was just barely okay instead of holding out for what I really wanted. I feel as if I let myself down. Those feelings of regret and self-recrimination are the result of having made an important financial decision unconsciously.

Rick: Our firstborn, London, is a girl. When I told friends that my wife and I were going to have a second child, the most common comment was, "Gee, I'll bet you hope it's a boy."

Actually, I hadn't spent much time considering what I "hoped" it would be, given that I had little control over the matter. While there was some allure to having a son, doing so would mean a costly upgrade in our housing. Our two-bedroom house, adequate for the three of us, feasibly could accommodate another daughter. But a boy in the house would mean we'd need a third bedroom after a year or two.

Well, we were blessed with a bouncing baby boy whom we named Davin. His birth made clear the undeniable fact that we would soon need a new house.

The prospect of finding new digs was not something that excited me. Unlike my wife, who is always up for a new adventure, I am a man of routine. I once frequented the same restaurant so often, ordering the same dish time and time again, that the maitre d' nicknamed me "Rut Man."

I had lived in that home for 24 years, which was half of my life. It was not lavish, but it was well located in a nice neighborhood and served my family's needs well enough. Besides, I am a city dweller. I vacation in places like London, New York, and Denver. I like the bustling life of the city. While I would not say that downtown Rapid City, South Dakota, is anything remotely like London's West End, it is still as urban as it gets for 300 miles in any direction. So I was thrilled that my house was located in the historic district of town, just three minutes from the heart of downtown and five minutes from my office.

Rapid City is located in the foothills of the Black Hills. The west side of the city is in the hills, while the east edge is rolling prairie. Now, I am a bit out of the mainstream in my choice of locations. I would venture a guess that better than three out of four local residents, if asked where they would like to live, would want to live west of Rapid City in a house that is "in the pines." Since almost everyone living here has that desire, the principle of supply and demand means that lots "in the pines" are expensive. They also mean a longer commute time to schools, restaurants, and work. How long a commute time? Somewhere between 15 and 30 minutes.

Yes, those of you in larger urban areas can laugh. Still, having once sold residential real estate in Rapid City, I was very much aware of the typical mistake made by people with children who moved to Rapid City from larger metropolitan areas. They would buy their dream home "in the pines" that came with a 20-minute commute into town. This was a relief to them, as they were used to commutes of 30 to 45 minutes. They would laugh at me when I would mention that the property was sure a long way from town and question whether they wanted to make the drive every day.

Once they bought the house, I would make a note to call them in two years. I knew that sometime between the second and third year they would make the transformation from big-city dweller to reality. That many months spent driving back and forth for work, school, soccer games, volleyball games, school plays, shopping, movies, church, meetings, etc., etc., would be enough to leave them seriously cranky about the long commute. Of course, the solution to the problem was to sell their house in the pines and move into a home in town.

For these reasons, when I bought my historic house in 1979, I made a very deliberate decision not to buy a home located in the hills. It was obviously a good choice, and one that served me well for 24 years.

Looking back on that decision now, I am pleased to realize how consciously I made it at the time. By the way, don't assume that making a conscious buying decision means you need to look at and analyze every possible prospect. I was not especially "looking" for a house when this one came on the market. But I was very clear about the area, style, and price range I was interested in. Within six hours after that house became available, I was its proud owner.

So, back to the story at hand, how does all this relate to buying the house my wife and I have just purchased?

Conflicting Goals

In June 2000 Marcia and I attended a two-day "Seven Stages Of Money Maturity®" seminar, created by George Kinder, CFP®, which was led by Marcee Yager, CFP®. As a part of that seminar, attendees are led through a series of exercises to help them identify their own integral goals and dreams. At the completion of the exercises, Marcia realized that her number one desire was to live on a hill, with a view, surrounded by trees, largely out of sight of any neighbors. This setting evoked memories of going to her family farm on weekends and spending hours walking through the woods. It was her refuge and safe place. She had never before consciously considered that living in such an environment, which she knew would be highly nurturing to her, was actually attainable.

Now, uncovering this unconscious desire was really cool—for my wife. I could see her excitement as she would describe living on a hill with a view, surrounded by trees.

The problem was that this goal was nowhere to be found on my top ten list. I knew that "hills and trees and a view" spelled "west of town in the pines," which spelled "more money." I liked my house payment just the way it was. I also knew that it spelled "commute." I liked my proximity to the cultural center of downtown Rapid City. I also knew that most west side, hilltop houses would be contemporary and open in style. I like living in formal, historic, Victorian or classic-type houses.

So, from a selfish position, I was not extremely motivated to see my wife's desire come to fruition. The birth of our son changed the landscape for me. I instantly realized that, one way or another, a move was in our near future.

Marcia started looking at houses in earnest. She would scout out the possibilities and then set up appointments for me to view the better candidates. One day it became crystal clear to me just how important a view was to my wife. She had called excitedly to let me know she thought she had found the perfect house. When I looked at it, I had to agree that it had a great view to the west of the Black Hills and a valley below. But the house was a disaster. It was built as a bachelor pad, complete with no doors on the bedrooms and an undersized staircase crammed into a space intended for a circular staircase. This, however, made me realize that Marcia would live in a condemned mobile home or a leaky tent, as long as it had a panoramic view.

One thing we agreed upon was that our new house needed space for the adults. To put it succinctly, I was tired of living in a toy box. Our current home had no playroom for the kids. The toys were jammed into a sun porch adjacent to the living room, which did little to contain their encroachment into other areas of the house. In addition, for Marcia's sanity, there was a small set of toys in every room, including our bedroom and the bathroom. Getting up in the middle of the night to make a bathroom run was putting your life in jeopardy.

Compromise and Reality

After a year of looking, we were beginning to wonder whether we would ever find a house that had the formality I needed and the view that Marcia needed. Finally, though, we found a house that had an acceptable view for her. She rated it an eight on a one-to-ten scale. It also had an acceptable floor plan for me that would put the children's bedrooms and playroom on the lower level, with the kitchen, living and dining rooms, an office and the master bedroom on the main level. I rated the house a seven. It would be an improvement from our current situation, but it was not a house and a location that really excited me.

This was a cause of concern to those closest to me, including Marcia. In my rating system, whether I am evaluating cars, clients, or employees, I try not to let anything below an eight into my life. Jack Miller, a real estate instructor from Tampa, Florida, once told me, "The cheapest eviction is to never let the bad tenant move in." It took me years to figure out that this principle applied to far more situations than real estate.

So most of my mentors were very concerned that I was "settling for" a house that was only a seven. I remember my financial planner (yes, financial planners need their own planners) and my business coach both recoiling from my lack of passion around the move and questioning my motives. Was I being co-dependent, thinking only of my wife's needs instead of my own? Would I resent the choice and hold it over her head? Was I settling for too little and selling myself short?

Why not wait until the perfect house came along that was an eight or higher on both our lists? Indeed, such houses do exist in our town. They are located in a subdivision called Carriage Hills. We could have purchased my classic type, two-story dream house on a lot with Marcia's million-dollar view. Unfortunately, such a house would have also come with a million-dollar price tag. Neither of us had a dream that included making payments on a mortgage with that many zeros.

We talked about our choices. I spent time, using the process we describe in this book, becoming clear about what I really felt about the idea of living in this house. After much processing with all my advisors, my wife, and myself, I came to the conclusion that I was indeed clear and clean about this decision. I was really very comfortable with the move.

No, it was not my dream house. Yes, that was okay.

Dreaming is important. In fact, it is essential to defining who you are and where your passions lie. But dreaming does not always make it so.

There is a place and a time where dreams meet reality.

My dream met reality when I made the choice not to be a slave to a house payment. I also made a conscious decision that, as a couple, my wife's need to have a view and dwell with the birds and the trees outweighed my desire to be in the middle of town in the historic district. I knew this house had the size we needed, along with the "kid-free zone" and some of the formality I wanted.

The important part of this decision was not whose dream house weighed more on the scale. What mattered was that there was no hidden resentment, no "whatever you want, dear," with a martyred sigh. Marcia and I made the choice together, carefully and consciously, with respect for our family's needs.

When we put all the dreams, needs, and boundaries into the blender of decision, what emerged was what we purchased. It was a conscious choice. I knew that moving into our new house need not be a decision for life. I also knew it was the best decision for now. Choices remain, circumstances change. As the kids get older and our needs change, we can make other choices. Heck, you never know—this book may become a best seller and I'll be able to afford one of those Carriage Hills mansions.

One day, six weeks after we moved in, my wife turned to me and said, "Have I told you yet today how much I love this house?" That would warm any husband's heart; it did mine. And it let me know even more clearly that our conscious choice had been the right one.

An added bonus is that our daughter says often that she is happier in the new house. Our son hasn't verbalized anything of that sort yet. His two-year-old way of showing his approval is the way he gleefully makes laps on his tricycle around the safe and roomy driveway, surrounded by the nature he has loved since he was a baby. Both Davin and London seem to do a lot of dreaming out there. Marcia's hope, and mine, is that we can teach them not to be afraid to dream or to make their dreams reality.

Exercise

What difficult consequences have you experienced as a result of making unconscious decisions around finances? Or what satisfactory consequences have you experienced as a result of making conscious financial decisions? Write some of them down, as briefly or in as much detail as you wish.

3

Money Scripts

Before you can begin making financial decisions consciously, you need to understand how and why you have learned to make them unconsciously. From both the direct and indirect messages you received as a child, you created your own set of unconscious or hidden beliefs about money that have shaped your choices.

Various authors have different names for such beliefs. Some counselors refer to them as "mottoes" or "life scripts." We use the term "money scripts," coined by therapist Ted Klontz and clinical psychologist Dr. Brad Klontz.

If you think of an unconscious belief as a "script," it's easy to understand it as a set of instructions written by someone else. Actors are given scripts, which they rehearse until they can follow them perfectly. In the same way, we blindly follow our money scripts. We've learned our parts well, and we faithfully act them out.

Where we get into trouble is when we unconsciously use the same script repeatedly for every financial circumstance in life. It makes no more sense than using the character of Romeo for every leading male role in all of Shakespeare's plays. That role fits perfectly in *Romeo and Juliet*, but would make no sense in *Hamlet* or *Richard III*. Yet playing Romeo over and over, regardless of whether that role fits the current situation, is exactly what we do when we blindly follow our early money scripts.

Each of us has hundreds of unconscious money scripts, many of them formed in childhood.

Children are constantly being taught—both consciously and unconsciously—by their parents and other significant people in their lives. Absorbent as sponges, little kids soak up the attitudes and beliefs around them even when they're too young to have any conscious understanding about what's going on. Messages are coming in all the time: do this, don't do that, behave this way, this is good, that is bad, this is true, that is not. Children take those messages, process them with the immature perspective and limited resources they have available, and internalize them into sets of "rules" that shape the way they view the world and the way they behave.

Many of the most powerful of these messages come from families. Some messages are spoken, but many others are communicated by family members' behavior. If Mom and Dad fight about money, the kids can learn that money is a source of conflict. If Mom and Dad give regularly to charities, the kids learn that giving is something "our kind of people" do. If Mom and Dad worry over paying bills and talk about never having enough money, the kids are likely to grow up to be adults with chronic fears that there will never be enough money.

Just to complicate things further, kids may get contradictory messages from their parents. Perhaps a father's behavior reflects a belief that, "It's okay to spend; I can always earn money." At the same time, the child's mother may demonstrate a belief of, "It's not okay to spend anything on myself, because everyone else in the family has to come first."

Those whose childhoods are filled with pain around money
are especially likely to develop money scripts
that cause them great difficulties as adults.

Charlie grew up in a large family on a South Dakota farm during the Great Depression of the 1930s. He saw his parents struggle to feed ten children during years of drought and failed crops. He saw his father treat the neighbors' ailing farm animals and not get paid for his services. He and his older brother did odd jobs for neighbors, sometimes getting paid and sometimes not. Neither of them was able to go to high school because there was no money to send them and they were needed at home. Charlie's father had co-signed a note for a relative and spent years paying off a debt that shouldn't have been his to repay. All of these circumstances caused Charlie to grow up with a deep and damaging money script of, "The world isn't fair. 'They' won't let you get ahead anyway, so you might as well not try." As an adult, he worked at a job he didn't like, supporting himself but never becoming successful. An intelligent and capable man, he frittered away his ability and creativity on oddball schemes and projects when he could have used his talents to create a meaningful career.

Messages from Outside the Family

We also receive messages about money from the larger world outside our families. Religion is one source of money scripts that can generate significant amounts of guilt. One of the most common beliefs that we see people pick up from Christianity is, "Money is the root of all evil." This message can leave a person thinking that poverty is a virtue. Actually, the Bible doesn't say this at all. The New Living Translation says, in 1 Tim 6:10, "For the *love of* money is at the root of *all kinds* of evil."

Other money messages might come from schools or influential adults such as teachers, coaches, friends, and neighbors. Memorable childhood events—both traumatic and beneficial—may also generate money scripts. A parents' divorce, for example, often leaves financial as well as emotional scars. An incident that leaves a child feeling shame might generate a money script seemingly out of proportion to the event. Being laughed at in school because of being dressed poorly, for example, might cause a child to vow, "When I grow up, I'm never going to let that happen to me again." As an adult, this person may follow money scripts such as, "To be accepted, you must always buy new clothes."

Then there are the broader messages from society as a whole. Just think, for example, about a typical evening's worth of television commercials. The overall message is simple: in order to be happier, buy more stuff. From the time we're small, we're bombarded with the notion that we need more, that we don't have enough. In fact, some of the most common money scripts identified by participants at Rick's workshops are "There will never be enough," "Money will give you meaning," and "More money is better."

Beliefs like these, ingrained as they are in the world we inhabit, promote a sense of scarcity and dissatisfaction that is the source of a great deal of pain around money. Parents who are consciously trying to teach their children to look at the world differently from this societal message face an uphill battle. And when parents unconsciously reinforce society's "buying equals prosperity" messages, it's no wonder that children get a skewed perspective on the proper place money should have in their lives.

How Money Scripts Are Created

As an illustration of how a money script may be created, let's take the example of a mother who yells at her two-year-old, "Take that penny out of your mouth! Don't you know money is dirty?" Well, it's true, physically, that money is dirty. It's been on the floor, in various people's hands and pockets, and who knows where else. So the overt part of this message is a simple attempt to keep the child from picking up germs and maybe swallowing that penny. But perhaps this is the umpteenth time the mother has warned her child against doing this. Maybe the child receives a time-out, a severe punishment, or even some physical abuse this time for his action. If that is the case, the toddler may absorb a deeper message along with the punishment: "The whole concept of money or wealth is something dirty, something to be ashamed of. You should feel guilty if you have money."

This example may seem extreme. Obviously, most children aren't going to make a leap from "That penny is dirty" to "Having money is something to be ashamed of," based on one incident. But depending upon the repetitions of such incidents and the trauma that may surround them, a message such as this could certainly be processed into a deep, firmly entrenched money script. How strongly embedded a money script may become will depend upon the degree and depth of trauma the child, not the adult, attaches to this issue or incident. An adult may not recall the event as being especially traumatic or memorable. While that may be true, it doesn't matter. The key is how any money message was internalized by the child.

Money scripts are anchored by emotions such as sadness, fear, and anger resulting from what counselors call "unfinished business." Brad Klontz, Psy.D., defines unfinished business as "painful emotion attached to an event from the past which one was unable to express or deal with at the time." This leftover and unprocessed emotion is transferred, unconsciously and often inappropriately, to events in later life.

Over time, as parents repeat their own beliefs and patterns of behavior around money, children internalize various money scripts with different degrees of intensity. Some scripts are primarily a matter of habit, of doing what we have learned and what is familiar. Others are much deeper behaviors, intended to help us avoid the pain of unfinished business.

The more you believe a money script applies to every situation, the more entrenched it is, and the greater the chance that it is causing discomfort or pain in your money relationship.

One reason money scripts create difficulties in later life is that children internalize them before they have the maturity to understand the circumstances that created them. Charlie learned to believe "they" were out to get him because he saw his parents' ongoing financial struggles and experienced being treated unfairly. He didn't have the perspective to understand the bigger picture: that the Depression was a time of hardship for everyone, including those neighbors who couldn't afford to pay for his father's help; that his parents were making the best choices they could in difficult circumstances; and that none of the unfairness was directed at his family personally. All he could see was that the world wasn't fair. This became a "truth" for him, a script upon which to base his actions and decisions.

As adults, then, we continue to operate according to those childish and incomplete money scripts. It doesn't occur to us to apply our adult judgment to what we took in so completely when we were five or six because we don't consciously realize that we even learned it. We build our financial lives according to unfiltered and unexamined childhood "truths" that we never question. We assume them to be just the way things are. In fact, such an assumption is one indication that you're following a money script.

Unconscious money scripts are so ingrained, so rooted in our own sense of self, that we have no idea even what they are.

Your particular set of money scripts was shaped by your own interpretation of what you saw and felt. Because of your personality, your birth-order position in the family, and a great many other factors, you saw your childhood world through your own unique set of filters. Those filters were what resulted in your unconscious childhood decision that this or that message was "the truth."

Your unconscious truths may be similar to those of your siblings, or they may be quite different. Charlie's older brother, for example, growing up in the same family in the same difficult times, internalized very different concepts around money. His money script was, "Life is hard, so you have to take action if you want to be successful." Despite the same childhood poverty and lack of education as Charlie, he learned a skilled trade, formed his own successful business, and used his creative talents in a fulfilling hobby that brought him considerable recognition.

Money Scripts Are Partial Truths

Many of the money messages we received as children were incomplete. They were partial truths. Most of them weren't lies; they weren't necessarily wrong. In fact, many of them were valid and useful for our circumstances at the time. The problem was the way we as young children swallowed them whole. We did not have the tools to examine them and modify the aspects that would cause us problems in the future.

It is sometimes said that perception is more important than reality. If you perceive something as true, it is true to you, regardless of the facts, and your behavior will be shaped by your perception rather than the reality of a particular situation.

We like to think of most money scripts as being true roughly one third of the time. For example, take a money script that says, "Always buy the best." In some cases, that is certainly true. If you want a pair of hiking boots for hard wear, getting the best makes sense. If you're going to have laser surgery to correct your vision, you want the best surgeon that's available. In some cases, the script would be completely false. If you are a student on a tight budget and need curtains for a rented apartment you'll live in for one semester, then getting the cheapest ones you can find would be the way to go. And sometimes the script would be partially true. If you're getting a new dishwasher, the "best" model might have features you would never use, so it would be silly to buy it. At the same time, the cheapest one probably would not work as well or last as long as a better one. So a model somewhere in the middle is likely to be the best choice. If you are blindly following a script of "Always buy the best," however, you will believe you have to have the finest boots, the best surgeon, the most expensive curtains, and the dishwasher with the most options. You won't see that you have the option of making your choice based on what you genuinely need in your particular circumstances.

Blame Is a Waste of Energy

The money scripts you internalized in your childhood may not be the ones your parents intended to give you. What parents intend to teach their children about money—the conscious message—may even contradict the unconscious message the children actually take in.

There are two reasons to emphasize this point. For one thing, knowing it may help your own money scripts make more sense. As you begin to identify your hidden beliefs about money, many of them will match what you remember consciously about your parents' teaching or behavior, but not necessarily all of them will. They don't have to. Your beliefs are a result of your own individual processing, shaped as that was by the countless factors which help make you the unique person you are. In addition, you may have received some of your deep money messages from sources other than your parents.

The second reason to emphasize the importance of each person's childhood interpretation is that we absolutely do not intend for you to use your money scripts as a way to blame your parents. Blaming your parents, your work, the government, or anyone else for any money woes is a good way to guarantee that you will stay stuck in the cycle of financial unconsciousness.

Chances are that your parents intended to teach you good things about money. They almost certainly wanted you to grow up to be successful and responsible. That doesn't mean they knew how to pass along that learning. Nor does it mean they knew what they were doing when it came to money. It's certainly possible that they didn't know how to make wise financial decisions themselves. They may have been irresponsible, unreasonably rigid, miserly, or manipulative about money. Their mistakes and misconceptions may have caused you some pain. Even what they intended to be positive messages may have resulted in pain for you.

Exploring your money scripts is almost certain to bring up painful emotions, including anger. Letting go of such resentment and anger is necessary for your own healing. This book provides tools to help you accomplish it.

*Choosing to blame your parents or anyone else for the circumstances
that created your difficult emotions, rather than choosing
to do the work of healing them, only keeps you stuck.*

Just as it is pointless to blame your parents for their failings, it is
equally unproductive to blame yourself for your past mistakes. Your
money scripts and unconscious behavior may have caused you to make
many financial choices you wish you hadn't made. In addition, like all
of us, you certainly have made some financial mistakes because of a
lack of knowledge or experience. Your past may include behavior
around money that caused pain for you or for people you care about.
You may have regrets for many reasons. You did the best you could do
with the skills and knowledge you had, but there were times when your
best fell short of what you wish you might have done.

If you feel guilty or ashamed of some of your choices, please take
those feelings as a sign that you're a better person than your errors. If
you don't like what you've done up till now, that means you're ready to
learn how to do things differently. The process of looking into the
shadows of your past money scripts and difficult emotions around
money will stir up enough painful memories and feelings. This is a
normal and necessary part of healing. Please, don't add a layer of self-
blame to those difficult emotions.

It may help eliminate blame if you think of money scripts as blind
spots. You don't even know they're there, you just follow them. They
operate on automatic pilot and are always running.

Blindly following the scripts you developed as a child may take two
forms. One is to act the same way your parents did. Suppose your
parents' belief was, "Money is to save, not to spend." So, following
that script, you don't buy anything for yourself even when you need it
or can afford it. Perhaps your family has a script that says, "Rich people
are all greedy crooks." So you sabotage yourself if you get too close to
financial success, because you certainly don't want to become a greedy
crook. Or you have been taught, "If you want something, you have to
earn it." So you suspiciously assume any gift has strings attached, or
you refuse to ask for help even when you need it.

What you may do instead is make the choice—just as
unconsciously—to do the opposite. You aren't really rewriting your
parents' money scripts at all, of course; you're just turning them inside
out. Suppose your mother's script was, "Don't spend anything on
yourself." Trying to do just the opposite, you impulsively buy whatever

catches your eye in an immature attempt to make up for your sense of deprivation.

This reversal is deeper than simple rebellion against parental beliefs. It is especially likely to take place if your parents' behavior around money resulted in pain for you. Suppose that you felt deprived, or your childhood was filled with fear that there wouldn't be enough, or your parents used money as a tool to control your behavior. You may have made unconscious vows to yourself never to subject yourself to such pain again. From those promises, you would have formed money scripts causing you to choose actions that were the opposite extreme from those of your parents.

What these two sides of the same coin have in common is lack of awareness. Neither is a deliberate, conscious choice. Both can lead you to make the same financial mistakes over and over without understanding why you seem unable to change.

Identifying Your Money Scripts

The first step toward conscious money behavior is to become aware of some of your own money scripts. That is the purpose of the exercise at the end of this chapter. To help you get started in identifying your money scripts, let us tell you about a few of ours.

RK

Rick: Remember the potholder loom? For those of you too young to have used one or too cool to admit using one, it was a cheap metal or plastic frame about six inches square with teeth on each side. You could hook loops of stretchy fabric from one side to the other, then weave more loops across the first ones to make a useful and sometimes even reasonably attractive potholder.

Well, potholders were my earliest venture into the business world. I was about eight years old at the time, and I wanted a watch—a $20 Timex, which in 1963 was entirely out of reach for a kid whose parents didn't believe in giving an allowance. My parents agreed to pay half the cost if I earned the other half. I decided the best way of doing that was to go door to door and sell potholders. My market research (I asked my mother) indicated the market would bear a sales price of 25 cents per potholder.

I developed a marketing strategy that, looking back, I'm rather proud of. How often in your kitchen do you use just one potholder? Usually you need two, one for each hand. So when I knocked on someone's door, I took two matching potholders with me, selling them as a set. I sold enough to earn my half of the $20, and I got my watch.

Now, in many ways not receiving an allowance, needing to work for what I wanted, gave me confidence and taught me the value of money. It helped me establish a good work ethic; it taught me selling skills and initiative. My childish processing of this lesson *and many similar ones*, however, also formed the foundation of one of my many money scripts. I took the message to mean, "You must labor hard to obtain money," and "Your worth is found in what you do."

The results of this unconscious belief showed up in adulthood in several ways. One was workaholism, which contributed to a lack of close relationships in my life and the failure of my first marriage. Another was a sense of financial insecurity—a lack of trust in myself and in a Higher Power, as well as a general sense of negativity. A third was the loss of a personal identity, an erroneous belief that who I was depended on the work I did, what I earned, or what I had.

The sense of financial insecurity was also based on the fact that many of the parental messages I received about money were conflicting. As a young child, the unspoken message I internalized from my mother was, "Don't spend money on yourself;" but from my father's actions I decided, "It's okay to spend money on yourself." From my mother's actions I internalized a constant fear that the money would run out, while my father was always confident that money would be there. My mother told us, "Money isn't everything;" while I concluded that my father's dedication to his work meant, "Working for money is life's top priority."

It is important to underscore that these money scripts were formed from my childish view of reality. What my parents actually said, did, or intended to communicate could have been completely opposite to what I concluded.

No parents need to blame themselves and feel guilty
over the money scripts their children have formed.

In fact, in many ways, a parent has only limited control over the money scripts internalized by a child.

This was brought home to me when my daughter London was five. I asked her one day what the word "rich" meant to her. London answered, "Rich is having a lot of couches." To this day I've never figured out where that came from. If London holds onto this money script, she may grow up despising those with couches and not having a couch in her living room because she doesn't want to be perceived as being rich, or she could have a couch in every room and live life quite happily with the perception that she is rich.

I also asked her what she thought of rich people. She replied that they are snotty. I was shocked at this money script coming out of my daughter's mouth. The Gallup organization found in January 2003 that the average American thinks "the rich" includes anyone with an annual household income of over \$130,000 or a net worth of a million dollars or more. Well, by that definition, I make my living helping the rich, I am rich, and some of the family members London loves are also rich. London was a little surprised to find out that not all "rich" people are snotty. Where did that money script come from? Again, I don't have a clue. But that isn't the point. The point is that she has that money script and it is as true to her as the sky is blue.

➳◈❧

Kathleen: Probably the most central message I received around money as a child was, "Don't spend any, because there might not be enough to go around—and you really don't need that, anyway."

I grew up on a farm, and I still snort in an unladylike fashion whenever I hear or read anything about "simple country living." Farming, especially running a small family farm, is an incredibly stressful business. You put in 15-hour days and seven-day weeks for part of the year; you borrow money for seed and the year's operating expenses and hope that after harvest you can pay back the loan. In a good year, you'll have a little bit left over. You are at the mercy of the weather, from frost to floods to drought to hail. And if you do produce a good crop, you have no control over the prices you get for it.

So I grew up with a sense of uncertainty about money and a constant awareness that there wasn't any to spare. At the same time, my parents taught us by example that integrity and self-respect included financial responsibility. We learned that honorable people paid their bills, kept their commitments, and took care of themselves. We didn't think of ourselves as poor and would have been insulted had anyone else called us poor. My mother sewed beautiful clothes for my sisters and me, we went to the dentist regularly, got glasses for our near-sightedness, made frequent trips to the library, and took piano lessons. One thing we didn't have was spending money. Chores were something we did as part of our responsibility to the family, not something we were paid for. We didn't get allowances. Our needs were provided for, so we didn't need money to spend on ourselves.

As a result, I never got into the habit of spending money. In addition, I internalized an attitude of uncertainty and fear around money. "Don't spend anything because there might not be enough to go around." There was a sense of futility, because having enough seemed completely out of my control. "Even if you work hard, even if you are careful and responsible, there still might not be enough."

I want to reiterate the point we made earlier that our parents don't intentionally pass along such negative messages. To underscore how unconscious this learning was for me, I don't remember ever being told, "No, you can't have that. We can't afford it." The message operated at a deeper level than that. What I learned was not to ask for or want anything in the first place. I created money scripts that said, "It is wrong to want anything, especially if it will cost money," and, "Don't ask for anything; if you're good enough, you will get your turn after everyone else has had theirs."

This was certainly not a conscious message from my parents. We were well taken care of, and in many of the most important ways we did have enough. Nor was I ever treated unfairly or differently from my sisters. Somehow, though, in my child's brain, I developed a belief that I shouldn't expect to get my share until everyone else had theirs. If I were only good enough and patient, eventually I would get my turn.

I took that script into my first marriage, which only reinforced it. As my alcoholic husband began spending more and more of the family budget on his drinking, there truly was never enough money to go around. My turn never seemed to come. The pain this caused pushed me right back into my unconscious belief that I needed to try even harder, so maybe I would be rewarded by getting my turn. I went around and around in that particular cycle of financial unconsciousness, one which kept spiraling wider with a growing, corrosive sense of unfairness, frustration, and anger.

One painful memory I have is of the time that the folk group Peter, Paul & Mary was going to be in town for a concert on behalf of a political candidate. My husband and I were both fans of their music.

Our son, who was four, thought of "Puff the Magic Dragon" as his own special song and would have loved the concert. Tickets were five dollars—cheap even in 1980. And we couldn't afford to go. We didn't have the extra fifteen dollars.

What is most painful about this as I look back on it is realizing that I didn't even tell my husband how much I wanted to go to the concert. Nor did I try to think of ways we might have found the money to go. I simply accepted as fact that we couldn't afford it. My unconscious belief that there wasn't enough for me to have something I wanted just kicked in automatically, and I didn't even question it.

Exercises

What are your money scripts? You may have already identified some as you read this chapter, but now put down the book and go get some paper. You are going to start a list of your money scripts. We want you to ask yourself the following questions. Write down whatever comes up for you after each question. Don't censor yourself; you won't be turning in your answers. Quickly write whatever comes to mind around each of the areas listed, no matter how ridiculous it may seem.

What do you believe about money and:

Investing?	The rich?
The poor?	Food?
College expenses?	Retirement?
Insurance?	Saving?
Budgets?	Spending?
Taxes?	Wills?
Giving?	Receiving?
Financial advisors?	Employers?
Employees?	Work?
Marriage?	Children?
Relatives?	Happiness?
Sex?	Spirituality?

After you've finished, look back over your writing and ask yourself what scripts you actually heard spoken as a child and what others you may have learned non-verbally. They may sum up beliefs your family held about money, even though no one actually spoke them. What scripts do you have that came from society, teachers, ministers, and other authority figures in your life?

Below we've listed actual money scripts of people who have attended Rick's workshops. This is certainly not a comprehensive list. It's only intended to give you a general idea of some common money scripts. Some of them may jump out at you instantly; others may not apply to you at all. Still others may remind you of something else that was true in your family. Write down anything that seems to fit for you.

Write as much or as little as you like, but keep your list handy. You'll find it useful as you go through the rest of the book.

Sample Money Scripts

- Money is evil.
- Only money made by hard labor is worth having.
- Most people who are very wealthy have inherited money.
- Don't spend money.
- There will always be enough.
- Taking risks is bad.
- There is only so much money in the world.
- There will never be enough.
- More is better.
- Don't go into debt for any reason.
- Don't trust anyone with your money.
- Trust everyone with your money.
- I don't deserve to inherit money because "it wasn't earned."
- Money brings you happiness.
- Not having money brings you happiness.
- The money will run out.
- You have to work hard for money.
- I don't deserve money.
- Money isn't important.
- If you have a lot of money, you got it unethically.
- People are poor because they are lazy.
- You are not smart enough to have money.

- If you have money, don't tell anyone.
- It's better to give than to receive.
- Money is unimportant.
- There will never be enough.

4

The Cycle of Financial Unconsciousness

Barry, a successful businessman, had no trouble earning huge sums. But he could never save, spending money as fast as it came in. When we discovered that some of his money scripts were, "I don't deserve money," "Rich people are pretentious," and "Money is evil," it made perfect sense that he was trying to get rid of his money as quickly as possible.

Every behavior around money, no matter how illogical, makes perfect sense when we understand the underlying beliefs about money.
Ted Klontz

We find the above statement to be profoundly true. All our behaviors around money are driven by our unconscious money scripts. Understanding and identifying our money scripts is just the first step. The next step is to understand how they shape our behavior around money and why we keep repeating the same hurtful financial behavior, with similar negative consequences, time after time, year after year, without any change. This cycle of financial unconsciousness includes both interior and exterior components. It consists of repeatedly making a financial decision based on a money script, which results in consequences that create emotional pain, which leads to another script-based money decision, which results in more painful consequences.

Typically, the cycle is started by a challenging experience or exterior circumstance around money. Most of us could easily make a list of these. You lose your job. You get your credit card bill and can't believe you or your spouse spent that much money last month. You receive your monthly statement from your broker and learn your investment portfolio fell 20% in one month. The transmission goes out on the car when you're 400 miles from home and don't have enough money to fix it. Your roommate moves out and leaves you with a month's unpaid rent and a three-figure phone bill. The list is unending.

Nor is this list limited to a lack of money. Even financial gains can bring difficulties with them. People who inherit money often struggle with feelings of guilt or anger—as if taking the money is a betrayal of the person who has died or a denial of the grief they feel. Sudden windfalls, such as lottery winnings or selling the family business, can completely disrupt someone's life. Any financial success, such as a new job with a higher salary, can create feelings of fear or inadequacy and trigger a money script that says, "I am a fraud."

So what happens when you encounter one of these challenging exterior financial circumstances? If you operate unconsciously, it will trigger a money script followed by a difficult emotion. This causes emotional pain—something we as human beings are programmed to avoid at all costs. Trying to get away from the pain, you unconsciously follow the money script, even if it is inappropriate to the situation. This may get you through the difficulty at hand, but sooner or later it almost certainly will generate a new painful financial circumstance that generates even more pain. So you grab another script, which may result in another inappropriate money behavior. You keep bumping up against pain, and every time you sheer away from it, you are propelled into another round of the cycle.

Cycle of Financial Unconsciousness

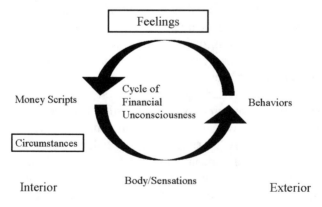

The driving force behind the cycle of financial unconsciousness is an intense, universal desire to avoid pain.

As an example, let's suppose that when you were a child, your parents routinely bailed you out when you ran out of money. Spending all your allowance was no problem—you could always just ask Mom or Dad for a little extra. From their actions you formed a money script of, "My parents will always take care of me financially."

For a period of time in your life, following that script served you well. You didn't learn to budget your income, because as a child you didn't have to. But you continued the pattern even after you grew up. You bought whatever you wanted, and if you ran short before your next paycheck you went to Mom and Dad for help. This was fine as long as they continued to follow the script and cough up the cash.

Eventually, though, the day comes when you ask them for money, and they say no. Regardless of how good their reason may be, their refusal causes pain for you. That pain might be a sense of betrayal—you have relied on this money script all your life, and now it has failed you. It might include anger toward your parents for not doing what you have learned to expect, anger that they care more about their own needs than about yours. It might be fear that you won't get what you want. In whatever way the particular situation plays out, you are going to experience some pain—anger, fear, sadness, or hurt.

Your involuntary reaction to any pain is to try to stop it, push it away, or soothe it. You aren't going to sit there and feel it. Instead, you will do one of two things: either try to fix things by grabbing another unconscious money script to follow, or else soothe your wounded feelings with some medicating substance (such as alcohol) or behavior (such as going on a spending binge with your credit card). In this instance, let's assume you choose to grab another script. While there are many money scripts you might adapt, the next one might be, "If a person has a lot of money, they will be loved and respected."

The trouble is, you don't have a lot of money, nor do you know how to get a lot of money. You've never worried about taking care of yourself financially. Besides, your anger and fear are pushing you to do something in a hurry. So you go and borrow as much money as you possibly can and invest it all into a risky startup company that promises to make you a millionaire. Predictably enough, you lose all your money and have nothing to show for it but a large debt that you can't repay. Now you're feeling some more pain. So you latch onto another money script. Maybe this one is, "You have to have money to make money." You conclude that the only way out of this tough place is to win the lottery. "When I hit it big, that will solve everything." So you secretly cash in your spouse's IRA and buy lottery tickets.

By now you're going around and around on a merry-go-round that's anything but merry. You don't know why things are going badly or why you can't just fix what's wrong. You aren't even aware that you're acting according to a hidden belief. You're just doing what you've learned unconsciously how to do. As long as you continue to follow your hidden money scripts and make unconscious decisions, you will be stuck in that cycle.

On the other hand, encountering difficult circumstances doesn't automatically mean you're going to wind up in a cycle of financial unconsciousness.

It isn't the circumstance that creates the cycle;
it's your response to the circumstance.

It's important here to distinguish between events and emotions. The event is a challenging exterior occurrence. The resulting pain comes from your emotional response to the event. The more that your interior response is based on an entrenched money script that is not appropriate for the situation, the greater the pain is likely to be and the harder you are likely to try to avoid it. It's trying to avoid the pain that pushes you into the cycle of financial unconsciousness.

Suppose you lose your job because of downsizing. You understand that downsizing can happen to anyone; it isn't personal. You'll certainly feel some difficult emotions, such as anger and fear. But because you won't have a sense of personal betrayal and shame, you're likely to get through the difficult experience without being caught in the cycle of financial unconsciousness. Your resulting behavior is likely to be constructive—actions such as asking for a letter of recommendation, examining your life and options, or calling industry contacts and informing them of your availability.

Suppose, though, you are in this same situation but you have an unconscious money script that because you're a good employee, you shouldn't ever have to worry about being fired. Your difficult emotions might include fear ("Will I be able to find another job?"), anger ("How could they do this to me?"), hurt and betrayal ("But I've done such a good job—it isn't fair!"), and shame ("This isn't supposed to happen to somebody like me."). This may result in behavior that even intensifies your pain. Maybe you decide to "get even" and sabotage your company's computer database or tell off your old boss. Such an action would only create another difficult circumstance and generate more pain. Or suppose the script you clutch at in order to ease the pain of losing your job is, "Employers can't be trusted." You think, "Why should I bother to try, when they won't let me get ahead anyway?" Operating with this attitude isn't exactly the best way to shine during job interviews. Every time you apply for a job and don't get it, your unconscious belief will be reinforced. This will add to the amount of pain you experience, make you try even harder to avoid that pain, and kick you right back into another round of the cycle.

Blaming and Medicators

One clue to realizing you are stuck in a cycle of financial unconsciousness, besides being aware you are in pain, is to become aware of the times you are blaming others, focusing on the unfairness, or chronically playing the role of victim. This focus keeps you pointing blame at "them," at circumstances, at anything external. This is one of the ways we all use to try to avoid pain.

A common way we keep ourselves stuck in the cycle of financial unconsciousness is by using medicators to numb emotional pain.

Medicators can be either behavioral or chemical. Medicating behaviors include blaming, compulsive spending, workaholism, sex addiction, hoarding, or trying to control one's environment or the actions of other people. Other medicators are substances such as alcohol, nicotine, prescription drugs, illegal drugs, or even food. As long as we are using medicators to block or push away feelings, it isn't going to be possible for us to experience and dissipate our emotions, which is the key to healing.

For many people, the use of medicating substances or behaviors is part of another and even deeper trap—the cycle of addiction. It works in much the same way as the cycle of financial unconsciousness: experience a difficult circumstance, unconsciously apply a script to the situation, encounter pain, medicate that pain with alcohol or another substance, exacerbate an unconscious belief that one is somehow not good enough, create more difficulties and chaos, encounter pain, and medicate some more.

Obviously, this is an over-simplified explanation of the disease of substance addiction. This book is not the place for a more detailed discussion, because we are focusing on financial pain, not alcoholism or drug addiction. Nor is everyone who medicates with substances or behaviors an addict. Many of them are, however. *In that case, recovery from the addiction is a necessary first step before someone can effectively look at issues around money.* For addicts, giving up those medicators may not be possible without substance abuse treatment, therapy, or the support of 12-step programs. Please, if you think you are addicted to medicating substances or behaviors, we urge you to get the help you need to overcome that addiction. You cannot heal your problematic money behaviors if you are numbing your emotions.

Some people, after a few rounds through the cycle of financial unconsciousness, learn from their mistakes and begin to make wiser choices. Others, however, with more deeply ingrained money scripts, can keep circling through the same territory for life without gaining any wisdom from their experiences. In some cases, money scripts and difficult circumstances follow each other around and around in an endless game of Ring Around the Rosy, and all the unconscious players can do is wonder why they keep falling down.

These are the people with so much pain to run from that they find it necessary to hide behind ever more medicating and illogical behaviors. These are the fearful hoarders, the addictive spenders, the enabling givers, the addicted gamblers, the workaholics, and the compulsive pursuers of wealth.

Ending Suffering By Choosing Pain

For those in such chronic financial distress and chaos, it is not an exaggeration to call the cycle of financial unconsciousness a cycle of suffering. That suffering, however, is unnecessary. Ironically, it's what we endure because we are trying to avoid pain. Compare staying in the cycle of financial unconsciousness to chronic physical suffering, such as the continual throb of a toothache or the nagging ache of a bad back. Ending the suffering would require experiencing more acute short-term pain—the root canal to take care of the tooth or the surgery to repair the damaged spinal disk. Often we stay in the suffering, even though it hurts, because it's familiar. We know how to handle it; we can stand it. We avoid the surgery, even if the doctor assures us it will help, because we don't know how much it might hurt and we're afraid of it. Yet experiencing the pain of the surgery is the only way we're going to take care of the problem.

You can choose the chronic suffering of continuing to avoid your deepest money scripts, or you can choose the acute but short-term pain of changing those scripts by confronting and feeling the difficult emotions surrounding them. Moving out of the cycle of financial unconsciousness requires accepting the reality that you cannot escape pain. Nor, ultimately, is it even desirable to do so. All you need to do to understand this truth is to see how poorly you have been served so far by trying to avoid pain.

By now you may already see areas in your life where you are stuck in a cycle of financial unconsciousness. Identifying with the cycle doesn't necessarily mean your entire life—or even your entire financial life—is a terminal mess. There may be aspects of your relationship with money that work very well, while others are less successful. Perhaps you keep your bills paid, but the load of debt you carry is becoming overwhelming. Perhaps you and your spouse are constantly at odds over money even though you should have enough. Or perhaps you manage your financial affairs well enough, but you lie awake at night worrying because you have so much fear around money.

For those in chronic financial pain, the cycle is one of continuing shame and struggle. For others, the worst consequence of unconscious behavior may be some discomfort, vague dissatisfaction, or unhappiness around money issues. Regardless of the level of the discomfort, however, the pattern of behavior is still the same, and the first step toward healing it is the same. Interrupting the cycle of financial unconsciousness will first require you to make a decision that you want to change. Making that choice means you are willing to do the work of reaching financial consciousness.

5

Moving Toward Financial Consciousness

Learning to make conscious money choices doesn't mean you have to throw out everything you've ever done and start over from scratch. In fact, doing so would almost certainly be latching onto another destructive money script, resulting in more pain and more illogical financial behavior.

Not all of your money scripts are necessarily bad or wrong. Some of them may be congruent with or working in your current circumstances.

The financial integration process involves becoming aware of your money scripts, understanding how they have affected your actions, and moving out of your pattern of unconsciously following those scripts even when they are not working. Financial consciousness creates flexibility; it includes the ability to decide whether a script is appropriate for the situation at hand. It also involves changing or modifying scripts that no longer serve a useful purpose.

By now, if you've done the exercise at the end of Chapter Three, you have identified some of your own money scripts. Get out your list and go back through it. Some of your scripts may be readily recognizable as flawed. You can easily identify that they are partial truths. In some cases, that recognition alone may have given you a powerful "Aha!" moment of understanding. Sometimes uncovering a hidden money belief in this way is all you need in order to change your behavior.

One man, for example, went to his financial planner because he was nearing 65 and it was time to retire. He wanted to arrange to start receiving income from his investments and take care of other details. During their appointment, she asked him what retirement meant to him and what he intended to do once he was free to do whatever he wanted. He thought for a few minutes, and then said, "Never mind. I don't need to do any of this." Her question had made him realize that the money script, "You have to retire at age 65," was not true for him. He loved his work, he was already doing exactly what he wanted to do, and he didn't want to retire.

There may be items on your list that could be changed easily by gaining some new exterior knowledge. Suppose one of your money scripts is, "You don't need a will if you don't have any property to leave anyone." You have no savings, you don't own a house, and you have small children. You talk to a financial advisor who tells you that one of the primary reasons to have a will is to name a guardian for your children, explaining that the courts will select a guardian if you should die intestate. With that knowledge, you understand why having a will is important and decide you will make one.

As you review your list, you are likely to find other money scripts that seem to you to be genuinely and absolutely true. These are the ones that make the most sense to you. They are the ones you assume everyone would agree with. Your reaction to them might be a thought such as, "Well, of course, everybody knows that."

Circle those scripts that to you are absolutely true. Most of them are likely to be your deepest scripts, the ones that influence your behavior the most. Some of them may have served you well. They might very well contain large elements of truth, but they most probably are also the ones that are causing you some of your deepest difficulties around money.

Exercise

You may be able to rewrite some of your money scripts by using the following simple exercise.

Take one of the scripts from your list that you have not circled. Let's use, "Never go into debt for any reason." Write down an instance of that script being true. Perhaps the situation might be using your credit card to pay for a vacation trip to the Bahamas when you are earning just enough for your day-to-day needs. So you could write a different version of the script: "Never go into debt for a vacation trip you can't afford."

Now write down an instance of that script being false. Buying a house, for example, is something very few of us could afford to do if we had to wait until we could pay cash for it. So you might write a new script reading: "It's reasonable to go into debt to buy a home."

The third step is to write down an instance where the script would be partially true. You might decide that using a credit card to pay for travel is all right as long as you can pay off the balance in full. Or perhaps borrowing money to help start a business would be a good decision as long as you have evaluated the situation carefully and realistically. This could help you write a third version of the script: "Never carry consumer debt, but it's okay to use debt carefully for convenience or as a business tool."

Try this exercise first with some of the scripts that you can quite easily see are flawed or that you don't have a lot of emotion about. Once you've practiced with those, you can move on to the scripts you circled as the truest and apply the exercise to them.

As you do this exercise, it's a good idea to treat yourself and your money scripts rather gently. The goal is to help you become flexible enough to move away from blindly following one "truth." You are adding to your money scripts and revising them, rather than trashing them completely. If you label them as wrong or stupid, you are in effect telling yourself you are wrong or stupid to believe them. Instead, it's useful to honor the part of the script that is true or that has been true in the past. You formed your money scripts in response to particular circumstances in your life. Even if as an adult you can see that a certain script never was literally true, you can still acknowledge that it was created in order to help you make sense of past circumstances. The intent behind the script was positive, even if the script has long since lost its usefulness.

∾∾

An exercise like this is not going to be enough to alter your more embedded scripts, especially the ones you cannot see any variation for, those that remain "absolutely true" even after you have done the exercise. These are commonly the scripts created out of painful or dramatic childhood circumstances, and they are anchored by difficult emotions resulting from unfinished business. For such scripts, change will require more emotional than cognitive effort. Uncovering them and recognizing the impact they have had on your life is just the beginning.

Knowledge alone will not be enough to help you shift to new behavior.

In fact, sometimes knowledge can make things worse. Knowing what we need to do merely adds to the shame when our actions don't follow our knowledge. We know what we "ought to do" in spades. We "ought to" be living within our means, save adequately for retirement, have a will, or be working at a job we truly love.

When we know what to do, but we aren't able to do it, most of us are accustomed to taking out our virtual baseball bats and beating ourselves up. We say to ourselves, "See, when it comes to money, you are as dumb as a rock, you know you should be doing better, and you just blew it again." This kind of self-blame isn't useful; it just intensifies the cycle of financial unconsciousness. Again, it's important to treat yourself with gentleness and respect.

What you will need in order to change your deepest money scripts is a combination of exterior knowledge and interior awareness. Because those entrenched scripts and behaviors are the ones causing the most significant problems in your life, they are the ones we focus on in the rest of Part I. You can only heal these scripts by working with the difficult emotions around them—by choosing to feel the difficult emotions that keep them embedded.

Pain as a Tool for Change

Pain is a teacher; it is trying to tell you something. You can learn to view pain as a signal that you are operating unconsciously and think of it as a gift that alerts you to the presence of a money script. Not only is it okay to feel pain, it is mandatory if you are going to let go of or modify your most entrenched money scripts and dissipate the difficult emotions that are trapping you in the cycle of financial unconsciousness. Once you learn how to do this, you will find that accepting painful emotions is ultimately less painful than is trying to avoid them.

Pain can be your ally and a tool for change. In order to use it as such, you have to pay attention to and befriend it. You need to choose to move into the shadows where it lives rather than keeping it shut away behind a locked door. Doing so can be difficult and frightening, but it can also provide some of your deepest healing and strongest growth.

Your more entrenched money scripts are likely to be protected by thick barriers of repressed or unfelt emotions. The more intense the emotions, the harder it is for exterior knowledge or interior awareness to penetrate them. This barrier needs to be dissolved or set aside before you can receive or apply new information.

Trying to change a deep money script with cognitive information is like trying to explain something to a person who is reacting emotionally. You already know the futility of this if you've ever tried to soothe a frustrated, screaming five-year-old; tried, with facts and reasoning, to change someone's opinion on a volatile political issue; or tried to end a heated argument with your angry spouse by offering a logical and sensible suggestion in the middle of the dispute. There is little sense in trying to reason with a frustrated or angry person until he has "settled down." Only after he has finished feeling his emotions will he be able to take in new information or become flexible enough to consider other options. You can tell someone a factual truth until you are blue in the face, but if he is operating from the emotion attached to his position or belief, he won't hear you. He simply can't take in this new truth as long as the emotion keeps him from objectively viewing his previously perceived "truth."

Since our most embedded money scripts are held in place by unconscious emotions, trying to rewrite them won't work until those emotions are dissipated or dissolved. This is not the same as ignoring them or trying to shut them off. Quite the contrary. It is accepting them, giving them the acknowledgement they need and deserve. Once you have done so, the emotions no longer need to demand your attention, and they can disappear or move out of the way.

Our experience shows the only way to dissolve an emotion
is to accept it and experience it.

Looking at the Shadows

Because we are wired to run from pain, embracing and feeling a difficult emotion is not something we will do unconsciously. It requires a conscious choice to experience pain in order to move toward healing and growth. Making such a choice requires you to look at the "shadows" of your interior relationship with money. *This is the most difficult part of the whole financial integration process.*

It's relatively easy to focus on exploring the "light side" of your relationship with money. Many financial planners and life coaches are beginning to do this, and there are quite a few books available which address this aspect. The light side usually involves a process of getting to your authentic goals and discovering what you really want to do and be. It includes learning to use money to help you live a fulfilled and satisfying life, to earn as much as you need by doing what you love, and to give wisely. Some financial planners refer to this as "life planning," "financial life planning," or "financial coaching." We define the light side of interior finance as looking from today forward.

This part of the interior work is important, and we include it as part of our process. By itself, however, it is not enough. In fact, it is getting the cart before the horse.

You can only look forward as you are willing to look backward.

The shadows of interior finance contain the unfinished business that is buried deep in your unconsciousness. These are the feelings, behaviors, scripts, and shame that you are either unaware of or unwilling to reveal to anyone else. They are dark only because you have been afraid to illuminate them with the light of consciousness. If you had been able to do so, they would no longer be unknown to you and operating unconsciously in your life. If you really want to heal your deepest difficulties around money, looking at the shadows is crucial.

There is disagreement about this approach, among financial planners and even among therapists. Some people even believe that looking at one's past is harmful in itself. We strongly disagree. Looking backward, being willing to face one's shadows, is an essential part of healing. We know this, because we have both done it and have learned from the experience how tremendously positive the results can be. We have also seen it work for hundreds of others. We understand from our own work that it's possible to go forward, into the light, only as far as one has been willing to go backward, into the shadows.

Let's clarify here that we aren't talking about the *Star Wars* version of "the dark side." We don't call this the shadows because it is "evil" or "bad." It's only murky because the light hasn't shone there. All we're urging you to do is go in with a good strong utility light and take a look. Thinking about doing that is probably about as appealing as the idea of going down into a dark cellar. Once you get started, though, you will find that the reality is far less frightening than what you may imagine. Yes, you may find cobwebs and dark corners and some rather yucky stuff. But there are no real monsters. And buried in the shadows, you will almost certainly find hidden treasure that will enrich your life.

Deciding to Change

This brings us to the next question. What will it take to get you to go into that dark cellar in the first place? Or, as Robert Bailey, Jr., put it in the movie *What The Bleep Do We Know?*, "How far down the rabbit hole do you want to go?"

If you have been going around and around in a cycle of financial unconsciousness, suffering serious consequences from your behavior, something needs to shift before you can escape. Something has to jolt you out of that uncomfortable but familiar rut and toward consciousness. Something must impel you to begin the hard work that change requires. What might that "something" be?

This will vary, because we all have different levels of tolerance for suffering and different degrees of fear of change. Everyone, however, needs some combination of three factors: an intervention or "hitting bottom," which often is an increase in your level or awareness of suffering; enough cognitive knowledge to become aware that other choices are available; and hope for something better on the other side of the pain. At some point, for some reason, you become conscious enough to realize that you have been operating unconsciously. Or it becomes apparent that it is taking more energy to stay in the cycle of financial unconsciousness than it would take to do the work of changing.

One crucial component is that you recognize you are suffering. This may seem obvious, but it isn't. In reality we often plod along unconsciously for years and years, never noticing that we're in pain, because we are so skilled at medicating and avoiding the pain. We cover it up with activity and busyness; we medicate it with chemicals; we run from it by hurrying to the next money script. We do everything we know how to do—nearly all of it unconscious—in order not to feel any pain. So, for a long time, we can avoid recognizing that we are suffering.

Remember that "suffering," as we're using it here, means staying in the cycle of financial unconsciousness when you don't have to. If that word seems exaggerated to you, think of it as "discomfort" or "difficulty" or something that fits better for you. Please don't get hung up in the semantics, which can be just another way of pretending you don't have any pain and don't need to change. Many of us have spent a lifetime "numbing out" our painful emotions, so recognizing we even have some discomfort can be challenging in itself and can be a significant step forward.

Acknowledging that you are suffering doesn't usually happen by waking up one morning and realizing, "Hey, what I'm doing here just isn't working." Or, "I'm numb to my unconscious pain, but I think I'll feel it today," or, "I want to make better money decisions, so I'll go feel my decades-old pain around my most engrained money scripts."

Generally what is necessary is some sort of triggering event, the exact makeup of which will be different for everyone. At times the right piece of exterior knowledge or insight at the right time is enough to create a shift. Simply reading this book and doing the exercises might be sufficient for some of you. For others, it may take an intervention from a loved one who presents an ultimatum, such as, "if you don't change this damaging behavior, I am leaving." The impetus for change may come from a life-shattering event such as a divorce or a business failure. For others, it may not be possible to point to a single event; over time they have reached a level of suffering deep enough to make them decide, "enough is enough."

The second component of change, enough cognitive knowledge to be aware of alternatives, is primarily exterior. If you're overwhelmed by debt, learning about a credit counseling service can help you decide it's time to get help. If you believe you are incapable of managing money competently, taking a personal finance class might give you the information you need.

The third component, hope for something better, is one reason that support and help from others is so important. You can receive a great deal of encouragement from the experiences of those who have been where you are and who have been able to change their lives for the better.

Regardless of the specifics of any individual story, there is one aspect they all have in common.

The decision to change must be made by the person involved.

Someone else can suggest alternatives, offer advice or help, beg, complain, or nag—none of which will make a difference until the cycle of financial unconsciousness becomes difficult enough that the person in it becomes willing to change.

Some of us can endure a great deal of suffering before we reach a change point. We know one man whose money scripts included so much deep shame that he spent more than three years trying to carry an impossible financial burden alone before he was able to ask for help. He developed a serious and disabling illness that was not covered by his health insurance, lost his small service business, sold nearly everything he owned, and was down to living in a two-room apartment with no heat. Only then was he able to accept the reality that he could not pay his medical bills and the necessity of filing for bankruptcy. His money scripts, "I should be able to take care of myself," and, "You're worthless if you can't pay your bills," nearly destroyed him.

Sometimes we are forced into changes by an event that we did nothing to create. A man in one workshop had a script of, "If I don't bother them, they won't bother me." When a lawsuit threatened his livelihood, he was forced to come out of his shell and defend himself. As he explained the change from his former passive behavior: "I had to. There was nobody else there to do it."

Kathleen: Something similar happened for me when Wayne was killed and I was compelled to deal with major financial issues on my own. I had always managed our family finances, so I knew what our assets were, knew how to do the taxes, and knew how to deal with attorneys and accountants. But this was much different. For one thing, I didn't have him there to discuss things with. There was no second opinion; I was the one having to make the decisions. I had always deferred to Wayne's judgment, particularly since he earned the majority of the income. Literally overnight, it was all up to me.

Dealing with life insurance and Worker's Compensation payments and settling the estate also triggered many of my existing money scripts—as well as generating some new ones. Some of the old ones were: "It's not okay to have money I haven't earned." "I don't want to be like people who have money." "I have to take care of everyone else before I pay attention to what I want or need."

As if these weren't enough, some new beliefs climbed on board as well: "Accepting the Worker's Compensation payments means I'm saying it's okay that Wayne died." "I have to make the same decisions Wayne would have made." "I have to be fair to everyone in the family and do everything perfectly around this money, because it was Wayne's."

The painful feelings created by these money scripts, on top of my grief, would have made it easy to just pull away and ignore everything. It also would have been familiar and easy to fall into unconscious behavior—to refuse to spend anything except on necessities, to keep the old vehicle I had been driving just because Wayne had bought it, to hoard the money or give it away because I felt I had no right to it.

So why didn't I? That's a good question. I'm not sure I have a complete answer. I do know that one factor was the same one we described in the previous example. There was nobody else there to do it, so I had to. My sense of responsibility wouldn't allow me to neglect the tasks that needed to be done. I also had the support and advice of a wise group of friends. I had advisors I trusted, including Rick, who told me things like, "If you start feeling a need to give all the money away, give it to me, and I'll take care of it for you until you're ready to take it back."

I also think a factor for me was that I was in so much pain already that facing the smaller pain of unresolved money issues simply wasn't big enough to worry about. Wayne's death hurt so deeply that other issues I had been afraid of became insignificant in comparison. Certainly, I would have had the choice of medicating all of that pain and grief rather than dealing with it. I did try that, actually, in some rather minor ways. I don't drink, I don't smoke, and I've never used drugs, so medicating with substances wasn't really an option. My chief medicating behavior has always been reading—avoiding my difficult feelings by burying myself in a murder mystery. In the first few weeks after Wayne's death, though, my brain was so scrambled that I couldn't even concentrate enough to read. So my chief medicator wasn't available to me.

In addition, I had been in a 12-step program of recovery for enough years to have learned some healthier patterns of behavior. I knew how to express my feelings, to let go of what I could not change, to ask for help when I needed it, and to live one day at a time. I had never had to practice those behaviors as thoroughly as I needed to right after Wayne was killed, but I had them available to me and was able to use them. I had been practicing conscious behavior in other areas of my life, so it was one of the choices I knew about when my money issues on top of my grief threatened to overwhelm me.

᠎ᡒᡶᡩ

ᎡᏟᏦ

Rick: For me the event that made me willing to explore my own shadows was a financially and emotionally devastating divorce. My conservative-Christian, gospel-singing wife ran off with a member of a rock band. This was the painful wakeup call that got me into a 12-step program for Adult Children of Alcoholics (ACOA). The first time I went to a 12-step meeting, I could not believe how ridiculous it seemed. There was no leader, there was no advice—just these people sitting around talking about their feelings. I could not see how one earthly bit of good would come out of attending a meeting like that. So I didn't go back until a friend told me how powerfully the program had affected his life. Then I started attending the meetings on a regular basis.

That was very painful for me. It was very shaming for me to consider even going to a 12-step meeting, because those were for drunks and people who lived with drunks. Those were for people that were really screwed up. Those were not for me. After all, I reasoned, I was a successful, intelligent, hard-working, and responsible human being. But my pain was deep enough for me to go through the shame of admitting I needed help.

Now, depending on the meeting, there's some feeling that goes on at a 12-step meeting. There's a lot of talking about feelings, which is certainly a first step and which helped me begin to understand that I at least had feelings. Then from there I progressed within a few months to deciding that maybe a counselor would be helpful, and after that it was just a natural progression of starting to thaw out, starting to feel, and starting to change my painful life scripts.

My wife had filed for divorce, but then hadn't taken further action. I was struggling to pay her monthly support payments, as we were separated but not divorced. The church I attended at the time taught that divorce was not an option. So I never thought about what I wanted. There was no consciousness around that. It was just, "so this is how it is;" I didn't even question it. This went on for about a year, and meanwhile I was going to 12-step meetings and going to counseling. I was starting to see that there was some dysfunction around what was happening. I was starting to find my voice.

The turning point for me came when I was at a professional conference, and on the last evening they had a dance. I was watching people dancing and having fun, when one by one several women came up to me and asked me to dance. I declined them all, because I had a belief that a married man shouldn't be out dancing with other women. Then I had the thought, "What am I? Am I a married person here, or am I a single person?" And I thought, "I'm a married single person. What is a married single person?" And it just hit me that, "this is screwed up." For the rest of the evening I became aware of what felt like an ocean of difficult emotions swirling around me. Running from them was no longer an option, as I became willing to feel.

After that experience I gained some clarity. I realized I didn't care about what anyone else thought about this topic; I really needed to get some definition around my marital status. So then I came back and told my wife we needed to get on with our lives. Either she could come back and reconcile, or we should get divorced, but I was tired of being in suspended animation.

During that year, I had been getting new information and insights, and I had learned how to feel my emotions. The combination led me to the clarity that, regardless of what others thought, it was not okay for me to stay in the limbo of a marriage that was no longer a marriage. It was not okay to be financially supporting a wife who was no longer my wife in any sense except the legal one. So once I had that clarity, in a relatively short time we finalized the divorce.

$\approx$

Becoming willing to do the work that is required for change is an essential step toward consciousness. Once you have done so, the next step is learning to find and use the tools you need for that work. The next few chapters provide some of those tools.

6

Difficult Emotions as Tools for Change

Before you can change your most damaging money behavior, you need to develop your interior skills. Before you can have a healthy relationship with money, you need to have a healthy relationship with your feelings. There is wisdom in your emotions, because they can guide you to clarity.

Nothing else is more authentically you than are your feelings.

There is little you can do or say that is truer than when you say, "I am feeling sadness, joy, anger, or fear." Someone else can argue with the circumstances, behaviors, or thoughts that may have caused the feeling, but the fact that you are feeling what you are feeling is a rock-solid truth.

In order to dissolve difficult emotions so you can objectively modify your money scripts and behaviors, you need the ability to first become aware of your emotions and then to feel them. When you know what you are feeling and you allow yourself to feel it, you are able to move through the emotion and let it dissipate. When the "fog" of emotion has cleared, you are able to view your money scripts objectively. This clarity enables you to decide whether any of your scripts are useful in a given circumstance, to reject others, and to identify other options. Then, instead of rigidly following your money scripts, you have the flexibility to make choices appropriate to the situation.

Rewriting a deeply imbedded money script to bring about a permanent behavioral change is next to impossible until the emotions attached to it are dissolved. The difficult emotions are to changing our behavior around money as autopilot is to an airplane. A pilot can make manual changes to the plane's course, but as soon as she lets go of the controls the autopilot takes over again and the plane moves back to the original course. The only way to permanently change the direction is to shut off the autopilot. The only way to take our deepest money scripts and most destructive behaviors off autopilot is to dissolve the difficult emotions that lock them into place. And the only way to do that is to identify and feel them.

For those of you who are not in the habit of paying much attention to your emotions, even identifying them can be a bit of a challenge. Many psychologists say there are four basic feelings: anger, fear, sadness, and joy. Counselors sometimes do a "four-corners" exercise with these emotions by designating each corner of the room as representing one of the emotions. As participants begin a session, they are asked to "check in" by moving to the corner that best matches how they are feeling.

You might find it useful to do this exercise, perhaps by drawing a square on a piece of paper and labeling the corners as anger, fear, sadness, and joy. It may also work for you just to visualize the square in your mind. Either way can help you determine which of the basic four emotions best fits what you are experiencing.

Obviously, not every emotion is going to fit purely into one corner. There are all sorts of combinations and variations. Anxiety, jealousy, envy, worry, depression, irritation, guilt, or loneliness would probably be mixtures of anger, fear, and sadness. Joy might be touched with various combinations of sadness, fear, or anger to give you mild pleasure, quiet happiness, or smug satisfaction. With practice, you soon learn you are often feeling several emotions at once, and you can put yourself in the location that best represents those feelings.

As you are learning to recognize your emotions, it takes some practice to realize that a feeling is not a sentence. As one man said when he was asked how he felt about an early money memory, "I'm really glad that I've learned the value of a dollar." That is not a feeling; it's a statement of an idea or a money script. A feeling is one word, possibly with a modifier or two.

There is a great deal of power in naming a feeling with that right word. Many of us tend to use euphemisms to downplay our difficult feelings. "I'm crabby today." "I'm a little irritated." "That makes me sort of nervous." How much more powerful to say instead, even if only to yourself: "I am sad." "I am angry." "I am afraid." It is freeing and healing to claim and acknowledge the genuine feeling instead of its paler shadow.

Just to be clear, we are talking about emotions, not actions. We don't mean to encourage inappropriate behavior around anger or rage. We're not advocating that you act out your feelings by calling your boss names or punching someone in the mouth. What we're saying is, if you are angry enough to do either of those things, admit it to yourself. After you have done so, you'll be better able to take whatever action might be appropriate.

Difficult Emotions

Once you begin paying attention to your feelings around painful money issues, you are likely to find many of them difficult. Sadness, anger, guilt, regret, fear—none of these are naturally comfortable emotions. It's tempting to label them as negative or bad. How many times as a child did you hear your parents refer to anger as bad, or something that only a weak or defective person would feel? Or you may have been told to "suck it up," when you would start feeling fear or sadness and begin to cry. Again, the message was that something was wrong with you if you felt these "negative" emotions. Yet emotions are neither negative nor bad; they are simply part of the reality of being human.

It's more accurate to call these intense emotions uncomfortable or difficult. Challenging as they can be, they are friends rather than enemies. They are there for a reason. They alert you to the fact that you have an unconscious money script at work. When you are brave enough to feel them rather than avoid them, the reward is that you move through the pain they may bring. On the other side of the pain, you will find clarity. By dissolving the feeling, you will open up some room to see more objectively, apply new knowledge, and create new energy.

Feeling your difficult emotions instead of ignoring, avoiding, or medicating them will create objectivity, clarity, flexibility, and the ability to see new options.

Being aware of a difficult emotion and feeling it are two different animals. You may be able to name an emotion; you may even be able to talk about the emotion being there. *But it is something altogether different to actually feel what you are feeling.* When you allow yourself to feel, you are choosing not to judge your emotions, discount them, or distract yourself from them.

Getting to clarity requires you to release the thoughts that keep you distracted, allowing yourself to get to the feelings that hide behind those thoughts. Until you let that thought go, you can't get to the feeling. When you are able to separate your money scripts from the emotions that anchor them, the feelings become powerful tools that will help you find clarity. Clinging to money scripts and their associated thoughts, or medicating them in some manner, only serves to intensify and justify them.

To understand this, just pretend for a moment that you're a kid, you've misbehaved, and you've been sent to your room. (Now we know you were a perfect child, so this is something that's never happened to you, but humor us here. Use your imagination.)

So here you are, shut up in your room, talking to yourself. "I'll show them, they can't do this to me, I'll make them suffer." As a kid, you don't have the maturity to be able to separate the thoughts from the feelings. So you mutter to yourself, you think dark thoughts of revenge and getting even, and you repeat in your mind some variation of, "This isn't fair. My parents are so mean."

The repetition and the justification, "they are so mean," is just hardening that thought, which serves to hide the feeling. As long as you continue to do this, you can stay in your room until next Tuesday and you aren't going to feel sorry for what you've done or want to mend the breach with your mom and dad. You're just going to get madder and madder. No wonder that when somebody knocks on the door after a couple of hours, your reaction is a sullen, "Leave me alone!"

If instead you could quiet your thoughts and access the feelings behind them, what might those feelings be? You might feel angry about being punished. You might feel ashamed of yourself if you did something you knew was wrong. You might feel sad about the temporary emotional separation from your parents. You might feel fear about your parents being mad at you, or about the necessity of doing something to resolve the situation. Depending on the circumstances, you might even feel relief about being caught.

Only by feeling those emotions are you going to get to a point of being able to let go of the thought, "They are so mean." Then you can begin to understand why your parents were angry. At that point you can think about making a sincere apology, trying to explain why what you did wasn't wrong, or doing whatever else you might need to do to make things right. That clarity, followed by the appropriate behavior, would mean you were practicing emotional competence.

When you dismiss the thought and just feel the feeling, you're not looking outward in blame, which is just trying to cover up the feeling with a thought and a justification. *But sitting with that feeling, you're going to have a relationship with it.* You break that pattern of blame and resentment, and you begin to move into the pain, toward consciousness and clarity.

Part of what we're trying to do here is learn to *be at ease with our feelings.* That doesn't mean enjoying them, it means being able to be comfortable with them. (The opposite of being at ease with a feeling is being "dis-eased." Think about that.) Being at ease with our feelings just means acknowledging and allowing ourselves to feel the difficult ones as well as the joyous ones. We get lots of unconscious messages that feeling sad is bad, that feeling anger is wrong, that feeling fear is weakness. Our society tells us it's not okay to have those feelings, so we get to a point of believing that there's something wrong with us if we experience them. That's one reason we try to avoid them.

Another reason we run from feelings is simple fear. A difficult feeling can be so intense that there's a fear of being lost in it. "This will never end. I'll never come out. I'll die here." That fear applies both to our own feelings and those of the people around us. We can be so afraid of and uncomfortable with our own feelings that we try to shut down others when they are having feelings. We want to make them feel better so we can feel better, so we say things like, "It's okay," "Don't cry," or, "Pull yourself together."

The way to move through difficult emotions is to accept them, embrace them, and feel them completely.

This doesn't mean wallowing in self-pity or getting stuck in painful emotions. It means treating those emotions with the respect they deserve. It means acknowledging and honoring them as a part of your being that can be a powerful healer and teacher. It means using them to get to the wisdom and clarity they have to offer you.

Pain Will Not Harm You

It's incredibly powerful to learn that you can become at ease with a difficult feeling. If you can learn to be at ease with pain, there's no longer a reason to run from it. There is no longer the need to medicate it or act out a destructive financial behavior. When you have once had the experience of releasing a thought or money script, feeling the difficult feeling behind it, having the feeling dissipate, and finding it replaced by peace and clarity, then you know what's on the other side. You know you can survive the experience and learn from it. You also gain an enormous amount of energy—energy that has previously gone into avoiding the feelings.

---

*The ultimate goal of feeling difficult feelings
is reaching clarity and serenity.*

Kathleen: A massage therapist I used to go to had a saying she used when she was working on an especially tense or sore area. She would dig her thumb or sometimes her elbow into a knotted muscle until it hurt enough to make me gasp, meanwhile repeating in a soothing voice, "Pain cannot harm you." By the time she was done, she would have worked out the knot and the pain would be gone.

Her mantra also applies to emotional pain. The prospect of feeling deep and painful emotions may seem frightening and overwhelming. The reality of doing so may be excruciating. But once you have gone through the experience of feeling intense emotional pain and have come out the other side, you understand that doing so may hurt terribly, but it does not harm you.

On perhaps the third day after Wayne was killed, I remember waking up at about 5:00 in the morning. By then I had gone through the initial shock and disbelief, had made those terribly difficult phone calls to relatives, and had cried and cried. That morning when I woke up, I experienced what I was already becoming used to—that first tiny moment of being okay, and then remembering that he was gone. And instead of tears, I felt a heavy, deep sadness just settle into my very bones. The grief right at that moment was beyond words, beyond tears.

It was as if the pain flowed into every part of my body and became part of me. There was nothing I could do except let it be.

That is the deepest experience I have ever had of just feeling an emotion. It's not one I ever want to have again if I can help it. That was, I think, the time that I accepted the truth that my husband was really gone. I realized that the heaviness and sadness were there to stay for at least a while. And they were, intensely, for the first weeks. Eventually, as I continued to grieve and to mourn, those feelings lessened. With time and healing, I grew lighter again, and by now what is left is a thread of sadness that has become part of who I am.

After experiencing the depth of the pain that came with Wayne's death, I have become much less afraid of all of my feelings. I went through that agony, and I survived it. So there is no reason for me to shrink from all the smaller things I used to be afraid of—speaking my mind, having someone mad at me, making a mistake, making the wrong decision. Those no longer seem too big to face, because now I know what real pain is and I know I can get through it.

Learning how to feel your emotions and reach the point of wisdom they can teach you requires time, attention, and practice. It takes learning new tools and doing something different from what you have done in the past.

7

Interior Awareness: Tools That Help You Feel

Learning to feel a feeling, with the goal of dissipating the emotion and moving on to clarity about your money decisions, doesn't come naturally. Learning this interior awareness, like building competence in any other area, takes time and practice.

Feeling difficult emotions comes as easily to human beings as obedience training does to cats.

Fortunately, there are existing tools and methods you can use to help you develop interior awareness. Some of these may be familiar; others will be new to you. None of them work completely and exclusively. You will undoubtedly need to use several or all of them on your journey to financial integration.

In this chapter, we consider individual practices or tools to help you access and feel difficult emotions. Unlike the other components of interior awareness, these practices are done by yourself. This is where you can begin to listen to yourself and develop a relationship with yourself. This can only be done by eliminating the noise of your life and turning an emotional ear inward. Two excellent methods of listening to yourself are journaling and feelings meditation. We have found both of these to be valuable aids to uncovering our money scripts and changing our behaviors around money.

Journaling

A simple, accessible tool that is useful for identifying feelings is journaling. This isn't a keep-for-posterity kind of journal or diary. Instead, it is more a stream of "top of the mind" thoughts and feelings.

For Kathleen it works best to write in longhand on paper, while Rick prefers the computer.

ℋ𝒻

Kathleen: I find it a valuable practice to spend about 15 minutes journaling at the beginning of my day. I use cheap lined notebook paper, giving myself full permission to throw it away if I wish when I'm finished. I write as quickly and freely as I can, not stopping to polish my sentences or even write in sentences, not paying any attention to grammar or spelling. What I find is that writing brings out my thoughts about whatever may be going on in my life, then the thoughts bring up my feelings.

When I get to that point, though, it's important to stop writing. Then it's time to just sit and let the feelings come. Otherwise I end up writing about the feelings instead of feeling them, moving right out of the emotion and back into my mind.

ॐ

ℛℋ

Rick: I used journaling early on in my interior journey to express and get in touch with my scripts and feelings. At that time it was the only tool I was willing to employ. Journaling seemed to be the least public, least threatening, and least embarrassing option. It was the easiest way for me to put my toe into the interior finance waters and test them. Between my journaling and attendance at 12-step meetings, I eventually developed the courage to even go near a feeling. I began to learn I indeed had money scripts and that—even though I certainly understood and practiced the exterior skills—my relationship with money was not healthy.

ॐ

Keep in mind that if you use journaling as a way to help you identify feelings, it can be useful to lead to awareness, but it is only a preliminary step. It can also be a way to intellectualize, to analyze and medicate your feelings instead of feeling them. At some point you need to put down your pen and paper, sit still, and let yourself feel. We can't tell you exactly what that point is; as you use this tool, you will learn to identify it for yourself.

Feelings Meditation

Journaling can be helpful in identifying money scripts and becoming aware of your feelings. What do you do when you are ready to feel them? One of the most effective—and we would suggest necessary—tools for that purpose is feelings meditation.

Feelings meditation is one type of meditation that has also been described as "body scanning." Walking can be a form of feelings meditation. Even forms of physical exercise, like yoga or tai chi, can involve a large degree of learning to listen to your body. The purpose of a feelings meditation practice is to release the stream of thoughts and noise running through your head and to learn how to listen to your body, focusing on sensations and feelings. We call it feelings meditation rather than just meditation because this method is not about relaxation, it's about being alert to what is going on in your body.

Feelings meditation is simply about sitting still for a few minutes, quieting your mind, letting go of all thoughts, and letting yourself become aware of the sensations in your body. Usually, when you find a sensation in the body you will soon be able to identify the emotion related to it.

Please, don't let the idea of a feelings meditation intimidate you. There's no need to pretzel yourself into the lotus position, chant something in an unfamiliar language, light candles, burn incense, hold a crystal, shave your head, or become a vegetarian. This isn't a religion. It isn't a New Age rite. It isn't a big elaborate lifestyle change. It's a small addition to your life that can make a big difference. You don't have to set up a special room, buy special clothes, or in any other way make a big production of it. You don't have to even use the words "feelings meditation" if you don't want to. You can call it focusing time, body scanning, quiet time, or anything else that fits for you.

Depending on your circumstances, it is best to do this in a manner that will allow you to be both physically still and aware. Maintaining a physically quiet posture with maximum mental awareness is best done sitting in a straight-backed chair or lying flat on the floor. Your overstuffed recliner or your bed may not be the best alternative. Getting too comfortable can turn the exercise into one of relaxation, rather than alertness. You can practice feelings meditation in your office at work, in an airplane, or even to a degree while driving your car. All you need is a place where you can be physically and emotionally quiet for five to 20 minutes when no one will interrupt you.

This chapter is not a complete course in how to meditate. We are certainly not qualified meditation teachers. If you'd like to learn more, there are many books available. In a way, though, our lack of credentials here is our chief qualification.

If a left-brained, number crunching financial planner like Rick or a restless, brain-buzzing thinker like Kathleen can learn to do this, so can you.

First, sit upright or lie flat on the floor, taking time to make sure you are comfortable. Don't cross your legs or curl them under you in a position where they might become cramped or go to sleep. If you're sitting in a chair, you might want to try putting a small pillow behind your head so your neck doesn't get stiff.

Next, let your body relax. Some people do this very deliberately, beginning at the toes and working upward, consciously relaxing first the feet, then the legs, and so on. If you do this, you may notice certain areas that are more tense than others—your shoulders, perhaps, or your jaw. Don't try to force them to relax; just notice the tension and begin gently to let it go. Let your shoulders relax. Let your teeth part slightly as you make sure your jaw is not clenched.

Now take some deep "belly breaths." This is done by inhaling and expanding your diaphragm downward toward your belly, then filling your middle and lastly your upper chest with air, and then exhaling as slowly as you inhaled. You may want to take two or three of these very deep, mindful breaths, inhaling and exhaling slowly. This can help you relax. But then don't try to keep breathing deeply; hyperventilating is not a help to meditation.

Begin to become more aware of your breathing. Notice the physical sensations of your breath. Does it feel warm or cool? Do you feel an expansion or contraction in your chest, or in your belly? Stay focused on your breathing for a while. The reason for this is simple. You are attempting to get your mind ready to shift from focusing on your thoughts to focusing on sensations in your body. Focusing on the breath for a while helps with this transition.

Now, become aware of any thoughts. Your mind is likely to be running around like crazy. Just like small children who clamor for attention the minute you sit down with the newspaper, your thoughts are likely to start bombarding you. Immediately you can think of six or seven important things you ought to be doing. Your mind may bring up questions, remind you of things you should be worrying about, and wander off in all sorts of unexpected directions. Don't fight this busyness. Instead, gently let go of each thought as you become aware of it.

We have found it helpful to visualize the thought as a helium balloon, releasing it and watching the thought float away. Others find it works well to allow the thought to drop gently deep within them or to the floor. Whatever may work for you, when you become aware of having a thought, just let it go without judgment or getting involved with it. Don't actively ignore your thoughts, but detach from them and let them drift away. This is easier said than done; it will take some practice.

Next, begin to scan your body for sensations. You can do this systematically, starting at your feet and working your way through your body to your head. Or you may become immediately aware of a sensation and go directly to the body location where you notice it. Noticing sensations may come quickly to you, or you may need several sessions to begin noticing them.

Eventually you will become aware of various sensations in your body. Maybe you will feel a tightness in your shoulders or a contraction in your arms. Maybe you will feel a throbbing in your neck or a knot in your stomach. Perhaps you'll notice a heaviness, coolness, tingling, or hollowness in your chest. When you find a sensation, ask yourself how it feels. Notice whether the sensation moves, throbs, or changes in any fashion.

Other sensations that some people notice are a hyper-awareness of their heartbeat or pulse, even a sense of agitation at first. You may notice the pressure of your body against your chair. You may become aware of tiny sounds in the room. You may feel that you are becoming tenser rather than relaxing. Many of these bodily sensations are related to your emotions. Some type of feeling will undoubtedly be "attached" to these sensations.

Now you might want to gently ask yourself the question, "What am I feeling?"

Perhaps your mind has brought up the fact that you had a fight with your spouse yesterday over a money issue. Don't replay the conversation in your mind, rehearse the things you wish you had said, or get into the "it's not fair, I was right" thoughts that justify your position. Instead, let yourself be aware of the emotions behind those thoughts. Release the thought and focus on the feeling, whatever it is. You may feel sad, angry, guilty, afraid, or various combinations of emotions.

Or you may not be sure exactly what you're feeling. We are good at disguising our feelings under polite euphemisms, pretending even to ourselves that we don't have those uncomfortable or socially unacceptable emotions. Fear, for example, is often hidden under anger. Anger itself is often minimized as annoyance or irritation. Sadness can hide out under boredom or grumpiness. It's going to take time for you to sort out what's going on inside.

That's okay; remember we call this a *practice*. No one is grading you. There is no passing or failing a feelings meditation. The important factor is that you set aside time every day to do this. Certainly, it will seem unfamiliar, perhaps even silly in the beginning. Don't worry; you didn't learn to read on your first day of school, either. What is most important is your willingness to sit quietly and let yourself feel. With practice, you'll be able to identify your body sensations and your emotions. "Oh, there's that knot in my stomach again; that's fear." "My jaw and shoulders are tight—I'm angry."

After a while, it will become easier for you to identify your emotions. A great deal of clarity comes with just naming what you feel. Saying to yourself, "I'm angry," or "I feel sad," is acknowledging to yourself what is going on internally. Claiming your emotions is an early stage of interior awareness, and therefore a step toward integrity.

Recognizing what you are feeling is a big step, but it's only the first one. The next step is to let yourself feel those feelings. Just sit with them. Invite them in. If you are sad, let yourself feel sad. If you are angry, just feel it. If you are joyful, let yourself enjoy the fullness of that emotion.

It's difficult to tell someone else how to find, embrace, and feel an emotion, because it can't really be done except by experiencing it. But you may find it helpful to think of approaching your feelings in three stages.

The first stage is simply observation. It's learning to pay attention to your body sensations, then becoming aware that those are related to emotions, then beginning to identify and name the emotions. Observation is usually done at a distance. You don't necessarily have to be near the feeling to recognize that it is there.

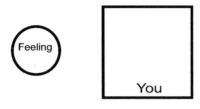

Observing a Feeling

The second stage is one of nurturing and compassion. It is moving closer to the emotion, supporting yourself as a parent may support a frightened child. Part of it might be described as detachment, as viewing that painful emotion from the perspective of a supportive, caring friend or parent. That is not the same thing as comforting yourself or trying to make the feeling go away. *Remember, the immediate goal is not to make yourself feel better; the goal is to feel.* Once the difficult emotion is felt and dissipated, feeling better will take on a whole new dimension. So you might imagine yourself in that supportive, parental role in much the same way you could support your child in doing something difficult. You don't say, "It's okay, that's too hard, you don't have to do it." Instead, you say, "I know it's hard, but I'm right here. I'll help you do this, I'll help you get through it."

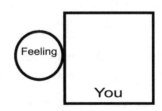

Nurturing a Feeling

The third stage is allowing, accepting, embracing, or entering the emotion. This is the tough one. It includes the welcoming and embracing of the emotion, and eventually, learning to become at ease with that feeling or sensation. The point is that you don't want to take away or avoid the pain, because that also takes away the opportunity to gain clarity and move into financial integration. What you need at this point is to respect yourself enough to allow yourself to feel that pain.

Embracing a Feeling

The goal in embracing the difficult emotion is to learn to be at ease with the feeling. This takes practice. *Once you learn that there is lightness and clarity on the other side of embracing fear or sadness, you will become more willing and less afraid to embrace difficult emotions.* After a while, you may even become excited when a difficult emotion appears, knowing that by feeling it you are about to become clear on how to modify or change an old money script, resulting in better money decisions and more joy in your life.

RK

Rick: The feelings meditation piece was hard for me at first because I had picked up the idea that meditation was either tied to Eastern religion or what is known in Christianity as contemplative prayer. Instead, I found out that it's really a very secular exercise. It's all about letting go of thoughts in a quiet space, so you can become aware of what's going on in your body.

An emotion can often first be identified by a body sensation. The first time I ever heard that, I thought it was nuts. How can you possibly feel an emotion in your body? But the more I thought about it, the more sense it began to make. I suffered from migraines for 20 years. Finally a doctor said, "I think you have tension migraines. You start by tensing your left shoulder, and that creates a vascular response, and it goes into a migraine."

Then I had to ask the question, "So why is my left shoulder tensed?" I discovered that my shoulder is where I tense up when I feel stress. And what's behind stress? Most often, at least for me, it's fear.

I started to understand that my body does play a big part in how I operate. I also learned to recognize that when things go badly for me financially, my stomach knots up. When I was going through one particularly stressful financial crisis, my stomach was so knotted I couldn't eat for 48 hours. Obviously, my body was feeling something. Was it because of a virus or bacteria? No, it was knotted up because there was a huge emotion there, which was evidence of an unconscious money script. Lots of thoughts were running around in my mind, so letting go of those thoughts and starting to feel the feelings actually released the sensation and finally brought me awareness of the money script. That resulted in my making a very unusual decision that resolved the matter quickly and with the least amount of financial damage. Without taking the time and effort to feel my feelings, I would have made a decision that would have perpetuated and deepened the crisis. But the first indicator I had of the level of stress was realizing that my stomach was in a knot. Then I was able to take the time to feel the fear behind the sensation, rather than stay in my head or turn to a medicator.

Usually, I notice the body sensation before the emotion. What I do, then, when I meditate is to begin by noticing what's going on and locating the feeling in my body. That can help make the process more complete. As I learned to pay attention to my body, I could eventually begin to note body sensations while sitting at my desk talking on the phone, visiting with a client, or executing a trade.

Perhaps my most vivid example of the relationship between a body sensation and an emotion occurred during a workshop I attended. At one point we were sent off separately to practice feelings meditation. I remember feeling a very light sky-rocket sensation in the left side of my chest. I just felt it fleetingly, a tingle, something really different that I had never felt before. But I was aware of it, and I paid attention to it. Behind it was a huge amount of sadness around a difficult loss in my life that occurred ten years prior to this time.

When I let go of the thoughts around that loss, incredible sadness just engulfed me. I was able to sit in the sadness and let the feelings be for maybe 15 minutes. At the end of that time, I felt lighter, had a sense of relief, and was able to let go of much of the sadness I had been carrying around the past incident.

That was the most powerful experience I've had of letting go of hurt and sadness. The point is that when I sat down to be aware of sensations in my body, that incident was the furthest thing from my mind. I hadn't talked about it or thought about it for years. There was just the physical sensation that brought it up. And behind the sensation was the feeling of sadness.

৵৶

𝒦ℱ

Kathleen: One day several years ago I was at a construction site with Wayne, waiting for him to finish what he was doing so I could help him do some testing. He watched me roam restlessly around the room for a while and finally said, "You just don't do nothing well at all, do you?" No, I don't. I can sit for hours as long as I have a book to read, a notebook and a pen, or something else to occupy my mind. But without any of those things, simply sitting drives me nuts. I find it hard to just be, rather than to be doing. So meditation is not easy for me.

The other problem I have with meditation is that as soon as I quiet my thoughts, the music in the back of my mind increases in volume. You know how you get a song stuck in your brain and it repeats endlessly until you want to scream? Well, I realized a few years ago that I always have some piece of music playing back there. Most of the time I don't particularly notice it. But let me get comfortable in my chair, close my eyes, quiet my breathing—and up comes the music, right on cue, just like the soundtrack of a bad made-for-TV movie. It's not so bad if the song is something halfway appropriate like "Amazing Grace." But "Louie, Louie" or "My Boyfriend's Back" tend to be a bit distracting. One recent morning, for some reason, it was "Yellow Submarine."

I've learned not to worry about this too much. Having some quiet external music playing usually helps. If necessary, I can replace the song in my head with something more meditation-friendly—change the channel, as it were. And after I sit for a few minutes the volume goes back down and becomes part of the background again.

Despite my restlessness and my background music, however, I can and do meditate successfully. It helps me focus on what's going on internally.

Another tool that helps me practice self-awareness is walking. A solitary walk can function much like meditation. The walking—the rhythm of my steps, the motion of my arms—keeps my body occupied but requires no real attention from my mind, other than looking both ways at street corners so as not to get run over by a truck. What happens for me is that my mind just floats. I don't make any conscious effort to control my thoughts or get rid of them. I just let them operate somewhere at the back of my mind without paying any real attention to them. This is more or less a stealth meditation—since it doesn't work very well for me to quiet my thoughts, I work around them. While the thoughts are busy doing whatever they do back there, I have a chance to notice and experience what I am feeling.

ॐॐ

Like any new behavior, feelings meditation is not something at which you will instantly be successful. The first few times you try this, nothing much may happen except that your stomach growls and your nose itches. But please, stay with it. The only way you can learn to be at ease with your feelings is to do it. It's difficult, because in your head you can say, fine, I'll let go of the thought. But that is still thinking. You can get so caught up in the thought of letting go of a thought that you think you've done it, when you haven't let go at all. That's why you can't read yourself well or do this overnight. It takes time and practice.

The heart of this process is being willing to experience the feelings once you are able to recognize them. That requires quiet time and solitude.

Taking time just to be alone and pay attention to your feelings may seem like a selfish thing to do. It may seem silly or unproductive. It may seem to be one more demand on your time when you're already too busy. Yet the benefits feelings meditation can give you in the form of increased clarity, focus, and peace of mind are well worth the small investment of time.

8

Interior Awareness: Working With Others

The individual practices we describe in the preceding chapter are essential methods of reaching interior clarity. There are limits, however, to the amount of awareness you can achieve on your own. Sometimes, as you work toward clarity, you will need to use tools that require the help of others.

Emotional Listening

A powerful way to become aware of feelings is emotional listening. This is not something you can do by yourself; it requires the very specific help of a supportive and wise friend. It is important to understand that emotional listening is unlike cognitive listening. It is paying attention, not to the content of someone's story, but to the feelings that go with the story. Emotional listening happens when the listeners only hear with their emotions, not their minds. Listeners are not to ask questions, relate a similar experience, or give advice. They will only relate the sensations and feelings that came up for them while you told your story.

George Kinder, in his two-day workshop, includes an emotional listening exercise that we have found to work miracles time and time again.

Emotional Listening Exercise

Tell a painful money story to someone who has agreed to be your emotional listener. Try to keep the story to five minutes or less. You don't need to tell them your life history. Keep it in bite-sized chunks so the listener can respond in a timely manner. You'll find you can get plenty of pain into a five-minute story.

Once your time is up or your story is completed, you will have one minute to identify and tell to the listener all the feelings of which you are aware. The listener is not to speak a word during your story or your one minute to identify your feelings.

Once you are done identifying your feelings, the listener will respond to your story using only this formula:

When you said (blank), I felt (what one-word emotion) in my (where in the body).

The listener will use this formula for as many points of your story as he or she responded to with a feeling. If the listener can identify where in her body she felt the feelings, that's great, but it is not imperative. The important thing is that the listener attach her feelings to the various parts of your story. Once the listener is done repeating this formula as many times as necessary, the listener *shuts up*. No questions, no advice, no responding with a similar story, no talking of any kind. We are emphasizing this for a reason; your listener is going to find shutting up to be inordinately difficult, as will you, but it is important. Your listener needs to do nothing to attempt to take you out of your feelings. Even a pat on the back can take you out of your feelings and back into your head.

Once your listener has responded to you, you will need to look for two possible awarenesses from the listener's response.

The first awareness is that the listener may have felt an emotion about something in your story that was different from your feeling. Perhaps you were feeling only sadness about your story. The listener's response may have been that she felt intense anger. You may not think you have any anger. But when the listener identifies her anger about your story, it may give you access to actually feel repressed or unidentified anger in yourself. This scenario is often the case. Don't dismiss lightly a feeling your listener has about your story. Our experience is that the feeling you don't think you have is often well medicated or hidden deep within, so you will need to be alert to what your body may be telling you. This is why you don't want the listener talking after the feedback. You need time to sit quietly and pay attention to your body sensations and emotions.

The second awareness comes from the listener having the same emotion as yours. Having your feeling validated by someone else serves to open and intensify the emotion, allowing you the opportunity to feel it. Validation from another person of your feelings is powerful. Again, you don't want the listener to be talking and potentially taking you out of your emotions. It is important that you feel comfortable and safe enough with your listener to feel the emotions that are coming up, and it is important for the listener to allow you to do so.

Perhaps the best way to explain this is to give you an example. As we were working on Chapter Six one day, talking into a tape recorder, we had the following conversation.

☙❧

Kathleen: Something I am wondering about is the step of nurturing a feeling, of learning to treat yourself with compassion around your painful money scripts. For example, one of my deepest scripts is, "You have to wait your turn. If you're good, sooner or later, you'll get your turn." Now that has nothing to do with money specifically, but it's very tied in to my money issues. So it seems to me in order to heal that, I need to nurture the difficult emotions around that script by having compassion around it, because there's so much pain there. It makes sense for me to look at that script from a nurturing adult or mothering perspective and say, "It's okay, you were just a little kid when you learned that. It's a belief that's not complete. But don't beat yourself up about it."

Rick: When you said you have a script that "if you're good, sooner or later, you'll get your turn," I felt sadness and hurt. That belief hasn't served you well, has it? Because you have waited, and you've still not gotten your turn.

Kathleen: And I still—there's sadness that comes up, just talking about it.

(A pause, with Kathleen experiencing a sensation of tightness in her throat and then tears beginning to gather.)

Rick: What you were speaking just then were thoughts. I sense there's a huge amount of sadness behind the thoughts. And just by me saying what I was feeling when you were telling me about your script, the hurt and sadness intensified in you.

Kathleen: So, when you responded to me by telling me what you were feeling, that let me know this is a safe place to admit how I feel, and to feel it.

Rick: And the reason those feelings came up for you was because I was listening to you emotionally. This is really a wonderful example that shows the thoughts aren't what's important, what matters is the emotion, in your case the huge amount of sadness that is behind it.

∂∞√

This conversation, which didn't start out to be "money therapy," is an example of emotional listening. Rick's feedback helped Kathleen intensify and feel the sadness behind her money script, resulting in increased clarity for her. His ability to empathize, to feel his own feelings in response to hers, was a demonstration of his interior awareness. Part of interior awareness is learning to recognize and feel your own feelings, and part of it is learning to listen to others emotionally, in turn helping them to recognize or validate their feelings. It includes being able to say, "When you said that, here's what I felt."

This is important for reasons other than just becoming a more empathetic person. If we want to help others be free of the money scripts that are giving them grief, we need to learn to respond from the interior rather than reacting from the exterior. We need to get out of our head and into our emotions. Even financial professionals would serve their clients well by practicing emotional listening.

The ability to listen empathetically and to be aware of your own feelings is also a useful aid in all sorts of interactions with other people. Whether you are listening to a child, discussing the month's budget with your spouse, or negotiating a business transaction, hearing the other person from an emotional as well as a cognitive level can provide valuable information to help the transaction go more smoothly for both of you.

It is important when practicing emotional listening to focus on your own emotions and body sensations. Often, in our interactions with other people, we respond unconsciously to what we sense or assume they are feeling. Yet we really don't know what another person is feeling; we can only be sure of what we are feeling in response to their words. So the ability to notice and communicate only what you are experiencing is important. If you can say, "When you said that, I felt this," the other person has a chance to tell you whether your emotion matches theirs. If, instead, you make assumptions about someone else's emotions, the result can be that person feeling discounted or unheard—the exact opposite of what you are trying to accomplish.

There is another benefit of having someone listen to you emotionally. That is the power that comes from simply being heard, accepted, and affirmed.

Just sharing a painful money story and saying out loud what you are feeling can help dissipate that painful emotion.

One reason this is important is that the cycle of financial unconsciousness can be shaming and isolating. It's easy to believe that somehow everyone else knows how to do it right, that you're the only one on the playground who wasn't given the rules to the game. When you begin to talk about how you feel, you may be amazed to learn that so many other people feel just the same way. This factor alone can be very healing and is an additional component of interior awareness.

Individual Psychotherapy

When you say the word "therapy" to ten different people, you are more than likely to get ten different definitions. Some will say therapy means talking to a counselor about your problems; others will equate it with being put in an intimidating group situation and confronted for hours on end; others will describe it as sitting peacefully in the woods or doing something they love.

Psychotherapy, by our definition, is a process that is not a lot different from having a friend be an emotional listener. The difference is that the psychotherapist has completed at least a master's degree and probably has many more tools than does your friend to help get you past the difficult areas.

For most of us, considering going to a therapist or counselor for the first time brings on a huge amount of difficult emotion. For many people, seeing a counselor is a foreign, frightening, or foolish idea. It may seem to be simply "washing your dirty laundry in public." Others may think it is treatment only for the mentally ill or seriously disturbed. Many people have unconscious scripts like the following: "Only people who are really screwed up go to counseling." "To go to a counselor means you are weak; it is an admission of failure." "A successful, healthy person does not need to go to a counselor." "Only emotional wrecks and people who just can't cope go to counselors."

The first time many people visit a counselor, they feel as much shame as they would going into a porn shop.

Telling the average person it would be helpful to visit a counselor will be met with the same enthusiasm you might receive if you told your spouse he or she was overweight and should make an appointment with a personal trainer and attend the next Weight Watchers meeting.

There is a common perception that, if you are going to a counselor, something must be wrong with you. Well, that is partially true, isn't it? So what's wrong with being wrong? Something is wrong with all of us, including almost everyone's relationship with money. Many things are right, too.

Therapy is as much about seeing what is right as it is seeing what is wrong.

Therapy is not magic that will heal you of your emotional or financial ills. Nor is it about the counselor controlling your thoughts or making you do anything you are unwilling to do. Much of therapy consists of supportive, skilled listening and feedback. The counselor may offer exercises to help you gain insights into past events or patterns of behavior. You may be given suggestions about changes you could make in your behavior or about new ways to think about circumstances in your life. You will not be coerced into making any of those changes. Therapy helps you uncover what is behind some of the behaviors or emotions in your life that are causing you difficulties. It helps you understand yourself and the significant people in your life more completely. It can help you reframe and heal painful experiences from your past, like money scripts, as well as cope with difficult times in your current life.

If you fell and broke your ankle, you wouldn't hesitate to go to a clinic or the emergency room. Nor, most likely, would you think twice about seeing your doctor for a pain in your stomach or a recurring infection. You know the doctor has the skills to help you heal a physical difficulty, and you don't assume you should be able to take care of it yourself. In the same way, counselors can help us heal our emotional difficulties. There should be no more shame around seeing a counselor than there is about going to a physician. They are professionals with the expertise to guide us through painful times.

Group Psychotherapy

Individual work with a counselor is a powerful tool for healing. So is group therapy. This kind of work comes in all different shapes, sizes, and colors. So let us be clear about the type of group therapy that we espouse. We're not talking about "encounter groups." We are describing healing groups led by professional therapists who are trained and skilled in facilitating this kind of work.

There are two basic classifications of group therapy: groups that are more cognitive or talk-based, and those that are more activity-based or what we might call theatrical. This latter type, often referred to as experiential group therapy, is the approach that we have found the most powerful in modifying entrenched money scripts and permanently changing behaviors. "Experiential" can be a scary word to someone unfamiliar with group therapy. Experiential therapy, however, simply means using techniques beyond just talking to access both the intellect and the emotions. Today we have dozens of approaches that are experiential in nature. Music, dance, theater, movement, exercise, yoga, art, animal-assisted therapy, meditation, books, movies, play, etc., are all being mined for their potential to help people live mentally healthier lives.

One of the goals of this kind of therapy is to find experiential ways to help clients understand a difficult concept. The idea is to engage as many of the senses as possible. Participants might be asked to draw pictures, move around the room, put charts up on walls, play music, or see a physical representation of a concept. They may be encouraged to express anger in physical ways that will not hurt themselves or others.

A powerful tool often used in psychotherapy groups is psychodrama or sculpting. Other members of the group assume the roles that relate to an issue that one person wants to work with. They might play this person's parents, spouse, boss, or children, for example. The therapist guides the role-players in representing an incident from the past or setting up a "sculpture" that represents the painful circumstance in the person's life. These dramatic representations can be sources of compelling insight, clarity, and healing.

Group psychotherapy takes advantage of the presence of the group members, who are untrained but who are on their own interior journeys. Those members contribute amazing insight and wisdom to one another. As long as a competent therapist maintains a safe, non-shaming, and structured environment, the participation and perspective of the additional "untrained counselors" is extremely valuable.

It is imperative that group members are never manipulated or shamed into participating in anything they do not want to do.

In a legitimate group, "No" and "I pass" are complete sentences. Another essential rule of group therapy is complete confidentiality about other members' work. Group psychotherapy only works when the participants know it is a safe and supportive place.

We have both participated in group psychotherapy at various times. Under the guidance of a skilled therapist, it is a wonderfully effective tool.

Anger Discharge

Anger is an especially difficult emotion for many of us. It may be hard to imagine letting yourself feel anger within the context of feelings meditation, journaling, emotional listening, or psychotherapy. After all, most of these imply calmness, serenity, and detachment. Surely there isn't a place there for anger. Shouldn't we be trying to get beyond anger?

Well, yes, eventually. But first we have to feel it. And sometimes, especially for those with deep anger that has been repressed for a long time, feeling anger may involve something more than writing, sitting quietly with our eyes closed, or talking to someone else.

There is disagreement even among counselors about the best way to deal with anger. An approach that both of us have found helpful is anger discharge work, which involves acting out the anger in a physical way that won't hurt you or anyone else.

One of the best ways to do anger discharge work is in an experiential group therapy session. Anger can be expressed in many ways, such as twisting a sheet, kicking a large pillow, or beating a pillow with a foam or plastic bat. A certain amount of screaming and swearing are often involved, as well. That may sound absolutely bizarre to you, childish or self-indulgent or just plain silly. Nice, adult people just don't do that sort of thing.

That is precisely the problem. We don't. Many of us don't allow ourselves even to feel anger. Our parents have told us we shouldn't, churches tell us that anger is a sin, and society tells us that anger is unacceptable. So what happens for some of us is that we build up a reservoir of anger and resentment that simmers and festers until it turns to rage. That rage colors everything we do. It may come out in the form of sarcasm, chronic complaining, bullying those around us, or outbursts of anger that are way out of proportion to the events that triggered them. Or it may turn inward, making us tense and edgy and even physically ill. Unresolved anger around money issues often results in unfortunate, knee-jerk financial decisions.

Sometimes the only way to get rid of that rage is to express and discharge it physically in a safe environment. Our experience suggests not everyone can meditate it away. We also have learned that no one can bury it successfully under a bandage of false serenity.

There's a difference between discharging anger and indulging it. Some use anger as a tool to manipulate and control others. You can use shouting, swearing, and beating on something to increase your anger or add to a sense of self-justification. Indulging anger in this way is destructive rather than helpful, and it isn't what we're talking about.

Anger discharge work is about getting through the anger so you can access the other difficult feelings (usually hurt, sadness or fear) that almost always lie beneath it. It is another way of dissipating the difficult emotions attached to painful money scripts. In the work that we have done or seen others do with the help of therapists, the process of discharging anger has almost always ended with clarity, compassion, or forgiveness. This is the exact opposite of indulging or fueling one's anger. It is similar to what parents try to teach small children about anger: yes, it's okay to feel angry; no, it's not okay to hit somebody or call them ugly names. This kind of work is meant to help you feel your anger in safe, non-destructive ways instead of taking it out on those around you.

Both of us, after learning how to do anger discharge work in group therapy situations, have also found it useful to do individually.

CRCK

Rick: Fortunately, I got into an experiential therapy group about a year before my first marriage ended. Learning how to appropriately and safely discharge anger is what kept me clear, almost kept me alive, during my divorce. My wife and I decided that rather than go through an ugly and expensive trial, we would use mediation. The experience was intense, and as you might imagine, the atmosphere was anything but friendly and supportive. Our biggest issues were financial: how to split up our assets. Quite often, the difficult emotions would become so intense that neither of us could continue, and we would take a recess. During the recesses, I couldn't exactly call an emergency group therapy session. Instead, I'd go home and find a cathartic way to release and discharge the anger I felt. In this way, I was able to express my anger privately and get it out of the way, rather than yelling at my wife or letting that anger push me into making impulsive decisions during the mediation. When I returned, I was empty, objective, and ready to negotiate.

Using the tool of anger discharge enabled me to stay focused on the goal of this process: working out a financial settlement that was fair to both of us. Had I not been able to keep my anger out of the negotiations, chances are we both would have succumbed to the temptation to use the money issues to manipulate or punish one another. We almost certainly would have ended up in court.

I am absolutely convinced that using this tool saved the mediation process—and saved us at least $40,000 in legal fees and other expenses. Assuming I spent a total of about two hours doing anger discharge, I made each of us about $10,000 an hour. Doing my interior work not only allowed me to participate in the mediation with more integrity; it also resulted in a practical, measurable financial benefit for both parties.

꙳

CKCF

Kathleen: A few months after Wayne's death, all the vehicles from his construction company were parked at a storage lot while his partner worked out the details of closing down the company. I went and bought a cheap plastic broom, and I took it out there and walked around among the trucks and cranes and Bobcats that had been so much a part of his life. I beat on some of them with the broom, and I kicked tires, and I had my own private temper tantrum. I was just so angry that he was gone, and I took some of that anger out on the equipment that was a representation of my loss. There was no way I was going to hurt any of those big vehicles with a little plastic broom, nor did I hurt myself with it. I ended up by leaning against an old blue and white pickup and just sobbing. The anger was just another aspect of my grief, and expressing it so physically helped me do what I needed to do, which was feel the sadness beneath it.

స్గ్

We're not necessarily advising you to go out and thump on things whenever you get mad. If, however, you encounter a lot of anger as you start accessing your feelings, and you don't know what to do with that emotion, it's possible that working with a counselor who understands anger discharge work could be valuable for you. This is especially true if some of your money scripts have been created out of traumatic events or abusive situations. In cases like these, we would strongly recommend doing some work with a therapist.

We also want to make clear that this kind of work is not necessarily something you need to do on an ongoing basis.

Discharging anger is most valuable when it is done to drain away and clean out a festering pool of accumulated rage.

Once that has been done, feelings of anger can be restored to their proper perspective. Then, if you're angry at someone in the here and now, for something they have done in the here and now, you are more likely to be able to express that anger appropriately. It won't be contaminated by all the old anger that you've stored up. In that case, you commonly won't have any need to go scream and shout and beat on something. You'll be able to deal with the anger cleanly, before it turns into rage.

12-Step Groups

Participation in a 12-step group is another tool that may be valuable in your interior journey. As we have said previously, a 12-step group is crucial if you find yourself addicted to alcohol, drugs, food, sex, or even work. If you are so locked into a cycle of suffering as to be addicted, chances are that not only are you unaware of your destructive behaviors and repressed feelings, you probably insist that your behaviors are normal, you have no repressed feelings, and that it is everyone else who has the problems.

Twelve-step groups are a wonderful way to find out that the millions of us with addictions and addictive personalities are not terminally unique and that others have the same struggles, thoughts, and behaviors.

℞

Rick: The first time I ever went to a 12-step group, I didn't go back for about six months. I couldn't believe I belonged in such a useless setting. Here were a dozen or so people, all sitting in a circle, taking turns talking about their problems and feelings. There was no moderator, no order, and worst of all, no one giving any solutions about how to fix the problem. This wasn't the place for me. I couldn't envision a worse waste of my time than waiting my turn to talk about problems that I really didn't believe I had, and then hearing no feedback or advice. When the speaker was done speaking, all you got was a collective group, "Thank you." Good grief!

I decided to try the 12-step program again six months later. My wife had left me, which of course deepened my pain. A friend whom I highly respected had just joined a 12-step program and said he had more insight and relief from "the program" than from his 20-year membership in his church. That got my attention. I started attending meetings and still do to this day.

⇝⇜

Typically, emotions are more talked about than felt at 12-step meetings, although feeling them is certainly not off limits in a meeting. You will want to shop around for a good, healthy group that is a good fit for you. Not all groups are the same, and not everyone in a 12-step meeting is mature. We recommend you attend six meetings before making a determination on the group and its ability to meet your needs.

If you are addicted to alcohol, drugs, or food, you can find help in Alcoholics Anonymous, Narcotics Anonymous, or Overeaters Anonymous. If you don't have an active addiction, we suggest you try Al-Anon, Al-Anon for Adult Children of Alcoholics, or Emotions Anonymous. Many people think of Al-Anon as only for spouses of alcoholics, but the only requirement for membership is "a problem with alcohol in a relative or friend." This will fit almost anyone. Many Adult Children of Alcoholics or Emotions Anonymous meetings include those who have been raised in dysfunctional homes or who are in relationships with people who have past or active addictions or compulsive personalities.

A crucial component of all 12-step groups is anonymity. Members identify themselves by first names only and are not to talk about other members outside of the group. Anything discussed at a meeting is absolutely not to be repeated. This powerful tradition makes meetings a safe place to talk about even deep and painful experiences and emotions.

While money is rarely discussed at any of these meetings, that is not important. The skills and perspective you can gain are tools that will help you with your journey to the interior, help you start uncovering your money scripts, and help you become aware of the feelings around those scripts. You have plenty of other scripts in your life that are not directly related to money. As you begin to understand how to identify those scripts, the money scripts will fall into place as well.

Twelve-steps meetings can be one of the most useful tools you will find for your own spiritual and emotional growth. They are also one of the least expensive. There are no membership dues or fees. Groups just pass the hat, and a dollar or two per person is sufficient to pay the rent for the meeting room.

Practicing Interior Awareness

There is one more piece around interior awareness. Once you've learned to identify a money script and to be at ease with a difficult feeling, you aren't magically healed and transformed. This isn't something you only do once. The same feelings and beliefs are going to come up again and again. The difference is that you will be able to recognize them and to use them; and you'll be able to do that more quickly and easily.

CR

Rick: When, in my morning feelings meditations, I started consciously practicing being at ease with difficult emotions, I became aware of a huge knot of fear in my midsection. It was way down in my pelvis. Every morning when I got up, I felt that fear. My big fear typically is around money issues and security. I have a money script that my funds will run out and I'll be destitute. So that knot of fear didn't just pop up, it had been there for a long time. I had only become aware of it through practicing feeling meditations.

Over a period of two or three months I'd get up every morning and spend five or ten minutes just practicing feelings meditation and being at ease with and embracing that knot of fear. It didn't go away. But over that time, I felt it move. It gradually moved up—to my stomach area, to my heart area, into my throat. One day I went into that fear, and there was just a rush of energy moving upward in my body. It was absolutely incredible.

And from that day forward, I have never had that chronic knot of fear. Have I felt fear around money issues? Yes. Have I awakened in the middle of the night, because income wasn't coming in, and felt fear? Yes. But have I let go the chronic fear that held that money script in place? Yes. Typically now I can move through acute fear associated with that money script in as little as two minutes, maybe half an hour at the most.

❧❧

Once you have identified a difficult emotion, learning to be at ease with it is the most difficult step. Just letting that feeling be, accepting and feeling it, is so important but so challenging. It feels unproductive, useless, and silly. This is the point at which you encounter all sorts of temptation to go distract your mind with something or to jump up and take some kind of action.

Instead, we want to emphasize again that what you need to do is to embrace the feeling, just feel it and let it be.

Let yourself feel, without doing anything about the feeling.

This is the "pause." This is giving yourself time. That time may be a few minutes while you're still sitting with the feeling. Or it may be a few hours or even a few days. Once the feeling begins to dissipate, you will have time to let your thoughts return and to think and collect additional information. This is the place where you begin to do something different.

This pause is the part of the process that helps you stop your former unconscious behavior. Once you have learned how to identify your feelings out in the "real world," the pause can keep you from doing something stupid.

To put this into a money context, suppose the market is selling off and you're watching your stock portfolio go down by one percent a day. Of course you're going to have the thought, "Oh, my God, I'm going to lose all my money; I need to sell."

If you are in the cycle of financial unconsciousness, you will react unconsciously to that thought; you will panic and sell. If you have learned to operate consciously, you will have that thought, let it go, feel the fear, and get through to clarity. You'll be able to pause. Then you can remember that markets go up and markets go down, and you want to buy when they're on sale. So the decision may be, "I'll go buy some stock."

The pause gives you a chance to acknowledge your feeling, absorb it, and make room for some logical thought and an understanding of what else you might need to find out about this situation. Then you can make a decision consciously.

Another aspect of practicing interior awareness is to communicate what you are feeling. Once you know what you feel, and you have learned to be at ease with a difficult feeling, then the next step is to ask, "Okay, what do I need to do with this?" We have said that a painful feeling is often a signal or a message that something is wrong. Well, if something's wrong, then perhaps you need to fix it.

Expressing your feelings or taking action is a matter of integrity and honoring yourself.

No matter how well you understand and can feel your feelings, if you don't have the courage to speak up or to do something different, all you will have is educated pain. You might have learned how to move into consciousness, but you haven't learned to change the behavior that is causing the pain.

By letting go of the money script (the thought) and feeling the emotions that keep it entrenched, by going through that process to reach clarity, you aren't necessarily done with having any emotion around that money script. For one thing, there could be a lifetime of emotions there that need to be released. For another, new situations can come up that generate new emotions. But there is something that shifts when you become conscious of a script and learn how to be at ease with the feeling. It doesn't have the same power over you because you know that you can get through to clarity. You're not unconscious any more.

The more at ease you become with a difficult feeling, the easier it is to become at ease with it the next time. And the less power it has. So this process is not about fixing a difficult emotion once, but about healing over a period of time.

Another part of practicing interior awareness, especially in relationship to other people, is the fact that your own clarity or serenity is always going to come from within. The world outside is always going to be chaotic. Your plate is always going to be full, and the world around you is always in chaos. Even if you became a hermit and went out into the woods to find serenity, you'd run into rain, hail, snow, ants, bees, and stickers—not to mention lions and tigers and bears—and you would still have money problems. You aren't ever going to be able to control your external environment. Living consciously is something you do from the inside.

9

Living Authentically

The larger purpose behind financial integration is learning to live authentically. This happens when you are doing what is genuinely important to you, and when your values and aspirations are aligned with your behavior. Living authentically naturally creates authentic energy, which is having the vitality, courage, and enthusiasm you need to achieve your life aspirations and authentic goals. It is speaking and acting in accordance with your beliefs so your behavior is congruent with who you are. It is finding your own voice and being able to express yourself fully. In the phraseology of one associate of Rick's, it is "going for the gusto."

There are two components necessary to create authentic energy: living in authenticity and removing exterior and interior barriers. This chapter covers living authentically, and the next one deals with barriers.

Kathleen: I'm writing this shortly after coming home from a Toastmasters meeting. I gave a speech this morning, and it was well-received. I got enthusiastic applause, a glowing evaluation, and a request to present the same talk at an upcoming conference. So at the moment I am on an oratorical high.

Giving that speech was great fun for me. Unlike many people, I enjoy public speaking. I like teaching people about a topic I care about, watching audience members react to what I say, and making people laugh. I like being in front of an audience, being onstage as the "star" rather than backstage as the support person.

Speaking is something I do well. I know I do it well, and I am recognized for doing it well. In front of an audience I feel competent, powerful, and as if I belong.

Even more powerful for me is the experience of reading something I have written and realizing, "Yes! This is good. It's clear and vivid, and it says exactly what I want it to say." Writing is my most important gift, the one I feel most compelled to use—and the one that for many years I hid away and neglected out of fear. Now that I have begun to use and practice it regularly, I can sometimes spend hours at my computer without any sense of time going by. At times like that, when I am "in the zone," it is absolutely clear to me that I am doing what I am meant to do.

∂∞∞

ℛℐ

Rick: I have just finished facilitating a Financial Integration Workshop where a therapist and I worked with eight people for five days, introducing them to the concepts in this book.

At the closing session I told the group that there is no other place, no other work that so totally satisfies me as does being in the room with those participants. During those five days, I've watched a lifetime of unconscious money scripts come into the light. I've witnessed the struggle, the tears, the difficult emotions, the joy, the hope—and the resulting life-changing transformations.

It is a sacred place to have other human beings trust you enough to open themselves and share their shame and vulnerability with you, and then allow you to witness their newfound enlightenment. It is like the feeling of watching my two children being born. Words just cannot explain the experience. I never feel more alive than when I am in that space, where my vocation of financial planning and my life aspirations all come together. I feel completely energized, confident, and peaceful; at one with myself and God.

∂∞∞

Another way to describe living authentically is being in integrity. When we use the word integrity, we are not talking about "being honest." We are using the Merriam-Webster definition of integrity as "the quality or state of being complete or undivided." Integrity as used in this way means wholeness. By this, we mean behaving in alignment with your most deeply held values, living your own dreams, and doing what you love and are meant to do. Living your life congruently with who you are, what you love, and what you are meant to be creates enormous energy and enthusiasm. The word enthusiasm literally means "God within." Nothing can be more energizing than to live life full of the enthusiasm of doing what you were created to do.

Discovering what you are meant to do is a journey. To make that journey, you need to know where you've been, where you are now, and where you are going. In other words, you need an integrated map.

Following the Right Map

Each of us is on a financial journey. The quality of that trip is largely determined by our consciousness of where we've been and where we are going. The more conscious we are, the more "present" we are for each step and the more we are able to apply the clarity we receive from interior awareness to our future decisions.

Some of us are wandering through life aimlessly, not sure of where we've been or where we are going. When a fork in the road appears, we flip a coin and head off in one direction or the other. As any good Boy Scout knows, the person who is wandering without a compass or map will tend to go in circles. This is a good description of the person caught in the cycle of financial unconsciousness.

Others know where they want to go, but just can't seem to get there. Every road they take is a dead end or comes out at the same place they began. This is what happens to those who, although they may have the necessary exterior knowledge about money, want only to concentrate on the future, without doing the interior emotional work necessary to reach clarity.

Conversely, others know exactly where they have been, but have no clue where they want to go from here. They're doing the tough work of looking at their shadows, but haven't looked into their future and determined what they want life to look like.

And then there are those blessed few who have acquired the exterior knowledge and have done enough of their interior work to figure out where they've been, where they want to go, and what they need to get there. They have an integrated financial map to help them find their way. You will benefit by creating such a map for yourself.

Any successful financial traveler needs a map. When it comes to obtaining a conventional map, you generally have two options. You can make your own map, which will take an enormous amount of skill, time, money, and energy. Or, for a few dollars, you can buy a map from someone who's already done the hard work.

Unfortunately, when it comes to mapping our own financial journey, it isn't that simple. There are no personalized maps we can buy that clearly chart our interior and exterior money journeys, so it is our responsibility to do a lot of our own mapping. Fortunately, we don't have to do all of it alone. We can enlist the aid of counselors to help us with the shadow work of our interior journeys. We can read books and take courses to learn the necessary exterior money knowledge and mechanics. We can employ financial planners to help us apply the mechanics and identify where we want to go.

While you would have trouble finding two financial planners who would agree on the definition of what they do, most would agree that financial planning, by its very name, implies working toward the future. More than any other profession, true financial planners help their clients create financial road maps. Yet, all too often, the clients don't follow the maps. You and your financial planner might agree on a list of tasks to do in order to reach what you perceive as your goals and aspirations: drafting a will, reducing spending, increasing contributions to a retirement plan, or whatever it might be. Yet many of those items never get done.

Why not? Because, no matter how well designed a map may be, you aren't going to get to where you want to go if it's the wrong map. Following a directional map that tells you every turn and highway to take that will get you from La Honda, California, to Oklahoma City, Oklahoma, will not do you a bit of good if you are actually in Denver, Colorado, and want to go to Carlisle, Massachusetts.

No matter how detailed a map may be, it won't take you where you want to go if it's the wrong map.

Maybe your financial planner has drawn a perfect financial road map to take you from point A to point B. That's great, except that really you don't want to go to point B, you want to go to point R. The problem is, you are not consciously aware of that fact. And to complicate things further, you aren't starting from point A, you're actually at point H. You are not aware of that, either. Until you do your own interior work around money, you aren't going to know what point you are starting from or what your desired destination is.

You may spend years trying to follow a map that doesn't take you where you really want to go. Even worse, you may be paying a financial planner to design and redesign that flawed map. You may have instructed the planner to draw a map that is designed to achieve what society says you "should" do. Your map may be for a journey based on what your parents wanted for themselves or for you. It may be drawn according to your spouse's or parents' dreams and goals rather than your own. You may be trying to follow your own map, but you're hauling such a heavy cargo of emotion-laden, non-functional money scripts that you can't make much progress. Or, as we said before, you may just be wandering around aimlessly without any kind of a map at all. Even worse, you may be in complete denial that you even need a map.

The point is this: as long as you are operating unconsciously, you aren't likely to be able to get to where you want to go. You may become angry with "them," the people or circumstances that seem to keep you stuck. You may become very frustrated or ashamed of yourself because you aren't following the map the way you think you're supposed to. Under circumstances like these, it's no wonder you aren't going to have much energy for your trip.

Life Aspirations

A crucial part of creating authentic energy, then, is beginning to draw your own map. The first step is to figure out where you are. That is the purpose of much of the work we have already discussed. The process we've described thus far—becoming conscious of your money scripts, becoming aware of the difficult emotions around some of them, and applying the tools of interior awareness to resolve them—is a major part of determining where you are now and how you have reached that point. The next phase is to start thinking about exactly where you want to go.

That, ultimately, is the purpose behind all the work we are asking you to do. The whole reason for financial integration is to help you do what you are meant to do and become who you want to be. It is being aware of your resources (both exterior and interior), and finding out what needs to be done to move you to where you really want to be. Learning to make conscious financial decisions is not necessarily an end in itself, but an important and powerful step along the path toward reaching your own aspirations. Money is a useful tool that can help you live the kind of life you want, one that is rich with meaning and purpose. Financial integration helps you use that tool effectively.

Let's talk for a moment about aspirations. We are using this word to describe your deepest and most authentic lifetime goals—what you aspire to do and the person you aspire to become. We've chosen that word deliberately, because another meaning of "aspiration" is breathing, especially breathing in. The most fundamental and essential life-giving activity we do is breathing. Our breath is life. So your life aspirations are the most essential, deepest elements of the person you are and want to be. They are as important to your living a full, successful life as breathing is to your living at all.

A life aspiration is a broad dream or purpose
that is authentically yours.

An aspiration is a life purpose, an aim or dream that is authentically yours. You probably will have several, if not many, lifetime aspirations. By our definition, an aspiration is bigger than a goal, which tends to be time-specific and measurable. An aspiration is a big-picture life intention. It is unlikely that your aspirations will be specifically related to money. Having money and making wise financial decisions can certainly help you achieve them, but aspirations are typically bigger than money. They are part of the "what I want to do and who I want to become" destination on your unique road map. Because these are so significant, achieving them is not going to happen overnight. You'll need to take purposeful actions along the way, as you follow the route that will lead you where you want to go.

A little later in this chapter we have several exercises that will help you begin to identify your life aspirations. Before we get to those, let's clarify some of the things that aspirations are not.

When people are asked to start setting goals related to the financial aspects of their lives, many of them will list some of the following: save more, spend less, earn more, plan for retirement, send the kids to college, build a new house, establish a budget, do estate planning, and draw a will. There's certainly nothing wrong with any of those, but they are not typically life aspirations. They are at best goals or, more often, tasks. Tasks are usually small, necessary chores that may or may not be enjoyable, but which move us toward completing a goal. Some of them certainly need to be done in order to achieve one's life aspirations, but they aren't aspirations in themselves.

This confusion over aspirations, goals, and tasks is one reason so many of us have dutifully written down "goals" we think we want to do, only to stick the list away in a drawer and disregard it except for the occasional pang of guilt when we think about the items on it that we've never gotten around to. All too often, these "goals" are lists of "shoulds" or tasks, those mundane activities we know we are supposed to do but don't have the energy to accomplish. They are often accompanied by the difficult emotions of guilt, shame, or fear. There is typically no joy or energy around a task that is not consciously related to a bigger goal or an even bigger life aspiration.

We don't mean to imply that tasks such as saving for retirement or making a will are unimportant. Quite the contrary. Taking care of them is part of being financially conscious and responsible. Many of these tasks are also important steps toward achieving your aspirations. The lack of energy around tasks comes in part because we see them as goals in themselves. What we need to do instead is see them as part of a larger whole. When you look at a beautiful building, you don't see the footings that support it. They are there nevertheless, a crucial part of the entire structure. In the same way, tasks may not be exciting, but they are essential. They are components that help you achieve the goals that support each of your life aspirations.

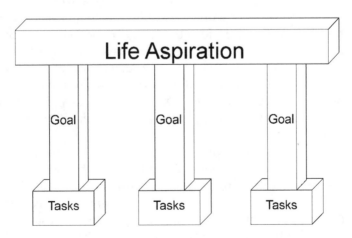

Both of us share a lifetime aspiration of being loving parents. Because Rick's children are young and Kathleen's children are grown, the goals and tasks each of us might have in order to support that aspiration would be quite different. Unlike a goal, aspiring to be a loving parent cannot easily be measured; neither does it have a specific date by which we want to achieve it. Conversely, a goal is something specific and measurable. Rick, for example, has a goal of spending Saturday afternoons with his children. That goal supports his lifetime aspiration of being a loving parent.

But a parent with such a goal will still need to complete certain tasks in order to spend every Saturday afternoon with the kids. Those tasks may be mowing the yard Friday night or cleaning the house on Saturday morning to make time for the children on Saturday afternoon. The lifetime goal would not be to mow the lawn or clean the house. These are typically not "goals" that energize someone, although possibly they could be. These are typically tasks that free someone to accomplish goals. Another example of a task may be ordering tickets to the Saturday matinee of a children's play one month in advance. The task is to order tickets in advance. The goal is to take the children to the play on a specific Saturday, which is another step in fulfilling the life aspiration of being a loving parent.

Part of being a loving parent is providing for children—emotionally, financially, and physically. The task of making a will fits into that aspiration. A loving father will not leave his children in chaos upon his death, having their future decided by a judge according to a sometimes rigid set of laws. Nor will a loving father leave his 18-year-old child several hundred thousand dollars in life insurance proceeds to spend in any manner he desires without also imparting some written or verbal instructions, guidance, or wisdom. Therefore, the task of having a will or a living trust drawn actually satisfies the larger life aspiration of being a loving father.

Acting in consciousness places a task in a different light. You may become willing to actually endure doing the task when you understand that it will be another stepping stone toward accomplishing your life aspirations. When you see it this way, you might experience joy and satisfaction in completing the task of making a will because you know you have just fulfilled a part of the aspiration of being a good father. Seeing the big picture that the task will help accomplish, rather than focusing on the task, can provide authentic energy to help you accomplish the task.

Here is another example. Probably nine out of ten people would agree with the statement that all of us ought to exercise regularly and eat sensibly. Given our country's current epidemic of obesity, however, it's obvious that far fewer than nine out of ten of us actually do that. "Losing weight" and "working out three times a week" are neck-and-neck competitors for the title of "goal least often achieved."

Let's face it—the initial prospect of changing one's lifestyle to include exercising and eating well isn't especially exciting. It's easier to watch television than to go to the gym, more tempting to have a piece of cake than a serving of broccoli. As a consequence, many of us don't have a lot of initial energy around these when we set them as goals for ourselves.

Suppose, though, that one of your life aspirations is to be a traveler. How necessary is good health to traveling? Essential, as anyone could tell you who has traveled or tried to travel without good health. In addition, the longer you remain in good health, the longer you are able to travel. Therefore, establishing good health habits as early in life as possible is fundamental to supporting a life aspiration of travel. In fact, maintaining good health is as essential to traveling as is having adequate financial resources to fund your traveling.

Maintaining good health would include establishing and following a specific food plan, having an annual check-up, and establishing and maintaining a specific exercise program three to five times a week. All of those can be goals that are measurable and have specific dates by which you want to complete them. In order to achieve your specific goals, you are going to have to carry out some ongoing, consistent tasks, which might include joining the health club, employing a personal trainer, buying an exercise video, rearranging your schedule to make time for working out, or reading books about food preparation. It will be easier to stick with those tasks when you are clear about the larger goal and the even larger life aspiration behind them.

In addition, because the aspiration is so important to you, you will put some care and effort into designing the goals and tasks in such a way that you are more likely to do them. You might try a martial arts or yoga class, you might set up regular walking dates with a friend or family member, or maybe you'll bring the treadmill in from the garage and put it in front of the television set. Maybe you'll learn to cook interesting low-fat meals or experiment with some of the exotic fruits in the produce section. When these tasks are building blocks toward one of your life aspirations, you may begin to view them as investments in yourself rather than "shoulds" that you are supposed to do.

One way to think of life aspirations is as the "why" behind the "what." You might list "becoming financially independent by age 50" as a life aspiration. We would suggest that this is a "what," which is closer to a goal rather than a life aspiration. It needs to be even more clearly defined. Don't stop there, but go on to ask yourself, "Why do I want financial independence by age 50? What would I do with that independence if I had it? How much money represents being 'financially independent' to me?" Before you can answer those questions you need to know what you want to do, where you want to do it, and how much money it will take. Answering those questions will take you toward discerning your life aspirations.

The remainder of this chapter consists of exercises to help you identify your life aspirations. The exercises have several sections and may seem at first glance to be overly complicated or long. Please, don't allow that to deter you. Take them one step at a time, but do the exercises. They are some of the most important and most rewarding ones in the book.

Life Aspirations Exercise

Part 1

Pretend you have a fairy godmother who can give you all the money, time, and talent that you can ever want. What have you always dreamed of doing or becoming—physically, mentally, emotionally, and spiritually? Write down whatever comes to mind or has ever come to mind. Dream big, be outrageous; reality is not important in this exercise. You have complete freedom. What you put down can be complete fantasy and can have nothing to do with the reality of your current situation. The more daring, the better.

The list may include items like these: building a new home on the beach, swimming with the sting rays, writing a best-selling book, going to the moon, becoming a world-class skater, directing a movie, singing with Garth Brooks, becoming President of the United States, living in Europe, or raising award-winning roses.

Part II

Life aspirations can be described as broad and important dreams that you hope to do or become over your lifetime. Most of us have several of them. Look at each item above and ask yourself, "Why do I want to do this? What desire will it satisfy?" When you figure out the underlying reason for each item on your list, write it down on a separate piece of paper that we'll call your life aspirations worksheet. Start each one with the words, "to be..." For example, if you want to take your kids to Sea World, this may satisfy your desire to be a good parent, so you would write "to be a good parent." You may want to travel to remote places or to the moon, so you might write down "to be an adventurer."

Part III

After a long and full life, you have passed away. Your funeral or memorial service is today. Imagine all of your family members, friends, and co-workers at that memorial service. Each of them has prepared an acknowledgment of you, describing all you did or became in your life. They are about to read what they have written. You will be taking notes on what they say.

One by one, the most important people in your life take the podium and speak about you. What do you *hope* each would say about you and your life, what you *did* and what you *became*? Be specific and write several paragraphs that summarize what you would want them to say.

Part IV

Boil down what the people at your gathering above said about you to brief phrases describing your characteristics. Again, on your life aspirations worksheet, write these phrases with, "to be..." For example, if someone said, "She was always so supportive of her co-workers," you might write, "To be a mentor." Some of these phrases may duplicate ones you already have from part II, so you won't need to write them down again.

Part V

Now go to your life aspirations worksheet and look at all your "to be…" statements. Which ones really reflect your intentions in life? Leave every statement that is true, whether you feel you have accomplished it or not. Cross out any that don't resonate with you. Add any additional ones that come to mind. You should now have a complete list of your life aspirations. You may feel free to modify this list as often as you need. In fact, we recommend that you do this exercise annually. Even though it may change over time, this list will become the foundation or the touchstone of every goal you set out to achieve.

It is not uncommon to struggle a bit with this exercise your first time through. You may be like Laura, who uncovered lifetime goals of becoming a missionary and going into nursing, but had some trouble finding a common life aspiration "to be a healer." Don't worry; it takes some time to reduce lifetime desires, goals, and intentions down to a simple, but broad, life aspiration.

Doing this exercise will help you become more conscious of your life purposes and what you are doing to achieve them. Once you have a set of conscious life aspirations, you can use them to generate and test your goals. Goals are specific objectives that will help accomplish or fulfill at least one life aspiration. Some goals will satisfy several life aspirations.

For example, some of Rick's life aspirations are to be authentic, to be wise, to be a student, to be a seeker, to be a healer, and to be a teacher. These aspirations are supported by many goals he has had, including obtaining his Master's Degree in personal financial planning, co-creating the Financial Integration Workshop, and writing this book.

Authentic Goals

Now you are ready to begin to develop your authentic goals, followed by the tasks that will be necessary to move you toward realizing your life aspirations.

Authentic Goals Exercise

Part I

Label a piece of paper your "authentic goals worksheet." Now, review your life aspirations worksheet. On your authentic goals worksheet we want you to list some actions or things you might want to do, be, or have that would move you closer to fulfilling your life aspirations. Don't worry about how much these things may cost or how much time they might take to get. Let the items come spontaneously from within you. Quickly write down whatever comes up, no matter how silly or frivolous it sounds. Again, this is no time to censor yourself. Try to list 20 to 30 specific goals. Here is a sample list:

- Learn to fly an airplane
- Take the kids on a vacation
- Buy a new house
- Remodel my kitchen
- Start a new business
- Buy a new car
- Learn to rock climb
- Buy a laptop computer
- Write a novel
- Take a class in marketing
- Buy a vacation home
- Join a quilting club
- Volunteer at the hospital
- Visit the grandkids more often
- Go dancing

Part II

Look at the goals on your authentic goals worksheet. Do these goals fill you with enthusiasm? Or do some of them leave you with heaviness or dullness? Cross off the goals that don't excite you, that feel heavy. That doesn't necessarily mean these are things you won't do. But these may be tasks: getting rid of credit card debt, making a will, fixing the roof, getting health insurance, etc. Notice how different tasks feel from authentic or heartfelt goals. One key for determining whether you have a task or a goal before you is to ask yourself: "Will I feel relieved when it is done?" If the answer is yes, chances are the item is a task.

Now, pick the goal that excites you the most, put the number one beside it, and circle the number. Look at your list again, pick the next goal that energizes you, put the number two beside it, and circle the number. Continue until you have prioritized all of your goals. Now, go back and assign a dollar cost to each goal, if any.

Part III

Now you are going to look at your prioritized goals on your authentic goals worksheet and test them for their authenticity and attainability. Select the goal that you marked as number one. Check it with the acronym TEST:

- Is it **True**? Make sure the goal fulfills at least one life aspiration on your worksheet. Then, on a scale of one (low) to 10 (high), rate how much you want to see the action item completed in an attainable amount of time. If it is a seven or less, cross it off the list.

- Is it **Exact**, explicit, precise? Being vague about what you want keeps you in the cycle of financial unconsciousness. You will accomplish this goal or you won't. Leave no escape routes; nail down your goal. Make sure your goal is not another life aspiration. Those are broad rather than exact. Authentic goals are exact and specific.

- Is it **Sensible**? A goal needs to be a stretch, but not impossible. Make the goal worth the challenge, but something that is attainable. If this goal will require money, you will want to work out a financial plan to assure that achieving it is possible.

- Is it **Time-based**? Pick a specific date by which you will obtain or start this action item in the next few months, year, five years, or 10 years.

- Now select the goal that you numbered as your second priority and go through this same process until all of your goals have been TESTed.

Part IV

The next step is to look at all your goals that have been successfully TESTed and assign any tasks that will help you reach them. Write each of the surviving goals at the top of a separate sheet of paper. On each goal sheet, make a list of tasks to support the goal. Include the date by which you will complete each of them. You may want to put these in a folder or binder so you can conveniently refer back to them. It may be helpful to put them in order of priority.

For example, you may have a life aspiration to be a traveler. Supporting that life aspiration, you may have a goal to take a Baltic cruise by August 1 of next year. Now you need a list of tasks that will move you toward that goal. You will need to select a cruise line, pick an itinerary, determine how much you will spend on the trip, create a plan to accumulate the money, get a passport, employ someone to feed the dog, ask your employer for the time off, and so on. Now you will have an action plan to reach the goal.

Part V

This is for couples. Once you have each listed and prioritized your individual TEST goals, take your top five goals and compare them with your partner's top five goals. Are some of them the same? Are some of them different? The assignment now is for both of you to combine your top five goals into "our goals." While you may have some similar goals, you may not have them in the same priority. Work on combining similar goals, and then on prioritizing all of your similar and individual goals.

This does not mean all of your individual goals need to be combined with your spouse's individual goals. It is important, however, to be able to work together toward mutual goals and also to support one another's individual goals. This may require some compromise and creativity.

For example, you may have a goal of retiring in London to support a life aspiration of living abroad. Your spouse may have a goal of retiring in Omaha, close to the grandchildren, to support a life aspiration of being closely involved with family members. Additionally, you may both have as part of your goals the desire to buy a $300,000 retirement home. The problem may be that it is not realistic to buy two retirement homes, especially if you want to be maintain the resources to travel between the two locations. How will you resolve this issue? Sometimes these resolutions come easily. Other times a lot of difficult emotions may arise, sending you back to uncovering new money scripts and applying our interior tools to reach clarity. Sometimes it requires the assistance of a counselor and financial planner to fully resolve the issues.

Why Wait?

Once you list and identify your life aspirations and their supporting goals and tasks, the question becomes, "Can I obtain today at least part of what I hope to have in my life at some point in the future?" Sometimes you don't have to wait until retirement to have the life you want—that's a real myth in our society. Many times you can have what you really desire much sooner, if you are conscious about it. We are continually amazed at the results that happen to people who go through the process of becoming aware of life aspirations and then establishing goals and tasks. In many cases, people actually accomplish their goals much sooner than they anticipated.

For example, Joe and Lydia went through this process and established a list of goals, many of which they intended to accomplish within three years. One year later they went through the process again and updated their goals for the next year. As Rick was going down their list of goals from the previous year, he inquired about a number of three-year goals from the previous year that did not appear on their new list. "What happened to your goal of giving a stained-glass window to the church three years from now?" "Oh, we did that already." "How about your three-year goal to begin your master's class?" "Oh, I enrolled in the program last year." "How about your goal to take a European vacation, I don't see that on the list." "Oh, we did that, too."

There is something powerful about writing down your life aspirations and the specific goals and tasks needed to accomplish them.

Much has been written on this, so we won't delve into the theory. But we do know that it works. Just the idea of getting a goal out of one's unconsciousness into consciousness is powerful. It sets the mind into action and unlocks authentic energy. When you become conscious, things are set in motion so that the goal tends to happen. The hardest part of this process isn't so much accomplishing the tasks that take you to your goals; it is becoming conscious of the deeper life aspirations.

CRCK

Rick: Three or four years before we began this book, I identified a life aspiration to be a healer and teacher. One of my goals to support these life aspirations was to write a book in five to ten years. Even though I had written a weekly business column in a regional newspaper for ten years, writing a book seemed like an overwhelming task given my "day jobs" of running a financial planning practice, a real estate firm, a mortgage company, and an appraisal practice. But had I focused on what was "practical," I would have never listed writing a book as a goal to support my life aspiration of being a healer and a teacher. I also thought the book I would write would be a very different book on a totally different topic. But just identifying that I wanted to be a teacher and a healer and to write a book set my conscious mind in motion to where it happened, differently and much more quickly than I originally had planned. That sounds a little metaphysical, but truly there is something that happens when we identify authentic aspirations. Going through this process can truly be a life-changing experience.

Getting down to authenticity around who I am and what my life aspirations are is one of the most difficult things I've ever done in my life. Five years ago, I didn't have more than a very foggy notion of what I loved in my life. Ten years ago, had you asked me what I would do on a day off, I couldn't have even answered the question. I was addicted to my work. At the same time, I only liked about 35 percent of my daily tasks. I didn't know that, and it took me about three years of working these exercises over and over to finally get clear. Now, you may say I am just slower than the average Joe, and that may be true. But my experience with my clients would suggest I am not alone. A lot of us get pickled with the notion that "This is just the way it is." Figuring out what it is you really love can be one of the hardest exercises you'll ever undertake as an adult. I know it was for me. And, like a lot of my clients, I suffered a lot of shame in doing these exercises. "I should know this stuff!" was one of my scripts. Well, I didn't, and getting down to authenticity didn't come quickly or easily.

Identifying your life aspirations and authentic goals is essential to living your life with authenticity and integrity. Beginning to do so can generate a great deal of authentic energy. Knowing where you want to go will help you start your journey with a burst of enthusiasm. But you may find that energy slowly subsides or wanes. That is normal and in most cases to be expected. In order to maintain your energy, you may need to get rid of some of the barriers that will make it harder to reach your destination.

Some of these barriers we've talked about before, like uncovering money scripts and applying the interior tools to dissipate difficult emotions. In the next chapter we discuss other barriers and suggest some ways to remove and get past them.

10

Authentic Energy

Inherent in becoming conscious around money is having the energy to take action. You can have all the exterior knowledge in the world about the mechanics of money; you can do your emotional work so you understand clearly what has created your unconscious behaviors and what is needed to change them—but if you don't act, your behavior never changes. You also need the energy to actually follow through and begin to do something different from what you have done in the past. Authentic energy is where you find the power to apply your exterior knowledge and your interior awareness.

Authentic energy is having the vitality, courage, and enthusiasm you need to achieve your life aspirations and authentic goals. It is speaking and acting in accordance with your beliefs, so your behavior is congruent with the person you are. It is finding your own voice and being able to express yourself fully.

However irrational your behaviors might be or may have been around money, they made complete sense in relation to the unconscious money scripts upon which they were based. By becoming conscious of these scripts and then applying the tools of financial integration to change and heal them, you can release yourself from the cycle of financial unconsciousness.

Once an ingrained money script is released from the emotion surrounding it, you set free the energy that was previously diverted to avoiding pain and repressing the difficult emotion.

That energy is now available to assist you in modifying the script and creating new, healthy money behaviors. Creating those new behaviors is foundational to "doing something different." Functional money behaviors allow you to correctly ascertain where you are and where you want to go. This is necessary if you are going to make sound financial decisions that will help you live a full and free life.

Even with your exterior knowledge and interior awareness, however, you may still have trouble tapping into or sustaining your authentic energy. Once you have experienced the initial enthusiasm associated with uncovering your life aspirations and authentic goals, you need the ability to maintain that energy. This is especially true because working against you is what we might oxymoronically call "the energy of entropy." Your natural tendency is going to be to move back toward the habitual and familiar behaviors you are trying to change.

An important part of keeping your energy alive is eliminating barriers, both interior and exterior, that can sap your energy around your goals. Some typical exterior barriers to authentic energy are: lack of the necessary knowledge or money mechanics, an overwhelming project, doing a job you hate, difficult exterior circumstances, poverty, wealth, addictions, and poor physical health. Next are some common interior barriers to authentic energy: insufficient interior work, dependence and victimhood, co-dependency, fear, shame, guilt, depression, blame, and resentments.

We have grouped these energy-blockers into categories, but it isn't possible to separate them completely into their own tidy little boxes. More commonly, several of them will overlap or be tangled up together. Co-dependency or fear, for example, could contribute to someone's staying in an unsatisfying job. Dependency could grow out of either wealth or poverty. So, as we discuss some of these blocks in more detail, keep in mind that they are unlikely to appear in isolation. Neither is this an all-inclusive list. You may well be able to add some specific blocks of your own.

Exterior Blocks

Lack of Exterior Knowledge

For some, this is one of the easiest blocks to deal with. For others, it's among the hardest. Part II of this book provides some basic financial information. You'll find that knowledge necessary to help you gain the energy to accomplish many of your life aspirations, authentic goals, and tasks.

Not having the exterior knowledge required to complete your tasks or goals is certainly a block to authentic energy. Wanting to take a trip to Russia to fulfill a life aspiration of traveling may never happen, for example, if you don't know that international travel is more complicated than just booking a flight. You may not realize you need to obtain both a passport and a visa. Even if you know that much, not knowing how to obtain these documents or what they cost could sap your energy for taking the trip. You might conclude, "It's just too hard."

It is typical either to be drawn naturally to the exterior mechanics of money or to really struggle with it.

If you find exterior finance uninteresting, difficult, and painful, you will need to uncover your hidden money scripts around this area.

This exterior information is a critical component of modifying your money scripts, so it is imperative that you apply the tools of interior awareness to understand how unconscious money scripts may be blocking your ability to get the knowledge you need. Choosing not to learn this information because you "aren't a numbers person" isn't a valid excuse. You don't have to become an expert on investing, but you are absolutely capable of learning the basic mechanics of taking care of your financial affairs.

A Job You Hate

The solution to this particular block is not necessarily just changing jobs. If it were, you would probably have taken care of it already. For many people, going through the life aspirations exercises helps them identify what they want to be doing and whether they are in the right job or profession. Then they can take steps to change what they do, either within their current field or by working toward a different career. For others, job dissatisfaction has more to do with the relationships around work or the circumstances of a particular job, rather than the type of work they are doing. Solutions for them may be focused less on what they are doing and more on how and where they are doing it.

An Overwhelming Project

Life aspirations without supporting goals and tasks are almost always overwhelming. Even a specific authentic goal can be overwhelming when it is not supported by bite-sized tasks.

When you're faced with the challenge of eating an elephant, it isn't always easy to remember that you have to do it one bite at a time.

Confronting a life aspiration, an authentic goal, or even a huge task that seems overwhelming—whether it is the life aspiration of being a teacher, the goal of writing a book by a specific date, or the task of finding a publisher—can drain so much of your energy that you can't even see how to begin. The process of breaking life aspirations into goals, goals into tasks, and even tasks into sub-tasks, can help you take that first bite, and then the second and the third. This can help you do something, no matter how small or irrelevant it may seem, to start your progress toward accomplishing your goals.

Incompletions

These are broken promises—promises made to yourself as well as others. Incompletions might include unmet goals and aspirations, such as wanting to go back to school but never getting there. They also encompass all those financial-maintenance tasks that will make your life easier or more organized. These are the things you know you need to do, but you keep putting off: making a will, setting up a spending plan, or beginning to invest.

One major incompletion can be debt. Living under a burden of high credit-card balances, student loans, or other debt can suck away incredible amounts of energy. This issue is so pervasive and so important that we discuss it in detail in Chapter 11.

Many incompletions deal with money mechanics or the "housekeeping" aspects of having your life in order. Here is a simple checklist to help you evaluate the financial incompletions in your life. As you read through it, you might want to make a separate list of those you have left unfinished.

1. I pay off my credit cards every month.
2. My spending is under control.
3. My checkbook is balanced.
4. I allow myself vacations and adequate play time.
5. I am saving enough for retirement.
6. I am saving for goals such as cars, a house, etc.
7. I feel good about my career/work path.
8. I have an emergency fund.

9. I have adequate life insurance (10 times my salary).
10. My risk of income loss from disability is covered.
11. I have adequate insurance to cover damages to my property.
12. I have adequate insurance or resources to cover possible long-term care costs.
13. I have a plan in case I live longer than expected and outlive my retirement income.
14. My beneficiary designations are current.
15. I have a plan for meeting my financial goals in the event I become incapacitated.
16. I have a spending plan.
17. I consistently follow my spending plan.
18. My educational saving (for myself or others) is on track.
19. I have clear financial goals for the future.
20. I am at peace with my estate plan.
21. I have discussed my estate plan with family.
22. I am satisfied with my current level of charitable giving.
23. My investment knowledge is satisfactory.
24. I have a current analysis of my investment holdings.
25. My investment allocation is appropriate to my goals.
26. My investment savings programs are in place.
27. I review my financial plan/status at least annually.
28. All my income tax payments are current.
29. I have an updated will or a living trust.
30. I have a financial planner or advisor.
31. I have an attorney.
32. I have a tax advisor.
33. My risk from lawsuits is covered.
34. I have a durable power of attorney.
35. I obtain regular medical exams.
36. My car is in good repair.
37. I promptly return items I borrow.
38. I am current on all my payments.
39. Any friends, family, or co-workers who owe me money have arranged to pay it back in a systematic way.
40. If I am self-employed, my billing is up to date and I don't have a lot of receivables.
41. If I am self-employed, I am charging enough for my services.
42. My personal space (house, closets, garage, desk, and kitchen) is in order.

If going through this list is difficult for you and reveals a great many incompletions in your life, you may want to do more work on this specific area.

Difficult Exterior Circumstances

These are the "life isn't fair" challenges that all of us have to face sooner or later—perhaps a job loss, a serious illness, a special-needs child, the need to care for a difficult elderly relative, or the death of someone you love. Sometimes, when you are faced with one of these, the only thing you can do is get through it. This may mean putting your authentic goals on hold for a while. In some cases, it may mean revising your goals completely. In other cases, it may mean taking time to recover before you continue on the path toward your life aspirations. Almost always, in these circumstances, you may need to use "borrowed energy" by relying on the help and support of those who care about you.

Kathleen: Until Wayne was killed, I always knew logically that life wasn't fair, but I had never fully realized at an emotional level that it could be unfair to me as well as to other people. Yet somehow, quite soon after his death, I was able to understand clearly that what had happened to him and to those of us who loved him was not fair, but it also was not personal. Paradoxically, because life is unfair, but it is unfair to everyone, that makes it fair. We were not being punished or singled out or tested. I took great comfort from a wise letter I received from my cousin Paul, who wrote, "As far as the Universe taking Wayne from you, nothing was meant. It simply must obey its own laws of physics, regardless of our dreams and hopes." In other words, sometimes bad stuff just happens, and all we can do is deal with it the best way we can.

Poverty

If you're a college student, living in a dump with rummage-sale rejects for furniture and really splurging if you put a can of tuna in the macaroni and cheese, you aren't in poverty. You're just broke. For now, you don't have any money, and you may be struggling, but you're on your way to something better. Chronic poverty, on the other hand, can engender a sense of helplessness and hopelessness. Families in poverty are those who live constantly on the edge of failure, with parents who may work hard and do the best they can or parents who may have given up a long time ago. Children who grow up in this kind of poverty need a great deal of energy and determination if they are to overcome the obstacles life has placed in their path. At the same time, they have few places to obtain the tools they need to tackle the job.

Wealth

For anyone who struggles or has ever struggled to pay the bills, the idea of wealth being a burden or a block to anything seems absurd. But ironically, wealth can impede energy just as much as poverty can. Elaine Walker, a wealthy woman with a great deal of wisdom and insight, once told Rick, "I don't know if it is more of a curse to have too little money or too much." There is little to create vigor if you never have to struggle, if you have no need to do anything useful in order to earn a living, if you feel guilty because you have so much, or if you wonder whether your friends are in your life because they care about you or because of your money.

Some of the deepest financial pain we've ever witnessed is the pain of those who inherited generational wealth.

Physical/Emotional Illness

Addiction. An addiction, whether to a substance such as alcohol or to a behavior such as work or spending, is an incredible drain of authentic energy and resources. The addict's primary relationship is always with the addictive substance or behavior, and eventually that leaves little room, time, money, or spirit for anything else in life.

Depression. We have listed this separately from other mental or physical illnesses because it is so strongly tied to a life without vitality or enthusiasm. It also is a hidden illness that people may have for years without recognizing what is wrong. If your life is affected by a pervasive sense of disinterest, sadness, fatigue, and inertia, which does not seem tied to specific difficulties or events, depression is one possible cause.

Poor Physical Health. The relationship between poor health and lack of energy is obvious. If your days are made more difficult by a physical illness, whether that may be arthritis or diabetes or migraine headaches, you will have more difficulty doing the things that you need and want to do.

Interior Blocks

Insufficient Interior Work

We have spent a significant amount of time discussing the importance of gaining interior awareness by doing your interior emotional work. Identifying money scripts and dissolving difficult emotions attached to those scripts is foundational to removing interior blocks and creating authentic energy. Keep in mind that doing interior work is not a one-time event. You can't do a week of journaling or a few months of feelings meditation, see a counselor three or four times, and proclaim yourself finished. Interior work is an ongoing process. We have both been on our own interior journeys for years now, and we're still learning. We hope and intend to keep learning and growing for the rest of our lives.

Financial Dependency and Victimhood

Being dependent for some people means literally that—being dependent on or addicted to alcohol or other drugs. Equally damaging can be dependence on someone or something else—such as parents, spouses, or the government—for one's financial well-being. Financial dependency is a source of great shame: "I can't make it on my own." At the same time, it fosters a sense of entitlement: "They owe me." The combination is a breeding ground for a toxic mess made up of resentment of the hand that feeds you and resentment of yourself for taking the food. That same combination of entitlement and shame also drives a great deal of overspending or undersaving. The money script is, "I am entitled to more."

Someone stuck in dependency typically has the attitude of a chronic victim. Genuine victims are powerless over their circumstances. This would be the case for children in traumatic situations or adults who are victims of particular events such as rape or robbery. However, that same powerlessness isn't usually true of those trapped in chronic victimhood, except in their own minds. The person who chooses to remain a chronic victim isn't able to muster the energy to break out of the cycle.

This is where having had to struggle becomes such an important part of financial integration. The lack of struggle is actually financially harmful in the long run. Children who grow up being handed everything they want or desire will eventually run into a wall of pain when their life script, "There will always be enough money," doesn't work in adulthood. Welfare recipients, of any kind (whether personal, governmental, or corporate), will eventually encounter that same pain when the family or entity providing for them ends its funding. Lynn Twist, in *The Soul of Money,* presents an excellent discussion of this concept as it applies to individuals and even to countries.

Actor and director Roberto Benigni, upon receiving the Best Actor Oscar in 1997 for his film *Life Is Beautiful,* said, "I want to thank my parents for the greatest gift—the poverty." He understood first hand that important lessons are learned in "the struggle." Susan Bradley, CFP®, in her book *Sudden Money*, calls this area of struggle the Neutral Zone. She describes the Neutral Zone as the undeterminable period of time that a person spends between an "ending" and a new "beginning." This is the time when we struggle with gaining the exterior knowledge, the interior awareness, and the energy we need to make a new beginning. Our natural inclination is to try to reduce the time we spend in the neutral zone, getting through it as soon as possible. This can actually be counter-productive. It takes courage to spend time in unfamiliar territory—confused, uncomfortable, disoriented, discovering what you thought was true is not, and developing new belief systems. The reward is coming out the other side with increased wisdom, strength, and clarity.

Financial Co-dependency

Financial co-dependency could be described as unconscious giving. The term "co-dependency" was originally coined to describe a person married to or otherwise in a relationship with an addict. It has since become more widely used to describe someone who focuses excessively on another person. Co-dependent behavior is essentially living one's life on behalf of someone else in ways that are detrimental to both parties. In financial terms it involves giving to others in ways that keep them from having to take responsibility for their own mistakes and behaviors.

For every dependent, there is a co-dependent. Financially, the role of the co-dependent is the person, institution, or government that is the source of funds for those that are dependent. For individuals, this usually means giving or loaning money repeatedly to family members, friends, or significant others, and thereby helping them continue a pattern of irresponsibility. A popular term for this in 12-step communities is "enabling." For institutions, charities, and government agencies, enabling destroys entire generations and industries with entitlements, grants, and corporate welfare. For countries, it means crippling whole nations with handouts, rather than giving them constructive help toward solving long-term problems.

Co-dependency also might mean living your life according to someone else's script, feeling as if you have no right to your own dreams and aspirations, and feeling selfish about putting your own needs ahead of or even equal to those of someone else.

Whichever role co-dependency may play in your financial life, it is founded in fear. One form it often takes is a need to be rigidly in control of your own behavior, the behavior of others, or your surroundings. For parents, this can mean being so fearful of seeing your children in any pain whatsoever that you try to "save" them from the very circumstances that are meant to be their teachers.

Financial planners tell us that parents enabling and bailing out their children and grandchildren financially is one of the most common issues they deal with. *It is also tops on most planners' lists of problems that they are least able to help their client resolve.* Nor is such enabling limited to parents who have enough money to need the services of a financial planner. One elderly woman, who worked hard at menial jobs all her life, was still working in her late 70s when she should have been enjoying some well-earned leisure. In large part, this was because she gave too much of her limited resources to children and grandchildren who continually took advantage of her. In this case, the taking continued even after she died. Her son, who had done little to care for her in her final illness, showed up at her house the day after the funeral with a rental truck and hauled away everything of value.

Fear

This is one of the greatest inhibitors to taking risks and one of the strongest blocks to energy. Fear can take many forms and is intertwined with most of the other interior energy-blockers. Among the ways it can be manifested are perfectionism, self-doubt, and indecision—all of which are simply different ways to describe being afraid of making mistakes. We fear failing, taking risks, looking foolish, not being able to live up to our own or someone else's expectations, or losing what we have.

One of the most paralyzing fears can be fear of succeeding.

Even when you know you are talented and capable, the idea of success can be more frightening than the reality of settling for mediocrity. Fear can suck up all the energy you might otherwise have available to work toward your own dreams and goals.

Shame

Shame, a pervasive and chronic sense of "I'm not worth it" or "I don't deserve this," is another huge energy-inhibitor. It is commonly a part of all the blocks we have already discussed. It especially goes hand in hand with dependency, co-dependency, and self-blame. In addition, many of us carry an incredible amount of shame around money generally—shame over having too much, shame over having too little, or shame over making financial mistakes.

No other topic, including sexual addiction,
carries more shame than does money.

One aspect of shame that is often related to finances comes from the money script, "I should know this." Either there is a hidden belief that managing money is easy, or a belief that if you're smart enough to earn a lot of money you are smart enough to manage it.

Most of us don't have any shame about the other aspects of life that we routinely ask for help with. We go to doctors when we're sick, we hire mechanics to work on our cars, we go to accountants for help with our tax returns, and we send our kids to schools instead of teaching them ourselves. In all of those areas, we need to know enough to know when something is wrong or whether the professionals we hire are competent, but we don't expect to be able to do it all ourselves. Managing our finances is really no different.

℟

Rick. I would say that 90 percent of my financial clients apologize or in some way are defensive about coming in and asking me for help with their finances, especially their investments. Almost all of my new clients tell me something to the effect of, "I know I should know this stuff. I know I could do this, but I don't have the time." They seem to believe it is somehow shameful not to have the skills to manage their own investment portfolios or not to have the interest in doing it. There seems to be a societal message that if you're successful, you will know how to invest your money and you will enjoy doing it. I have learned over the years that one of my first tasks is to address that shame and to help them reframe it.

Suppose this new client is a physician. I'll say, "Well, that's funny, from what I hear you saying you feel kind of ashamed about not wanting to or being able to do your own investments. Yet I'm sitting here, and I don't feel any shame that I don't know how to take out an appendix."

∽∾

Guilt

Guilt is sometimes described as an awareness that, "I have done something bad," while shame is a sense that, "I am a bad person." The guilt that blocks authentic energy around money may stem from past failures and mistakes around money. It can also be deeply entangled with shame. Guilt often comes with having "too much." It's easy to assume that having plenty of money should increase someone's authentic energy. In fact, the opposite is often true. This is especially the case when money is inherited or wealth comes suddenly, but it can also apply to someone who earns a lot of money. Guilt is commonly involved when people give out of obligation rather than a genuine desire to give. It can play a huge part in financial dependency and co-dependency among parents and children. Guilt can also prevent someone from making money; a prime example would be self-employed people who consistently charge less than their services are worth. There are entire professions that have guilt around earning money at their core, such as ministers, therapists, social workers, and many others in the helping professions. At the base of this guilt is a money script that "money is bad."

Blame

Blame and resentment focus attention outward, away from one's own possible failings. If you are stuck in a low-paying job or didn't get a promotion, it's because "they" won't give you a break. If you blew this month's budget by eating out way too much, you "couldn't help it" because you were so stressed at work you didn't have time to cook. If you have made mistakes and poor financial decisions, it's "not your fault," it's because your parents were so messed up and didn't teach you better.

R&

Rick: In September 2003, *The Wall Street Journal* ran a story on the original Healing Money Issues Workshop (later renamed the Financial Integration workshop) that Ted Klontz and I led at Onsite Workshops. The reporter, Jeff Zaslow, attended one day of the program and sat in on a lecture that included a discussion of how blame and resentment block authentic energy. Two days later I was horrified when I picked up the *Journal* and read the headline to his story: "Money Hang-ups: Another Thing to Blame on Your Parents." It was exactly 100 percent opposite to the message of the workshop and the lecture.

Having been a columnist for over ten years, I knew that reporters don't write their own headlines. That is the job of the copy editors. Jeff's story was excellent and accurate, but apparently the subject matter triggered an unconscious money script in the copy editor, who wrote the headline according to something other than the content of the article.

ॐ∽ॐ

While outside factors and other people certainly are elements in anyone's difficult circumstances, blaming your difficulties on someone or something else keeps you from taking responsibility even for what is legitimately your part of a problem. It also wastes much of the energy you could be using to help make things better. Most of the time, we participate to some degree in creating our own difficulties, and concentrating on changing the things we can is a far more constructive use of energy than is blaming others for the things we cannot change.

The opposite face of blame is self-blame, which is focused inward and is no more accurate than focusing outward. Assuming everything is your own fault is just as skewed a perception as is assuming "they" are out to get you. In its extreme forms, self-blame can even be just another way of avoiding responsibility for your own actions.

Creating Authentic Energy

If we look at the flip side of all these energy-blockers, of course, we will come up with a list of factors that create authentic energy. We won't go over most of these in any detail, but just reading through the list can give you a sense of optimism and vitality to counteract the previous list.

Exterior Energy-Builders

- Knowledge
- Identifying money scripts
- Doing work you love
- Taking overwhelming challenges one step at a time
- Knowing life aspirations
- Having authentic goals
- Completing unfinished tasks
- Having support in stressful circumstances
- Freedom from poverty
- Managing wealth responsibly
- Physical/Emotional wellness
    - Recovery from addictions
    - Recovery from depression
    - Maintaining optimum physical health
    - Self-care
    - Exercise
    - Healthful diet

Interior Energy-Builders

- Continuing interior work
- Modifying money scripts
- Feeling difficult emotions
- Contemplative exercises
- Ability to mourn and accept losses
- Healthy independence
- Courage

- Speaking authentically
- Authentic relationships
- Self-acceptance
- Self-confidence
- Sense of balance and perspective
- Knowing your life aspirations
- Making amends and taking responsibility
- Keeping promises
- Forgiveness and letting go

Forgiveness and Letting Go

Because the last item on the above list is so important, we've chosen to discuss it in more detail. Understanding that blame and resentment will block authentic energy is exterior knowledge. Actually letting go of them is a function of interior awareness. Letting go of baggage from the past involves compassion and forgiveness.

We've said that identifying your childhood money scripts should not be used as a reason to blame your parents. Like many desirable behaviors, this one is easier to say than to do. Perhaps you grew up with chaos and fear around money. Perhaps you felt pulled between divorced parents who used money as a weapon or tried to buy your loyalty. Perhaps as a child you didn't get basic medical or dental care because your parents couldn't afford it or didn't take the time to provide it. Perhaps you felt ignored or neglected by parents who were so focused on financial success that they didn't spend time with their children. Perhaps money was used to manipulate or abuse you.

If your money scripts are rooted in painful experiences or circumstances such as these, it isn't realistic to expect you to dismiss that wrong easily or lightly. Nor is that what we are suggesting. We aren't asking you to say, "Well, they didn't know any better, so it's okay, I forgive them."

Letting go of blame isn't quite that easy. Because almost always, when you "forgive" someone that quickly, it is a false or surface forgiveness. It is a "should." Maybe your religious tradition teaches forgiveness. Maybe you believe that it's wrong to feel anger. Maybe you think that if you want to be a good person you have to forgive. But saying, "I forgive you," is meaningless if behind the words you are still carrying hurt, anger, and resentment.

False forgiveness actually just exacerbates the harm that was originally done, because it adds a layer of guilt and shame. If a good person shouldn't feel angry, and you ought to be forgiving, then there must be something wrong with you if you can't forgive and forget. It's also possible that you aren't even conscious of your own feelings of sadness and anger. Maybe you think you have forgiven someone who wronged you, and you don't realize you are still angry.

Or maybe you do know that you're angry, and being told you need to forgive your parents is the last thing you want to hear. If we were to tell you, "Your parents didn't know any better; they did the best they could," your response might be, "Well, the best they knew how to do was still a damned lousy job."

You would be exactly right. And, without knowing it, that statement would be your first step toward genuinely forgiving your parents for their mistakes.

You can't forgive someone until you first admit to yourself that there is something to forgive.

Yes, it may be true that your parents did the best they could to make good money decisions and to teach you to do the same. Yes, it is also true that their best fell far short of being good enough. Regardless of the intentions or the level of knowledge behind your parents' behavior, harm was done. Accepting that reality is your first step toward letting go of blame.

You have been harmed in some way. You deserved better. The anger and sadness you may feel as a result of that harm are perfectly understandable and legitimate. Don't discount yourself by pretending those feelings don't exist. Instead, honor yourself by allowing yourself to feel them. Let yourself be angry, or give yourself time to feel sad. This goes back to the process of accepting and feeling your difficult emotions that we have described earlier. It is an essential element in letting go of blame and reaching genuine forgiveness.

Accepting the reality that harm was done and acknowledging your feelings around that harm also means becoming willing to put the harm into proper perspective. One aspect of false forgiveness is minimizing, pretending that the wrong was smaller than it really was. "I know my mom always borrowed the money out of my piggy bank and never got around to paying it back, but that doesn't matter." Yes, it does matter. Stealing from your children is wrong.

The opposite of minimizing, of course, is justifying your resentment and blame by maximizing the offense. "My mom borrowed my money and never paid it back. Do you know how much I would have had in savings by now if she hadn't done that? She owes me thousands of dollars, and I'm going to get it back—I don't care what it takes." Yes, her theft was wrong, and in a perfect world she would pay it all back, with interest. But focusing so much of your attention on this relatively minor crime that you can't realistically do anything about is only using up energy that would be far better spent in other ways.

Once you have acknowledged and felt your emotions, you can begin to recognize another powerful truth about blame and resentment. The person harmed the most when you cling to blame and resentment is yourself. The persons who wronged you might well be going on with their lives, having forgotten what they did or having no idea that they even did anything wrong. Your focus on their transgressions doesn't necessarily touch them at all. You are the one lying awake nights over it. You are the one with the pain in your stomach or the headaches. You are the one devoting precious energy to it. Letting go of that burden is a gift to yourself much more than it is a gesture of charity toward the other person.

Once you have allowed yourself to accept and feel your anger and sadness about the wrongs that were done, you can make the choice to begin to let go. You don't let go of blame and resentment simply by becoming willing to do so, but that willingness is an essential part of the process. After you decide that you want to forgive, you can work your way toward accomplishing that goal.

One good first step toward healing resentment toward your parents is quite a simple one. It can be useful to think about the influences that shaped your parents' money scripts. Did they or their parents grow up during the Depression of the 1930s? Were their early years marked by family difficulties such as alcoholism or illness? Did they have a lot given to them financially, or did they struggle to have enough? Would they have chosen different careers if they had felt free to do so? Taking time to think about the factors that affected your parents' money choices can give you a great deal of insight and understanding. Just be careful, as you do this, that you aren't using it as a way to minimize your own emotions and fall into the trap of premature forgiveness.

Knowing something of your parents' backgrounds can help you think of their behavior, as well as your own, with more compassion and a more detached perspective. "Detachment," in this context, does not mean indifference or lack of caring. Instead, it is separating yourself from someone else's actions. Detachment is choosing not to take others' behavior personally, understanding that what they did or failed to do was not necessarily about you. You may certainly have been affected by what someone else did, but that doesn't mean the action was directed at you.

It may also help to realize that, most of the time, there was a positive intention behind your parents' behavior. The choices they made may have been intended to teach you responsibility or protect you from harm. Or perhaps they were just getting by from day to day in the best way they knew. But when you were born, they didn't look at you as a tiny, helpless infant and say to themselves, "I'm going to do my best to really screw up this kid's life by making stupid decisions about money."

As a child, you didn't have the power to change your circumstances. You were stuck with the situation you lived in, good, bad, or indifferent. As an adult, you are no longer helpless. You have the ability—as well as the responsibility—to make your own choices. Your parents taught you a pattern of behavior around money. That doesn't mean you are forced to follow that pattern for the rest of your life. Perhaps your parents didn't have an opportunity to learn how to do things better. You do. You have tools and choices that were not available to them.

Your task is to become conscious of your own money scripts and unconscious behavior, then to change your own relationship with money in order to have a healthier and more successful life. Blaming someone else has no value in helping you carry out that work. All it does is drain your energy. *Letting go of that load of resentment frees you to move toward your future.*

The end product of genuine forgiveness is compassion. This is not pity or condescension, but a sense of equality. It is understanding that you and the other person are both human beings, capable of making mistakes. True forgiveness is not a gift graciously bestowed from a higher being to a lower, but is a recognition that both of you are on the same level. False forgiveness results in the perception, "I am a good person over here, and you are a bad person over there." Compassion does away with that separation. It is the understanding—or at least the willingness to understand—why the other person did what they did. It is also the acknowledgement that, shaped by the same circumstances, you may have done the same thing.

We have focused in this section on forgiving your parents. The same process and principles, of course, apply to other people in your life. Perhaps you have felt manipulated and controlled by the way a spouse or ex-spouse handled money. Maybe some of your painful money scripts were formed by shaming experiences from a religion. Perhaps you have been cheated or taken advantage of by employers, employees, business partners, or friends.

Another point we want to emphasize is that forgiveness and compassion are not the same thing as letting someone take advantage of you a second time. Protecting yourself from being injured again is not lack of compassion, it's common sense. Yes, it is right and freeing and compassionate to forgive someone—but that doesn't mean you invite or allow them to harm you again.

CRCR

Rick: A few years ago I went into partnership with a friend. We each put up $30,000, borrowed $240,000 more, and bought a service business that he was going to manage. After a few months, we were a little behind where we had expected to be, but still at a point where we could quite reasonably expect the business to succeed. We had a temporary cash-flow crunch, so we each needed to come up with another $25,000 or $30,000. And my partner couldn't do it. What I didn't know was that he had borrowed on a credit card to come up with the initial $30,000, and he was so stretched financially that he had no way to get any more. Even with that, we could have been okay. We could have eliminated the position of our field foreman, and my partner could have taken that role himself for a time. The business could still have succeeded.

He was not willing to do that. He saw himself as a white-collar manager, and he wasn't willing to put on a hard hat and spend time in the field. Instead, he went into a panic and bailed out.

Did this ever give me a chance to get in touch with difficult feelings! I felt betrayed, I was angry, and I was fearful. This was one of the first times I was able to just sit with my feelings, accept those intense emotions, and reach clarity. And believe me, I was not grateful for the opportunity. By doing the emotional work, however, I was able to become very conscious of what action I needed to take in this situation. I was also able eventually to let go of the painful feelings and to see clearly my own responsibility and mistakes in the venture. I had helped to create it by failing to verify his financial status and by failing to reach a clear understanding about what responsibilities he was willing to assume. In time, this work helped me to reach a point of forgiving this man.

A couple months after his initial panic, my partner called me and said he had changed his mind; he was "ready to climb back into the saddle" and to continue managing the business again. Because of the interior work I had done, I was able to recognize that he had not changed his fundamental reluctance to be a hands-on manager. I was clear in my own mind that this was not an acceptable option for me. I told him no, that we would sell the business and deal with the consequences. We were able to sell the business at a significant loss. My partner declared bankruptcy, but also made a commitment—which he kept—to repay me over several years for his half of the loss.

Now I still consider this man a friend, or at least a friendly acquaintance. We still have some social contact, and it is cordial. I do not feel that I am carrying resentment toward him that makes it uncomfortable to be in his presence. But neither am I ever going to go into business with him again. Nor, in other ventures, will I neglect to confirm someone's financial status or fail to have a clear understanding of responsibilities. I have learned from the mistakes I made in this case.

The final point about forgiveness and letting go of blame is to apply the same process to yourself. You have almost certainly made financial mistakes and unwise choices that may have harmed others as well as yourself. As part of your commitment to changing your behavior so you don't continue making those mistakes, it is important to forgive yourself. Becoming conscious means choosing to have some compassion for yourself as well as for the other people in your life.

By the time you have finished this chapter, you may be beginning to wonder how we got so far off the topic of money. It may seem that we are saying you need to work toward healing practically every difficult area in your life. Is that really what we mean?

Well, actually, yes, it is. Because money is so intertwined with every aspect of your life, you cannot "fix" money difficulties by isolating them. Bringing your financial beliefs and behaviors into consciousness will inevitably involve becoming conscious of other areas of your life that are not functioning as well as you wish they were. The reverse is also true. Recovering from addictions or co-dependency, becoming able to let go of blame, and the other aspects of self-growth that we discuss in this chapter are all involved with your relationship with money.

The ability to make conscious financial choices and the energy to take action according to those choices are tools. The function of those tools is to help you make progress toward becoming your best self and doing what you are meant to do. Yes, we've come a long way beyond the topic of money. That's precisely where we intended to go.

Part II

Exterior Finance

11

Day-to-Day Money Management and Eliminating Debt

So far most of our emphasis has been on the interior aspects of your relationship with money. We've talked about money scripts, about unconscious beliefs, about pain, and about interior awareness. Now it's time to move to the exterior. The next few chapters focus on money mechanics.

However, that focus is not going to be so strong that it excludes the interior. It is simply not possible to completely separate the two. These chapters have plenty of information about the mechanics of money—budgeting, investing, estate planning, and protecting your assets. But as you will see, many of those exterior functions are inseparable from interior beliefs and emotions. You will be using the interior skills you have learned thus far as you apply this exterior knowledge.

Even though we are not leaving the interior completely behind, these next chapters may come as a welcome shift to those of you who are more left-brained and logical. You may be thinking, "At last! Finally, a little information with some substance." Those of you who are right-brained and intuitive are more apt to think, "Good grief! Do I have to do this? Maybe I'll just skip these chapters and come back to them later."

For those of you in the latter group, please don't skip this material. Yes, as we have established, feeling your emotions is essential. Learning to identify and change your money scripts is essential. Discovering your life aspirations and authentic goals is essential. *So is the cognitive information about the exterior aspects of money.* You may be aware of your own money scripts, fully in touch with your feelings, and willing to feel and learn from difficult emotions. You may be very clear about your life aspirations and have a list of authentic goals that energize you. But unless you have the applicable exterior knowledge to bring your goals to completion, you're still going to make reflexive financial decisions that will keep you stuck in the cycle of financial unconsciousness.

Making choices based on feelings alone is just as ineffective as making choices based only on numbers and logic.

Remember, our goal is balance and integration. Exterior knowledge is part of that balance.

This is true for any money decisions you need to make, from buying a house to deciding to open an IRA. Whatever the particular issue, it's important for you to do some research, ask some questions, and get the necessary information. This is part of taking responsibility for your own financial affairs and decisions.

This doesn't mean you have to become an expert. It does mean, however, that it's up to you to learn enough so you can make sensible decisions. These chapters certainly won't give you all the information you will ever need about financial planning, but they do provide the basic financial literacy that every financially integrated person needs.

You may think such financial knowledge doesn't apply to you because you have very little money. Or you may think you don't need this knowledge because you employ a gaggle of attorneys, accountants, business managers, and financial planners. Neither assumption is true. If you don't have money, you need this information because it will help you learn how to get and keep enough money to financially support your progress toward your life aspirations. If you have a host of financial advisors, you need this information so you can better relate to and direct your advisors and so you can be sure your financial affairs are being managed competently.

You might find the following analogy helpful: It's your responsibility to take care of your car. That doesn't mean you have to become a mechanic. But it's a good idea to at least read the owner's manual. Seeing that the car is maintained is up to you, and the more you know, the more intelligently you can hire a mechanic to maintain it for you. This next section might be considered an owner's manual for money, your guide to keeping your financial affairs running smoothly.

Interior Aspects of a Spending Plan

Let's start with the mother lode of exterior knowledge, how you spend your money. Historically, we've called the tool we use to manage our expenditures a budget. The word "budget" is not politically correct anymore, so now we use the terms spending plan, map of intentions, and other creative names. Despite the hint of sarcasm in the previous sentence, we aren't being facetious about this. The words we attach to actions and items can be very powerful.

For example, one physician attended a Financial Integration Workshop because he could not follow a budget and was constantly overspending. After discovering his money scripts and working through the difficult emotions connected with them, he was able to receive new information about the process of budgeting. For him, renaming a budget a "spending plan" completely changed the way he viewed the process. He said it was worth the cost of the workshop. Perhaps using the term "spending plan" for an overspender is similar to calling a diet a "food plan" for an overeater. The focus is not on what you can't eat, it's on what you can eat. Similarly, a spending plan focuses on what you can spend, not what you can't. With a spending plan, even savings becomes a monthly expense, or something to spend.

At first glance, putting together a spending plan or budget may seem to be a very left-brained exercise. You make a list of all of your income, then another one of all your expenses, add them up and compare them. How hard can it be?

The answer to that question is, "Very hard, indeed." This apparently straightforward, exterior assignment can generate huge amounts of interior pain. Putting in writing the way you allocate and spend your money is an incredible tool for accessing and identifying money issues. This is why so many of us run away screaming at the mere mention of the word "budget."

Whether you call it a budget, a spending plan, or a savings plan, setting down in black and white the way you spend your money is an emotional version of having an MRI. It can be a powerful diagnostic tool to help you identify some of your most significant money scripts. In fact, therapist Bari Tessler gave up her therapy practice in favor of what she calls "Conscious Bookkeeping." Creating a spending plan, which she calls a "map of intention," is a core component of the work she does with clients. Before Bari helps clients create their map of intention, however, she advises that they get "Financial Therapy," which she describes as exploring your relationship with money and addressing any associated obstacles, secrets, patterns, and "unfinished business." If that sounds familiar, it should. Tessler's concept of financial therapy is exactly what interior finance and the first ten chapters of this book are all about.

Part of this chapter deals with the mechanics of creating a spending plan. As you go through this section, monitor your body sensations. Without a doubt, some difficult feelings may arise as you go over this information. Be aware of the money scripts and feelings that come up. If you need to, put down the book for a while and practice what you've learned about letting go of your thoughts and embracing and feeling your emotions.

There are as many ways to make a spending plan as there are mutual fund companies. We don't have "the way" to design one. We will offer an outline that can help you create your own. If this doesn't work for you, hundreds of books on this topic are available.

One of the reasons for having a spending plan is to make sure that you are not spending more than your income. Another common goal of a spending plan is to set up a strategy to ensure that you save enough toward retirement. There is also one more important purpose behind a spending plan: becoming conscious of where your money is going so you can be sure that the way you spend your money is in alignment with your life aspirations and goals.

For many people, a major reason for establishing a spending plan is to control or reduce spending. However, it is almost always a mistake to go "cold turkey" and drastically cut out every creature comfort. For example, you may eat out five times a week. That may clearly be a discretionary budget item that you can reduce. Yet, eating out to you may represent far more than mere convenience. It may represent relationships, a celebration, or entertainment. In that case, eliminating eating out from your budget would be as foolhardy as an overeater going on a 500-calorie-a-day diet, or a drug addict trying to quit by "white knuckling" it with no help or support. It probably won't work, and you will soon be "busting the budget" and beating yourself up because you failed to follow it. You will soon find yourself right back in the cycle of financial unconsciousness.

Ron Gallen, an addictions counselor and financial counselor, is the author of *The Money Trap: A Practical Program to Stop Self-Defeating Financial Habits so You Can Reclaim Your Grip on Life.* His contention is that destructive money behaviors such as compulsive spending are attempts to make up for what is missing emotionally or spiritually in one's life.

A spending plan that doesn't provide anything
to nurture yourself is a setup for failure.

Gallen has clients, even those on a strict budget, list as the first thing on their spending plan a modest amount for self-care. He describes this amount as how much you would spend if you were taking care of yourself, but neither indulging yourself nor depriving yourself.

These self-nurturing items are more than just indulgences or conveniences. Having a three-dollar latte every morning or getting your nails done wouldn't necessarily qualify for this category. Its purpose is to nurture you at a deeper level, to support your life aspirations. Genuinely self-nurturing budget items might be art supplies, a dance class, books, dinner out with friends once a week, or something else that helps you express and become who you are. This category is perhaps best described by the following poem:

If thou of fortune be bereft,
And in thy store there be but left
Two loaves—sell one, and with the dole
Buy hyacinths to feed thy soul.
            James Terry White, Not by Bread Alone *(1907)*

One way to identify the areas of spending that "feed your soul" is to go back to your life aspirations and goals. What do you need to include in your budget to help you achieve those? Another tool is to pay attention to your feelings as you create your spending plan. What are the expenditures that bring a feeling of joy and energy to you? Or when you think about eliminating items, do you feel angry or sad? Expenditures that feed your soul will be aligned with a life aspiration and evoke feelings of lightness.

Whatever your "hyacinths" category may be, put it down as one of the first items on your spending plan. Despite the poem (which itself, of course, is a money script), we are certainly not suggesting that you devote half your income to this category. At least initially, keep this spending to 5 to 10 percent of your income. If your budget is designed around paying off excessive debt, you might have to spend less than this on self-care. Or if you've been overspending on these items, cutting back on them may take some time. In either case, you may need to go back to the basics of identifying money scripts and dissolving difficult feelings. Then you will begin to be able to see other options and methods where you can feed your soul within the constraints of your spending plan.

A second essential category is savings—building a safety net for the present and a source of income for your future. We discuss that more fully in the next chapter.

Next, many people feel it is important to allocate an amount of their income to give away to charity or as a tithe to their church.

Some financial advisors cover these three categories with the "10-10-10" plan. Ten percent of your income is for saving, ten percent is for giving, and ten percent is for fun and self-nurturing. The other 70 percent is for all your basic expenses: food, housing, transportation, and so on.

The big problem with a spending plan, of course, comes when the amount left for necessities is less than your current level of spending. If you find yourself in this position—and many do—you will need to analyze every expenditure. This is tough work and the step where most spending plans fail. Why? Because you run into too many expenditures that "just cannot be reduced." Pay close attention to those expenses. These are the expenses you believe to be absolute, which you just couldn't live without. Just like a money script that is "absolutely true," the expense that is non-negotiable is most likely loaded with emotional dynamite. These represent hidden money scripts.

It's particularly difficult when your budget tells you it's necessary to cut an expense that is related to an authentic goal. After all, we've told you throughout this book how important it is to support your life aspirations. How, then, can we tell you one of those expense categories has to be reduced?

Suppose you have a life aspiration of traveling and experiencing different cultures. Corresponding to that life aspiration, perhaps your authentic goal is to take two major trips a year. If your travel budget for those trips is consuming 25 percent of your income and you are unable to save for retirement, keep up with debt payments, or afford the repairs on your car, your travel spending is most likely entangled with a bevy of money scripts held in place by difficult emotions. When you run into one of these, it is time to apply the tools of interior finance. It may help, as well, to pay attention to the ways that life aspiration is supported by your other budget categories. Saving for retirement, for example, would be a way to ensure that in the future you can fulfill the life aspiration of being able to travel.

Other difficult categories in your plan may be related to "shoulds."

Pay attention to any "shoulds" that are in your spending plan.

The most common and problematic shoulds usually involve family members. Spending for children's college education is a typical one. While your money script may scream otherwise, you have no obligation to fund your children's education. Your kids, your parents, your friends, the university, or society may tell you that you should, but there is no law that says a child's formal education is the responsibility of the parents. A college education may not even be in your child's best interest or something all of your children want. Putting that as an automatic obligation ahead of your or other family members' needs or wants is likely to create resentment and anger. It is an example of acting unconsciously.

As you go through your expenses for the purpose of reducing them, it is often best to reduce spending in categories, not eliminate the category completely. There is, however, one exception. The only category in your spending plan that you want to completely get rid of is consumer debt. We discuss that in more detail later in this chapter.

Believe it or not, some people have a problem of not spending enough. Even after setting aside enough for self-care, retirement, charity, and all the necessities of life, they still have a surplus. Our experience is that many of these people have money scripts that say, "Money is to be hoarded, not spent." Usually they will have little or nothing in the self-care category. Ron Gallen describes these people as "financial anorexics" or "anorectic spenders."

Spending little or nothing to support your own dreams is just as unconscious as is compulsive spending. A person in this situation needs to do the same work as an overspender in applying the interior tools. Some underspending results from fear, a sense that there might not be enough. Other underspenders struggle with feeling that they are not good enough or with an exaggerated sense of responsibility for giving to others.

If this latter description fits for you, an important step may be to go back to the life aspirations exercises. Look again at what matters the most to you, at what you most want to do and to become. Then ask yourself one more question: If you don't honor yourself by using the resources you have to reach those life aspirations, how will that serve others? How will it help the world for you to be less than you could be? Ironically, you may find that exactly the opposite is true. If giving and service are important to you, often you are able to do those most effectively when you first support and fulfill your own deepest dreams. Money is a tool you can use to help you function in the world as authentically as possible.

Designing a Spending Plan

Now it's time to get started on your own spending plan. We aren't going to give you a detailed fill-in-the-blanks form because there is no such thing as one spending plan that fits everyone. What we are going to give you is some typical categories, just to help you remember all the items that should be included on your own.

So get out a sheet of notebook paper or a legal pad, or open a spreadsheet file on your computer, and start putting together your spending plan. There are many software packages that can help you with this. QuickBooks and Microsoft's Money Plus are two popular programs. You can learn more about them at quickbooks.intuit.com or moneycentral.msn.com.

The first thing to do is list all your sources of income—salary, self-employment, investments, alimony, social security, pension plans, illicit drug profits, and so on. It is best to use the after-tax amounts you actually receive, not the gross wage. If you do decide to use your gross income, make sure you include local, state, and federal income taxes as an expense item. Include in your income any bonuses or gifts only if you can be absolutely sure that you will receive them. Most people do a monthly spending plan, which is easy if you are paid monthly. If you are paid weekly or every two weeks, however, you will need to adjust the income amounts to fit a monthly schedule. Just multiply a weekly check by 52 (or a bi-weekly check by 26), then divide by 12 to get a monthly amount.

Now you need to list your expenses. Typically, the best sources to find out exactly where you spend your money are your checkbook register, credit card statements, and cash receipts. Don't forget items such as car insurance or real estate taxes that are paid once or twice a year. And don't underestimate incidental cash expenses. We strongly recommend that you keep track for a period of time—two weeks to a month—of the "little things" you may buy regularly. Those cups of cappuccino, the snacks or sodas from the office vending machine, and other seemingly minor purchases can add up to a significant monthly amount.

Here are some of the items that you may need in your spending plan. You can categorize them in whatever way works best for you.

- Self-Nurturing – The items that support your life aspirations, that give you the sense of a mini-vacation or real comfort and fulfillment
- Gifts – Charities, church, birthdays, Christmas, and other occasions
- Savings – Emergency fund, retirement, goals such as car, vacation, house
- Housing – Mortgage, rent, property taxes
- Utilities – Electricity, water, gas, phone, trash, cable, Internet
- Food – Groceries, meals out, school lunches
- Transportation – Car payments, gas, oil, licensing, public transportation, maintenance, parking fees
- Insurance – Health, disability, life, car, homeowners or renters, liability
- Repairs – Home, car, computer
- Debt – Credit cards, student loans, consumer purchases, personal loans
- Clothing
- Child Care – Day care, occasional baby-sitting
- Medical – Prescriptions, doctor visits, dental, eye care
- Personal – Allowances (for adults as well as kids), toiletries, haircuts, salon visits, manicures, other incidentals
- Entertainment – For adults and children
- Miscellaneous – School supplies, subscriptions (newspaper, magazines) organization dues and memberships, books

Other possible categories might be child support, alimony, tuition, health club memberships, care of an elderly parent, cost of a vacation or second home, payments and maintenance for a boat, lawn care, or house cleaning.

The idea of writing down everything you spend may seem overwhelming and be intimidating. Even reading through the list of possible categories may bring up difficult emotions. But, please, do this for yourself. The first step toward creating a realistic spending plan is to identify what you actually are doing now. You may want to keep track for a month or so to determine what you really spend in some areas. It's entirely possible that you will not be pleased at what you discover. You may find out that you are spending more than you're bringing in. You may be surprised at how much you spend on incidentals. You may become uncomfortably aware that you are saving too little or that you have more debt than you had realized. Such awareness is an important step toward consciousness around managing your money.

Once you know the truth about your spending, regardless of how uncomfortable that truth may be, then you can begin to work toward a spending plan that will serve you better. As you do so, we strongly recommend the following:

- As difficult emotions arise, use the financial integration tools you've already learned. By now, you understand that doing this work is important if you are going to change self-destructive behaviors around your spending.
- For couples, it is essential to work together on creating and following a spending plan.
- For couples, each spouse needs to have a personal allowance to be spent any way they choose. That may be five dollars a week or five hundred, depending on your budget, but it is important.
- If you and your spouse can't talk about your spending plan, consider getting professional help. This ideally would include scheduling sessions where a therapist and financial planner work jointly to help guide you over the rough spots. If that is not feasible for you, working with either a planner or a therapist may be valuable.
- If you are struggling with debt, a valuable resource is Dave Ramsey's Financial Peace University. Check out his website at www.daveramsey.com for detailed spending plans, books, and his "snowball" plan for spending down debt.
- Lasting solutions to money problems such as debt or overspending can be achieved by using the tools we have already described. Remember that a spending plan is just one of many tools for helping you reach financial integration.

Richard E. Vodra, CFP®, is the author of *Enough Money!*, an excellent resource for lifetime money management. Here are some of the financial rules of thumb that Dick suggests, modified with a few suggestions of our own. These rules have helped many people manage money wisely.

1. You can use a credit card, especially for convenience and to keep track of business expenses, but pay it off monthly.
2. When paying off debt, concentrate on the most expensive debt first.
3. Don't borrow more for a home than twice your annual income. Banks will lend you more, but we find it is often a setup for the failure of your spending plan.
4. Control your automotive appetite. Buying a late-model used car is often your best car buy, because the original owner has borne the expense of the high initial depreciation factor. It is a good idea to make a monthly "car payment" even if you have no car loan. Cars depreciate annually and eventually need to be replaced. Don't spend more than four percent of your income for one car, or more than seven percent for two cars.

Debt

As we said earlier, the one category that you want to eliminate from your spending plan is consumer debt. This is any debt that is not secured by an asset (such as real estate) that either appreciates in value or produces income. Consumer debt would include any revolving credit cards, department store cards, or financing on any household item. It would also cover larger consumer items like cars, motorcycles, and college tuition. Consumer debt is a trap that can sabotage your journey to financial security and success.

Including car loans in this category may seem a bit extreme. Many people view a car loan as a modern necessity. Yes, the car is certainly a necessity for most of us. But the loan is one automobile accessory you are better off without. Once you have your spending under control, your goal is to have the only car payment you ever make be the one you pay into your savings account toward the cash purchase of your next vehicle.

Now, it's easy for us to tell you that you should get rid of your consumer debt. Chances are you even agree with us. However, if your unconscious money behavior has taken the form of overspending, you may have a crushing burden of debt. Even if you are beginning to understand how and why you accumulated the debt, and even if you know clearly that you want to eliminate it, you may not have any idea how to get the job done.

In this section we'll give you some suggestions for getting started, as well as some resources to investigate if you need additional help. Freeing yourself from debt is not easy, but it is possible and achievable. Accomplishing that task can generate an incredible amount of energy, in two ways. One, it frees you from the worry and the struggle of coping with the debt. And two, it gives you the powerful sense of accomplishment that comes along with knowing you have tackled something difficult and have succeeded at it. That feeling of competence is worth far more than any "bargain" you've ever bought with a credit card.

Stop Creating More Debt

The first step toward eliminating debt is simple and straightforward, but is probably the hardest one to actually do. It is to *stop creating any more consumer debt.*

Do not borrow another penny from this moment on.

If you are in trouble because of excessive consumer debt, that may mean cutting up your credit cards. For many people, this suggestion generates fear and even panic. What if there's an emergency? How would you manage without a card to fall back on? Besides, doesn't everyone need a credit card for travel or paying for things online?

Well, no, novel as the idea may be in our society, you don't need a credit card. Yes, it is useful and convenient to have one. But for any situation that requires a credit card, like renting a car or buying something online, you can use a debit card that will take the amount directly out of your checking account. It is true that a credit card offers some protections against loss or theft that are not available for debit cards. Once you have your spending under control and are making your financial decisions consciously, having and using a credit card is certainly an option as long as you pay off the balance each month. But you absolutely do not need a pocket full of plastic. And if you have a pattern of compulsive spending and a long-standing struggle with debt, you do not need a credit card in your wallet any more than a newly sober alcoholic needs to carry around a pocket flask of whiskey.

If you have absolutely no cushion for emergencies, some debt counselors suggest a compromise that might at least get you started in the right direction. Destroy all of your credit cards except one. Make a solemn commitment in writing that you will only use that card for real emergencies, and write down a list of qualifying emergencies. Then either give that card to a trusted relative to keep for you, or put it into a large container of water and freeze it. (No cheating by writing down the number first, either.) Then you'll have it for a genuine emergency, but it won't be available for impulsive spending.

We offer this alternative with some trepidation, because as long as that card is available, it is too easy to fall back into the habit of using it. The definition of "emergency" has a sneaky way of expanding. If you do go this route, we suggest you make a further commitment to destroy the card as soon as you have saved one month's income as an emergency fund.

Once you have begun a new pattern of not creating any new debt, you can turn your energy toward eliminating your current debt. The first thing to do here (which you may have already done if you've written down a spending plan) is to make a complete list of all your debts. What is the total amount of each one? The interest rate? The minimum payment?

If you haven't already created your spending plan, now is the time to do so, because your next step is to determine how much money you have available to pay off your debt. You will need to continue doing your interior work as you do this. Some of you may not see anything in your budget that you can reduce. Others may want to devote every possible penny to debt reduction, even at the cost of depriving yourselves of necessities. Either extreme is almost certain to be unconscious behavior.

Talk to Creditors

Sometimes a person's debt load will be so large that there is little left for even the most basic necessities of life. If you find yourself in this situation, obviously you need to take care of your most basic survival needs first. If you simply do not have enough money in your budget to make full payments on all of your debts, one of the first things you need to do is talk to your creditors. The worst thing you can do if you can't pay a bill is to ignore it.

Creditors are more likely to work with you if you pick up the phone and explain to them that you cannot meet your obligation, but you can do something. Even sending in a fraction of the payment is better than sending nothing at all. Many times creditors, once they see that you are struggling but are still making an effort to pay what you can, will forgive the interest accrual or even a portion of the principal. It is generally in their best interest to work with you, rather than have you completely default on your debt.

Talking to your creditors doesn't mean simply calling them and saying, "Sorry, I can't pay this bill." It requires coming up with a plan to pay the debt. Whether you offer your own plan or ask the creditors for their suggestions, it's important that you communicate your acceptance of responsibility for the debt and your willingness to do what you can to repay what you owe.

Certainly, doing this will evoke some difficult emotions. Again, employ the interior tools to identify money scripts, dissolve any painful emotions, and apply any new knowledge you have gained. If the thought of negotiating with your creditors is too intimidating, you may need to ask for help from a third party. Perhaps a family member or trusted friend could help you; someone else who can look at your situation with a fresh eye may have ideas you have not thought of.

There are also consumer credit counseling services available in many places. These agencies generally charge modest fees to negotiate with your creditors and help you set up a repayment plan. Many of them are nonprofit programs funded in part through donations. They may also offer classes to help you learn better money management skills.

Beware, though, of loan-consolidation services. Read the fine print carefully and get some independent advice before you commit to one of these. Often they do nothing more than move your problem from one set of creditors to another.

Getting Debts Paid Off

There are several ways to accomplish the mechanics of actually paying off your debt. Some advisors recommend paying off the debt with the highest interest rate first. Ron Gallen's suggestion is to figure out what percentage of your total debt is allocated to each creditor, then pay that percentage of whatever amount you have available for debt payments each month. In *The Money Trap,* he offers guidance for creating your own "recovery spending plan."

Dave Ramsey offers a "snowball" plan: pick your smallest debt and put everything you can afford toward paying that off, meanwhile making minimum payments on the others. When you have the first one paid off, go to the next smallest, and work your way up the line. The advantage of this is that you can get one debt paid off relatively quickly, which generates a sense of accomplishment and helps you maintain your energy around the debt-elimination effort. He has several books available, including *The Financial Peace Planner*, a detailed workbook; you can find out more at www.daveramsey.com.

The specifics of your plan, of course, will depend on what arrangements you are able to negotiate with your creditors. If you owe money to the IRS, for example, it's possible that you won't have much room to negotiate and will have to make that debt your highest priority. Regardless of the details of your plan to eliminate debt, the crucial thing is to make a commitment to become debt-free, have a plan, and keep moving.

It may take from a few months to a few years to free yourself from debt. As you make progress, one important thing to keep always in mind is that *this is a temporary situation.* You need to determine what you can do, not what you can't do, and stick to it. Being unable to meet your obligations, with the consequence of ruining your credit rating, is not the end of your life. It is a temporary consequence of having made unconscious financial decisions. You will be given another chance and another opportunity to become conscious around your spending.

In the meantime, you can do much more than you might have believed possible to get yourself out of this trap. You may need to severely cut back on your discretionary spending. You may need to find a temporary second job. You may need to sell your expensive car and buy a much cheaper one. You may even need to move to less expensive housing. As long as you are making those decisions consciously as part of your debt-elimination plan, they can give you a sense of pride rather than generating feelings of failure or shame. As long as you are moving toward your goal, you are succeeding. You won't have to do this for a lifetime—in fact, you may be astonished at the relatively short time it can take to work your way out of debt. The more progress you make, the easier it will become. And when you are finally out of the consumer-debt trap, you will have given yourself a gift of tremendous empowerment and energy to help you move toward your life aspirations.

K&

Kathleen: I can testify to the relief and freedom that come with being debt-free. In my first marriage, we did not buy "stuff" and did not accumulate a great deal of debt. Neither did we ever manage to save anything or plan for the future. We got by from month to month, taking care of our responsibilities but never getting ahead.

When Wayne and I married, we were both dealing with financial fallout from divorces. He and his former wife had owned some rental property that was heavily mortgaged and in need of maintenance. He had a couple of personal loans and lots of credit card debt. I had very little debt, but my credit rating was in disgraceful condition because the bank had foreclosed on the house my former husband received in the divorce settlement.

We needed a house with space for five kids, and our financial situation was so bad we couldn't buy one. So we settled for renting a house that was smaller than we would have liked. Our youngest, who was four at the time, slept in the downstairs laundry room; he was the only kid we knew with a refrigerator, washer, and dryer in his bedroom. We drove old cars. We bought furniture at second-hand stores and clothes at rummage sales. We ate a lot more hamburger and tuna casserole than we did steak. And we paid off debts. And paid off debts.

It took a few years, but eventually the personal loans were paid off, the rental properties were sold and those debts out of the way, and the credit cards were down to small amounts that we could pay off each month. We started shopping at the mall instead of the neighborhood garage sales. Wayne was able to fulfill one of his lifelong dreams and buy an airplane. We bought a nice house. We kept driving the old cars, though—by now we were really attached to the idea of not having car payments.

After several years of hard work, Wayne's construction business was doing well. We paid off the mortgage on the one rental house we still owned. We stopped using our credit cards. We started building up some decent savings. Then we paid off the mortgage on our house. We traded up to a faster airplane. We were debt-free, with savings, freedom, and plans for the future.

A year later, Wayne was killed. Among the things I have found to be grateful for in the aftermath of that loss has been the fact that we had no debt. All of a sudden my income has gone from upper middle class to lower middle class. But because there was no mortgage, I could afford to stay in my house until I chose to sell it and get a smaller one. I had been driving a company vehicle and had to buy a car, but because we had savings, I was able to pay cash for it. The insurance company paid nothing for the loss of Wayne's airplane. Yet because the plane was paid for, I was able to walk away from that loss. Wayne's estate consisted primarily of the share he owned of the business, which the kids and I received in full because the company had no debt.

My monthly expenses are minimal, because I have no credit card debt, no mortgage, no car payment, and no loan payments. I can afford the health insurance I now have to buy; I can travel; I can give to causes I believe in. Above all, I can continue doing the freelance work I love and want to do. Because the life insurance and the estate were not swallowed up by debt, I have the security of knowing those funds are invested for my future.

∾∿

RK

Rick: I am much different from Kathleen. I have lived my entire adult life in debt up to my eyeballs. However, the debt I have accumulated is not debt from credit cards, consumer loans, car loans, or personal items. I have always abhorred borrowing for anything except real estate. And when it comes to borrowing for real estate, I've gone for the gusto. I started my career in the 1970s and attended every real estate investing course and read every book on the topic I could get my hands on. One of my favorite books was Robert Allen's *Nothing Down*. I became a disciple of creative finance, and I applied it well. It didn't take me too many years to own over a million dollars of real estate. That was the good news. The bad news was that I had over a million dollars of debt.

Buying real estate with nothing down works really well, as long as you have a constant stream of paying tenants or a large enough monthly salary to cover the payments if your tenants stop paying or the real estate market goes into the tank. Since I did not have a large salary, I relied on tenants and luck. Both ran out in the mid-1980s when 4500 military jobs left town overnight and our area fell upon hard times. With the economic slump came a fall in real estate prices. I quickly found myself owing more on my real estate than it was worth. I spent the next ten years working as hard as I could to earn enough money to cover the mortgage payments on my rentals. It was not until the mid-

1990s that my rentals began to break even again and real estate prices started to rise.

I haven't only borrowed against real estate; I've also borrowed to start businesses and fund expansions. Three different times, failed business ventures have given me the opportunity to stare bankruptcy in the face. Fortunately, I was able to work my way out of every situation without going bankrupt.

You could certainly say I am a risk taker and entrepreneur. But, for the most part, I am not an unconscious risk taker. In looking back at my successes and failures, I can truly say that 80 percent of my borrowing was conscious. Don't be misled, however. Some of my conscious borrowing didn't turn out so well. Borrowing consciously is no guarantee that your venture will be successful. It just means you have applied the interior and exterior skills and are seeing the situation objectively, fully aware of the upside and downside risks. Taking risks inherently means that there will be failures. I try to remind myself of that every time one of my ventures fails. Fortunately, for every failure, I've had three successes.

Today, I am still relatively leveraged. I have a plan to become debt-free, and that plan still relies on a relatively healthy economy and paying tenants. I am still accumulating assets with the intention of funding some of my life aspirations and authentic goals. I am doing this consciously. The odds are in my favor that I will reach most of my financial goals. But I also understand there are no guarantees, and I am comfortable with the level of conscious risk I am taking.

෨෬

12

Investing and Planning for the Future

Planning for the future includes taking care of yourself by investing for your own future needs and for retirement, possibly taking care of some of your children's educational expenses, and taking care of your family by making a will and doing estate planning. In this chapter we cover the first two of these topics. We concentrate heavily on exterior knowledge, which may seem intimidating if you are unfamiliar with investing. If this is the case, remember, you can take your time. There's no need to try to take in all the information all at once. You can refer back to this section whenever you need to. At the same time, don't give in to a money script that says, "I can't learn this." You can. It isn't quantum mechanics, it's just money mechanics.

Investing 101. The Basics

The first thing you need to know about investing is that it's not as difficult as you might think. There is no "one-size fits all" in investing, but there are some basic principles that you need to know and that anyone can learn.

First of all, saving even small amounts regularly can add up to significant numbers. This is due to the magic of compound interest. If you save $100 the first month, you earn interest on that $100. If you add another $100 the second month, you are earning interest on the first $100, plus the interest already earned on it, plus the second $100. Because the interest you earn is added to the principal amounts you contribute, your account grows relatively quickly.

How much can you save toward retirement if you contribute regularly to an IRA or other savings plan? To use some very conservative numbers, suppose you save even $3,000 at the beginning of each year at an average return of only 4%. At the end of 10 years, you would have contributed $30,000 and have a total in your account of $37,459. After 20 years, with a contribution of $60,000, your investment would be worth $92,908. After 30 years and a contribution of $90,000, you would have $174,985. These are simplified calculations, not taking into account factors such as inflation, but they are meant to give you an idea of how much even a modest but consistent investment can grow.

Owning and Lending

There are two basic categories of investments—owning and lending. Among the things you can own are real estate, art, gold, commodities, or businesses. Among the types of lending you can do are loans to individuals, banks, businesses, insurance companies, or governments.

First, let's take a look at the various methods of loaning money. When you loan your money to a bank, it is called a deposit, savings account, or certificate of deposit. A loan to an insurance company is called a fixed annuity. When you loan your money to an individual, it is most often secured with a promissory note. Some promissory notes are secured by real estate. These are called mortgages. If you loan your money to a corporation or government, it is called a bond or debenture. Bond investments extend to the bonds of foreign companies and governments, too. These are often referred to as international bonds. Regardless of the type of lending, the entity using your money is going to pay you interest for the use of your money. In normal economic conditions, the longer they get to use your money, the higher the interest rate.

You may have never thought of putting money into a bank savings account as loaning money to the bank, but that's exactly what you're doing.

If you have a savings account, the bank agrees to pay back your loan any time you want it. If you invest in a certificate of deposit, you agree to loan the money for a specific term, usually a year, though some CDs are as short as three months and as long as five years. Because your money is tied up for a certain term, the bank will pay you a higher interest rate than it will for a savings account. That is also why there is a penalty if you take the money out before the term is up. When you invest in a bond, it will also have a specific term, from perhaps as short as 30 days to as long as 30 years.

Now let's explore the various methods of owning. We've already mentioned that one method of earning money is to own a business. For some people, this means the ownership they have in their own company. To most of us, it means owning a portion of a very large company represented by buying shares of the company's common stock. Common stock is commonly referred to as stocks or equities. As a shareholder, you become part of the group of people, the stockholders, who own a publicly traded company. The stocks of public companies are traded on exchanges. Most of the largest companies in the U.S. are traded on the New York Stock Exchange. Another popular exchange is the NASDAQ exchange, which is known for trading shares of smaller companies. Stock ownership may include international as well as U.S. companies.

A common asset that many people own is real estate. Almost everyone in this country lives in either a multi-family complex (duplexes, condos and apartments) or a single-family house. In the past, one of the best long-term investments people could make was to own their own houses. Average Americans have more of their net worth represented by equity in their homes than anything else. With that said, we don't like to consider home equity as a part of a person's investment portfolio. While a house is an asset, its primary purpose is to provide a home.

Investment real estate can take several forms, like owning single-family dwellings held for investment or owning income-producing property such as apartments, office buildings, retail strip centers, and industrial properties. Owning direct real estate investments such as these is not for the uninformed or beginners. You need to obtain a lot of knowledge before jumping into the real estate game. One of the best places to learn is from Jack Miller and his network of mentors, located at www.cashflowconcepts.com.

The majority of investors have no business owning real estate directly. However, an indirect way to own real estate is by investing in a real estate investment trust (REIT), which is a business that does nothing but own real estate. There are over 200 REITs traded on major stock exchanges and many mutual funds that specialize in REITs. Another way to indirectly own real estate is via limited partnerships, which are typically for institutional investors or individuals with a high net worth.

Natural resources or commodities represent another type of ownership. This would include precious metals such as gold or platinum, lumber, oil, grains, and other natural resources. Owning these rarely includes actually taking possession of the asset; adding commodities to your portfolio does not include turning your basement into an oil-storage tank or a grain bin.

Understanding Investment Returns

As an owner of common stock, real estate, or natural resources, you earn money in two ways. The first is through dividends paid to you as your share of the profits the company or real estate earns. As the profits or rents from your company or real estate increase, the value of the asset will typically increase as well. So the second way you earn money on stocks or real estate is through appreciation. Of course, if you hold an asset (such as raw land, metals, commodities, or art) that does not produce income, dividends are non-existent. In that case, the only way you can make money is by appreciation.

As a lender, you primarily earn money through the interest you are paid for the use of your money. In some economic environments, you can also earn money if your bonds appreciate in value, because bond values can fluctuate.

The interest or dividend you are paid is referred to as the *yield*. For instance, if you own a share of stock and get a 3% dividend, that is known as the stock's yield. But if the value of that stock also goes up 7%, your total *return* is 10% (3% dividend + 7% appreciation = 10% total return). If the value of the stock goes down 7%, your total return is minus 4% (3% dividend – 7% depreciation = -4% total return). So *total return* is the yield of the investment—the stock dividend or the interest on a bond—plus the appreciation or minus the depreciation of the asset.

This difference between yield and total return is important for you to know and understand.

Focusing only on yield may result in a disaster.

For example, you might see an advertisement for a bond offering a yield of 12%. Yes, you may be getting 12% interest, but if the value of the bond falls 8% in the first year, you'll have a total return of 4%. In contrast, a certain stock may have a yield of 1%, but appreciate an average of 6% a year, for a total return of 7%.

Most people are surprised to learn that bond values fluctuate. They think of the value of a bond as being stable. If you loan a company $1,000 for 10 years at an interest rate of 4%, how can the value of the bond possibly fluctuate? The fluctuation in bond value works like this:

When you loan a company or a government money through buying a bond, you will get your principal back on the date the bond matures. Until the date of maturity, you'll get the agreed-upon interest rate. The fluctuation comes if you have to sell the bond for any reason prior to the maturity date. You can't go to the corporation or government and say, "Sorry, I need my money now, even though this is a ten-year bond and I've only had it for three years." It doesn't work that way. You have to go out and find someone else to buy your bond. This is done through a broker, who sells your bond on the secondary market. If interest rates have gone up since you bought your bond, it will be worth less than the face amount. If rates have gone down, your bond will be worth more.

This teeter-totter concept is tricky for most people to get. Suppose you bought a $1,000, ten-year bond at an interest rate of 6%. After three years, you need to sell it. At that time, interest rates on bonds are 8%. So investors aren't going to pay the face amount of $1,000 for your bond, which only yields 6%. Why? They could get an 8% yield if they bought a new bond in the current market. You will need to sell your bond at a discount, so the buyer's *yield to maturity,* or total return, is 8%. Rising interest rates are an inherent risk of investing in bonds. You can also lose money on bonds if the borrower defaults or if inflation erodes your purchasing power.

Just as you can lose money in bonds, you can also make money on bonds when interest rates fall, which results in the bond appreciating if you sell prior to maturity. Using the example above, if interest rates have gone down to 4%, buyers would be willing to pay more for your bond, or give you a premium. This is because the 6% yield is higher than the market yield of 4% on new bonds. The premium will give the buyer a yield to maturity or total return of 4%.

Which Has More Risk, Stocks or Bonds?

Lending your money is a defensive strategy rather than an active attempt to increase your capital. For one thing, before you can lend money, you first have to have some. So lending investments provide stability to your portfolio. They help decrease price fluctuations. Having a high percentage of CDs and bonds might be more appropriate for someone who has enough and wants investments to provide a very secure income. When you retire and need more income, you might choose to put a larger percentage of your portfolio into bonds. However, we recommend against ever having your entire retirement portfolio in bonds or CDs. You will want to keep a portion of it in various forms of ownership: stocks, real estate, and natural resources. The reason is that the typical retiree turning 65 has a life expectancy of 20 or more years.

You will want your portfolio to include a mix of assets that can provide real growth to offset inflation and the reduction of your purchasing power.

The biggest threat to lending money is *inflation*, which is a general increase in prices across the economy over a period of time. If you're getting a 4% interest rate and it's locked in for 10 years, you have to subtract inflation from any return in order to determine how much money you're actually making. So if you're earning 4% and inflation is 3%, your real return is 1%. Any time you see the term *real return*, that means inflation has been factored in.

Most professional money managers are very pleased if they obtain a real return of 3% to 5% from a portfolio. If inflation is averaging 3%, this would mean an overall, or *nominal*, return of 6% to 8%. Obviously, if you have a 4% bond and inflation pops up to 5%, you can't go back and ask for more interest, so your real return is minus 1%. This was a problem back in the late 1970s and 80s when inflation was high. Retirees who had invested their portfolios into bonds (also called *fixed income securities*) were seeing their purchasing power fall almost daily.

This may be a little confusing to you if you have a money script that says, "Bonds are safer than stocks." Like all money scripts, this one is only partially true. Its validity depends on the period of time. If you are investing money that you will need within a very short period of time, a short-term bond (one that matures in less than three years) or a certificate of deposit can be safer than stocks. That is because the price of a short-term bond or CD fluctuates very little over a year, while stock prices can fluctuate greatly. When a person or talking head says, "Stocks are risky and CDs are safe," the unspoken part of the sentence is, "if the holding period is short-term, such as a year." But not all bonds would be safer than stocks for short-term periods. A long-term bond, such as one that matures in 30 years, could experience price fluctuations even greater than those of stocks. The reason is *volatility*, or the degree to which the price of an investment fluctuates. Stocks tend to be more volatile than bonds in the short term. When you know you will need a certain sum of money in a very short period of time, you want to put it in an investment vehicle that has low volatility. That usually means a savings account, certificate of deposit, or short-term bonds.

If you are investing money that you will not need for 30 years, stocks are almost certain to be safer than bonds. In this case, volatility is not the important issue, because you don't need your investment funds for a long time. Short-term volatility or fluctuations aren't an issue, unless another money script pops up its head that says, "Oh my God, my investments are losing money, I better sell now before it goes to zero," and you sell prematurely. This is part of the unconscious "buy high, sell low" cycle. The key factor in a long-term investment is the total rate of return. There are few, if any, 30-year periods where bonds produced a higher return than stocks. And in almost every 30-year period since 1926, the worst return on stocks still was greater than the best return on bonds. Even if you examine any ten-year period of time going back to 1926, stocks have generated higher returns than bonds in about 80% of those ten-year periods. So, over a 10-year period or longer, you can make a reasonable assertion that the majority of someone's investments ought to be in equities. This would be a general rule if you are under 50 and saving for retirement. Of course, the exact makeup for an investment portfolio is going to vary, depending on the age of the investor and the goals that person has.

Diversification:
What People Think They Understand About Investing, But Don't

An absolutely essential concept in investing is *diversification*. You've probably heard the old cliché, "Don't have all your eggs in one basket." Like all money scripts, there are times this doesn't work, such as when you are investing in your own business. But, for most investment portfolios, diversification is crucial. Diversification is an important part of your portfolio's *asset allocation*.

Now using both of those terms in one paragraph may make some of you think we're starting to get too technical. Please, before your eyes start to glaze over and you decide you'll just skip this section, give us a minute to explain. We've often heard financial advisors explain that diversification means you don't put all your eggs into one basket. Well, that's true enough, but it's only part of the picture.

Dividing your eggs among a variety of similar baskets might work perfectly for eggs. That same approach doesn't work for investments.

To be a diversified investor, you must put your money into the investment equivalent of several different types of containers. As well as baskets, this would need to include Tupperware bowls, buckets, boxes, and egg cartons. We call these differing containers *asset classes.*

You achieve the greatest reduction of portfolio risk by dividing your money among various asset classes.

Asset class diversification can be compared to the ingredients that go into making a cake. Flour, milk, and sugar, all of which are necessary, still won't make a cake. You also need other ingredients, such as eggs, baking powder, salt, vanilla, and butter. And you need the appropriate amount of each one. If you were to use equal amounts of each ingredient, what you would pull out of the oven would be a big mess rather than a cake. So, when putting together your portfolio, you not only need the right combination of asset classes, you also need to allocate appropriate percentages of your portfolio to each asset class. As economic conditions change, some asset classes earn more and others earn less. If you have a good mix, you might lose money in the short term in one asset class that is doing poorly, but at the same time you'll be gaining on another asset class that is doing well.

To illustrate this principle, let's assume there are only two asset classes from which to choose, and over a long period of time each will return 8%. The difference is that these asset classes move directly opposite one another, so that when one is going up the other is going down an equivalent amount. If you invest all your money in just one, your portfolio will rise and fall. If you happen to need money at the bottom of a downward movement, you will significantly reduce the amount of money available to you in the future. Or more probably, the huge drop in your portfolio could trigger a money script, and you may make "the big mistake" and sell precisely at the wrong time.

What would happen if you placed half of your portfolio into each asset class? You may ask, "Why would I want to own two investments where I am guaranteed one will always be losing money?" To reduce your volatility. Remember, both asset classes will earn 8% over a period of time. So if you place 50% of your portfolio in each asset class, you will never have any volatility. The teeter-totter will stay perfectly balanced. In other words, your total portfolio will be increasing at a steady 8% annually.

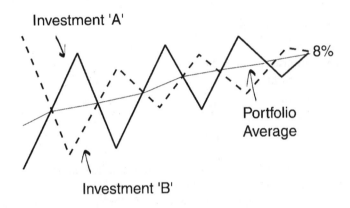

The bad news is that there are no two asset classes that move directly opposite of one another and that earn the same return over time. If, however, you diversify your portfolio with enough asset classes that move independently of one another, you will reduce the price fluctuation of the portfolio as a whole and actually lower its overall risk and volatility.

Studies show that to enjoy optimum asset class diversification, you must have five or more asset classes in your portfolio.

Investors who had more than five asset classes in their portfolios lost very little, if anything, during the market crash of early 2000. We know of many investors who saw no decline in their portfolios for a three-year period following the peak of the NASDAQ on March 11, 2000. They had a total return of 0% during one of the worst market crashes of modern times. And they did it not by timing the market, but by being diversified among five or more asset classes. Those who lost more than 15% during the three-year period following the peak of the market in March 2000 probably were not diversified among asset classes.

Most investment portfolios need to have five or more asset classes. This is crucial for successful long-term investing. Various investment advisors will differ on what constitutes an asset class, but here are our categories:

- U.S. Stocks
- International Stocks
- U. S. Bonds
- International Bonds
- Natural Resources
- Cash
- Real Estate
- Market-neutral Funds

Just to keep things interesting, there are subcategories within those classes. For example, in either U.S. Stocks or International Stocks, you can invest in mutual funds that own the following types of companies: large, medium, or small. The size of the company is referred to as its capitalization. So, the industry lingo for the size of a company's stock is *large-cap*, *mid-cap*, and *small-cap*. Some mutual funds will specialize in just one capitalization, while others will own a combination of large-cap, mid-cap, and small-cap stocks.

We've just introduced a term—*mutual fund*—that we need to explain. A mutual fund is simply a pool of money, contributed by shareholders, which is managed by an investment company. The company is charged with investing the money according to the directions of the shareholders. Most mutual funds invest in stocks, bonds, hedging strategies, commodities, or money market securities. For the most part, we believe average investors should invest their money with mutual fund managers, rather than investing directly into stocks or bonds.

Just to complicate things further, mutual fund managers typically have a *growth* or *value* bias when selecting companies. Some managers select companies that are likely to grow quickly, without giving much weight to the profitability or ability to pay a dividend. Others choose companies that have a high intrinsic value: lots of cash and assets, a high dividend, and a low amount of debt. Other managers will combine equal amounts of value-based companies and growth companies, or blend them together. So that gives you the possibility of having nine different categories within the asset class of U.S. or International Stocks:

Large-Cap Value	Large-Cap Blend	Large-Cap Growth
Mid-Cap Value	Mid-Cap Blend	Mid-Cap Growth
Small-Cap Value	Small-Cap Blend	Small-Cap Growth

The same is true for bonds. You can invest in high-quality, medium-quality, or low-quality bonds with long, medium, or short maturities. This gives you nine categories of bonds that can be owned within the asset classes of U.S. or International Bonds.

A bond that is considered low-quality, meaning that the company is encountering credit problems, is also called a *high yield* bond or a *junk* bond. Why would anyone want to own such a bond? Remember our discussion about discounting? A bond backed by a company with credit problems will usually sell at a steep discount. The object of the investor buying such a bond is to eventually sell it at a higher price once the company turns its credit problems around. Of course, buying such a bond requires the mutual fund manager to do a lot of investigation, or due diligence, on the company and be convinced that its financial woes will improve.

Additional classes of bonds would include mortgage bonds, typically backed by a pool of FHA, VA, and conventional mortgages; bonds that can be converted into stocks, called convertible bonds; and Treasury Inflation Protected Securities (TIPS), which are indexed to inflation so their yield increases if inflation rates increase.

One asset class we haven't said much about is market-neutral funds or funds that use hedging techniques. *Hedging* can be defined as strategy that reduces investment risk by using a variety of investment strategies like options, short-selling, or futures contracts. The purpose of hedging is to lock in profits, and therefore reduce the risk of loss or volatility of a portfolio. Funds that engage in hedging techniques are sometimes classified as hedge funds. However, we want to be clear that we are not talking about the high-flying limited partnerships of the rich and famous that have garnered so much negative publicity. We are talking about mutual funds that apply hedging techniques.

Examples of funds that use hedging strategies are merger or convertible arbitrage funds, long/short funds, and event-driven funds. Some investment advisors even define real estate investment trusts and commodities as being hedging strategies.

The point here is that even though these strategies are complex and exotic sounding, they are not necessarily risky. In fact, merger arbitrage has about half the volatility of the normal stock fund, being about equal in risk to a junk bond fund. The benefit of hedging techniques is used by some of the most successful pension funds in the United States. The state of South Dakota, which for the last 30 years has ranked in the top one percent of most successful public pension funds in the U.S., has allocated 5 to 10 percent of its retirement fund to arbitrage investments since 1986. Fortunately, mutual funds that engage in hedging strategies are available to even the small investor.

We want to reemphasize that many people, unfortunately including some financial advisors, think diversification means owning several different stocks or putting their money with several different stock mutual funds. That's one type of diversification, but it isn't enough by itself—and it is not adequate asset class diversification. For example, you might have three different mutual funds, but all three of them invest primarily in large growth U. S. stocks. That's no different from owning a Ford pickup, a Dodge pickup, and a Chevy pickup. They're still all trucks, so you aren't diversified. If you had a Ford mini-van, a Dodge pickup, and a Chevy convertible, then you'd be a little more diversified, but you would still only own one type of transportation. However, you would achieve asset class diversification if in addition to those you owned a helicopter, a train, a jet airplane, and a bicycle.

So we have talked about having actually three levels of diversification. First, you want different asset classes, ideally at least five. Second, you want different categories within each asset class. We talked about the fact you can have up to nine categories in stocks and bonds. Third, you want a lot of different companies or bonds within those categories, which can be obtained by investing in a mutual fund or several mutual funds.

Once you have selected the asset classes for your portfolio, you need to determine how much of your portfolio should be invested in each asset class, a function we call *asset allocation*. Just as it is important to have five or more asset classes, it is important to have significant parts of your portfolio allocated to the different asset classes. If you have 90% of your money invested in U. S. stocks, 2% in cash, 3% in natural resources, 2% in market-neutral funds, and 3% in real estate, that isn't going to give you much asset class diversification.

Here is a simple example of what a diversified portfolio might look like.

The portfolio above has 35% in U.S. stock funds, 20% in bonds, 15% in international stock funds, 10% in market-neutral funds, 10% in REITs, 5% in natural resources, and 5% in money market funds. The particular asset classes and percentages would vary, of course, depending on factors such as the age and the goals of the investor. Younger, more aggressive investors need more allocated to stocks, commodities, and market neutral funds. Older or more defensive investors will allocate more to fixed income and market neutral funds.

It's important for you to understand asset class diversification, even if you aren't a beginning investor and you already have a financial advisor managing your portfolio. The reason for this is that your financial advisor may not understand it.

*Too many financial advisors either don't understand
or don't practice asset class diversification.*

We aren't sure why. Asset class diversification is a part of any investment curriculum. Still, even some of the largest investment advisory firms in the nation just don't offer it. So if you as the customer know what asset class diversification means, you're able to monitor whether the people managing your money are practicing it.

Investing 102. How To Get Started

We've given you what we might call the theory of investing. Now let's talk a little bit about the mechanics. Suppose you are ready to start saving for your future, and you have maybe $200 a month to invest. You can't walk into the office of a financial planner who has a minimum annual fee of perhaps $10,000, and say, "I need some help with my $200 a month." At the same time, you do need some financial advice. Where are you going to get it? How do you get started?

We're assuming you've read the previous section, so you have an idea what a good investment portfolio should look like. Obviously, you aren't going to get there right away, but you know what you need to work toward. We're also assuming that by now you have some money in a regular savings account as an emergency fund. If you don't, then that's where you need to start stashing your $200 a month until you have perhaps three months' salary.

Retirement Plans

Your best option to begin investing is a retirement plan that is sponsored by your employer. There are many types of employer-sponsored plans. Some plans promise you a specific amount every month after retirement (defined benefit plans) while other plans will provide a lump sum amount (defined contribution plan). The defined contribution plans are the most popular with employers today, especially the 401(k) option.

Under a 401(k) plan, you can contribute a percentage of your earnings, according to guidelines set by your employer. There are several advantages to these plans. Perhaps the biggest is that you don't pay taxes on the amount you contribute, since it is taken out of your paycheck before your withholding and FICA taxes are computed. The maximum annual amount you can contribute before taxes is also quite high ($14,000 for 2005). In addition, many employers match a percentage of the employees' contributions.

A 401(k) plan is not managed directly by your employer. This means your retirement fund is protected against creditors should the company go out of business. (That doesn't mean your money is protected against risk, just that if your employer goes bankrupt it can't take your retirement account with it.) While your employer has selected the investment options from which you must choose, your allocation to each investment option is not determined by your employer. Within the investment options offered by the plan, you can choose how to invest your money. The choices are usually somewhat limited, but if you use the information in the preceding section, you can get at least some asset class diversification. All retirement plans have some restrictions; the most common is that if you take any money out before you reach age 59 and a half, you'll have to pay a 10% penalty in addition to the income tax you'll pay on it.

Depending on your income, the amount you are able to invest, and the makeup of your employer's plan, putting the maximum into your such a retirement plan may be all the investing you need to do. Because the amount you contribute is before-tax income, and because of employer matching, it certainly is the place you should start if you have such a plan available.

If your employer doesn't have a retirement plan available, or you're already putting in the maximum amount allowable, then the next place to go is an IRA or a personal account. A personal account is simply any investing you do that is not in a retirement account.

An IRA, or individual retirement account, is not in itself an investment. It's just a type of account that holds investments. You might think of the IRA as a bucket or container; the investments are the contents of that bucket.

When you open an IRA, all you do initially is deposit your money. Then you need to decide how to invest that money. You generally can buy anything in your IRA that you can buy personally. There are some restrictions on real estate, precious metals, and other investments not traded on a public exchange. The most common investments we see in IRAs are stocks, bonds, or mutual funds. The depth and breadth of the investment selection will depend on the choices offered by the company that is the custodian of your IRA.

As of 2005, as long as you have earned income, you can contribute the lesser of your total income or $4000 a year to an IRA ($4500 if you're over 50). Because you must have earned income, parents can't open an IRA on behalf of children who don't have earned income of their own. However, for a married couple, if only one spouse has earned income, each can open a separate IRA.

There are two basic types of IRAs: the traditional and the Roth. With a traditional IRA, your contribution is tax-deductible. The trade-off is that you pay taxes on the amounts you eventually withdraw, and there are penalties for withdrawing money early. Your contributions to a Roth IRA are not tax-deductible, but you don't pay taxes when you withdraw the money. The younger you are, the better the chance that the Roth IRA is the way to go. Even though you don't get the immediate tax deduction, you will come out ahead in the long run because you won't pay taxes on what you withdraw.

Many companies—from your local credit union or bank, to online discount brokers, to your insurance agent—can set up an IRA for you. Keep in mind that many of these institutions have limited choices for your IRA investments. Some of those choices, like an annuity, are downright awful. One thing you don't ever want to put in an IRA is a fixed or variable annuity. Like an IRA, an annuity is a tax-deferred bucket to put investments in. Since your IRA investment is already tax-deferred, it makes no sense to put another tax-deferred investment inside it—especially since fees for annuities are high because you're paying for insurance protection. There is really only one reason we know of to put an annuity in an IRA, and that is so the salesperson can earn a commission.

Paying a commission to a salesperson isn't bad in itself;
it just means you need to be conscious and cautious.

Before you set up an IRA, ask plenty of questions about fees and options. Demand to know exactly how the company's salespeople are earning their money, how much money they are earning, and for how long they will continue to earn it. No one is going to be helping you out for nothing, not even a discount broker.

Investing on Your Own

Now that you have decided which retirement plans to use and how much you can stash away in them, you will need to understand the mechanics of setting up an account. If you are using your employer's 401(k), this has already been done for you. Your employer has also selected your investment options, so all you need to do is determine your allocation among the options. The downside to this, however, is that you must live with the investment options within your employer's plan. Since most employers don't understand asset class diversification, you'll probably find the asset classes offered limited to U.S. stocks, U.S. bonds, and possibly international stocks.

If you have established an IRA or have additional funds to invest personally, you will have much more control over your investment selection. Of course, with more control comes a little more homework. Where do you start? To begin with, make sure you have put your emergency funds in a bank savings account or a money market fund. While the rate of return will most likely be dismal, you don't want to take any chances of your principal not being available on short notice.

When you begin investing, you'll probably need a minimum of at least $1000 to open a personal account and $250 for an IRA account. Once you have that minimum, where do you go to open an investment account? One option would be to head for your local bank or credit union. There are two things to be aware of before you go this route. First, the choices offered and the advice you get are likely to be limited. This is a bank or credit union, not an investment firm. Second, it is likely that the investment advisors there are paid at least in part through commissions on products they sell. This certainly does not mean those products aren't worthwhile investments. It does mean you should keep in mind that the advisor is primarily a salesperson with a vested interest in selling you one product over another.

Another option is to call one of the large discount brokers such as Schwab or TD Waterhouse. *Smart Money* magazine rates the discount brokers on an annual basis. You can get a list of twenty or so discount brokers and their ratings at www.smartmoney.com. All of these brokers have websites that will help you establish an account and give you basic information on investing. You can also call their toll free number and have one of their representatives help you open an account. Remember, though, that these are discount brokers. The person you talk to will answer basic questions and help you open an account, but his or her primary job is not to teach you the basics of investing. This is the "do it yourself plan." You need to do your homework before you call.

Let us give you one word of warning. If you establish an online account, you will soon see how easy it is to buy and sell stocks and mutual funds. You may become tempted to start investing in, or worse yet, trading in individual stocks. *Please, please, don't do this.* There are 20,000 or so publicly traded companies. A professional stock analyst who makes a living following those companies will typically track 30 to 50. So it's foolish to think that someone just starting out could analyze and pick wisely from all 20,000.

The best choice for all but the wealthiest investors is to buy open-ended mutual funds.

These are pools of money managed by a fund manager. Since there are 15,000 mutual funds out there, how do you pick one? Assuming that you are going this alone without professional advice, we will first narrow the choices. What you want are several *index funds* or one *asset allocation fund.*

First, let's talk about index funds. These are mutual funds that seek to produce the same return that investors would get if they owned all the securities in a particular "index." An index is a group of companies chosen to reflect a certain market. The most popular index is the Dow Industrial Average, which is made up of one share of stock from each of 30 very large companies. Another popular index is the S&P 500, made up of the 500 largest companies in the U.S. Because these funds are passively managed, they are not constantly buying and selling. This low turnover keeps fund costs down. It also means you won't have a huge list of transactions to cope with when you file your income tax return. Another benefit of a S&P 500 Index fund is that over time it will beat 75% of all actively managed large-cap funds.

While an S&P Index fund probably belongs in most portfolios, you will most likely want a mid-cap and a small-cap index fund. But don't make the mistake of stopping with index funds invested in only US stocks. You will remember that in most portfolios, we want several asset classes to reduce the price fluctuation and risk. This will mean you want index funds representing many of the other asset classes listed previously in this chapter. Vanguard, for example, offers low-cost index funds in U.S. stocks, U.S. bonds, and REITs. They also offer reasonable mutual fund choices for international stocks and bonds. Another easy way to invest in index funds is to buy an Exchange Traded Fund (ETF). These are closed-end mutual funds that trade on most major exchanges. They tend to have some of the lowest management costs of any mutual funds. The drawback is you will pay a flat fee, usually less than $25, to purchase an ETF, regardless of your investment amount. This makes ETFs a poor choice for the investor who is buying small amounts of the fund periodically.

You can purchase index funds from all the major discount brokers, such as TD Waterhouse and Schwab. Beginning investors want to purchase an index fund that doesn't incur a transaction fee for buying and selling, because you'll be buying small amounts every month. Most discount brokers have a list of "no transaction fee" funds, where the fund will pay the discount broker's trade fee. While these funds have a higher management fee (remember, there is no free lunch), they are well suited for the small investor. Most of these funds will have a $250 to $2500 minimum purchase when you start out. After that, you can invest as little as $50 each month.

Suppose you have set up an account at one of the discount brokers. Then all you have do to is call and say you want an S&P 500 index fund with no transaction fees, and the advisor can help you select one. After your initial investment, you can even set up automatic withdrawals from your checking account into that fund.

Obviously, when you're just starting out, you can't create a portfolio that is diversified among several asset classes by buying $50 worth of one asset class and $75 worth of another. What you can do is buy an asset allocation mutual fund that splits its funds among a variety of asset classes. Ask about the asset mix in the fund before you buy. You will find very few, if any, that have five or more asset classes, but they will probably have at least three, so you'd be moving in the right direction. Almost every family of funds has an asset allocation fund, so look around and do your homework. A great resource you can use is Morningstar (www.morningstar.com). This is an independent research company that compiles information and ratings on mutual funds.

Once your asset allocation fund has $15,000 or more, you'll have enough money to control your own allocations and select specific index funds. By investing consistently and paying attention to the basics, eventually you can build your $200 or $300 a month into a truly diversified portfolio. You don't have to be a big investor to be a wise investor.

Paying for College

"College Tuition." When it comes to sending cold financial chills down a parent's back, those two words are right up there with "orthodontia" and "I really want a pony."

As we discussed earlier, paying for your kids' higher education is often a "should." For some families, there simply isn't enough money to make paying for college even an option. Other parents assume that tuition is their responsibility. Still others believe that kids will benefit most by paying at least part of their own way. There is no one "right" choice; what matters is that you make those decisions consciously by doing your own interior work and by working in partnership with your spouse.

If you do intend to help your kids with college expenses, one of the best ways to save for that purpose is a 529 plan.

This is an investment plan operated by a state, designed to help families save for future college costs. Plans can be set up by parents, grandparents, siblings, aunts and uncles, or other relatives. Contributions to the plan are not tax-deductible, but no federal tax is due on any funds—including earnings—that are withdrawn to pay for college. The money can be used for tuition, books, and room and board at any accredited college in any state.

One big advantage to these plans is that they are flexible. Suppose you have two kids, and you've put money into a 529 plan for each of them. Your son graduates from high school, but decides not to go to college because he's earning so much money from the Internet tattoo-design business he's been running from his bedroom. You can shift the money from his 529 plan into the plan for his sister, who wants to become a doctor and will need all the college money she can get.

If the money isn't used for the original beneficiary, it can be rolled over into a new account, as long as the new beneficiary is related to the original beneficiary. Many states' plans define family very broadly, including in-laws, stepkids, sisters, brothers, aunts, uncles, and cousins. Beneficiaries do not have to be residents of the state.

A second advantage is that the donor retains control over the plan's assets. If you've been saving for the benefit of a grandkid who, at age 18, is making some less-than-responsible choices, you retain the right to decide what to do with the kid's 529 plan. It isn't automatically handed over.

Or suppose over the years you have put away a considerable sum of money in 529 plans for your kids. Suddenly you're hurt in an accident and will be unable to work for a year, and the family is going to have a hard time putting food on the table. You can withdraw that 529 money yourself, paying a relatively small penalty of an extra ten percent tax on only the accumulated earnings portion of what you take out.

A third advantage is that the funds are considered to be outside of your estate. Resource-rich individuals can contribute up to $55,000 every five years to each child's 529 plan. Obviously, a lot of money can be transferred out of a parent's estate, yet parents can still control the funds. This is the estate planner's version of having your cake and eating it too.

The specific provisions of 529 plans vary from state to state. Some states shield the assets in a 529 account from creditors of both the donors and the beneficiaries. In many states there are no income limitations, such as those applying to education IRAs, and no age restrictions. Even though the donor retains full control over the plan's assets, contributions are considered in most states to be completed gifts, and thus are not included as part of the donor's estate. The minimum for opening an account is generally about $1000, with subsequent contribution amounts as small as $50. Upper limits are typically quite high, perhaps $300,000 on the total balance per account—not likely to be a problem for the average donor.

Almost any financial advisor or bank will be able to tell you where you can find out more about your state's 529 plan. There is also information available at a website called www.savingforcollege.com. But, like everything, 529 plans are not a one-size-fits-all solution to saving for college. They may not be the best alternative for your situation. There are other vehicles that can be used for college savings, including Coverdell education savings accounts (formerly called education IRAs), prepaid tuition plans, custodial accounts (Uniform Gifts/Transfers to Minors Act, or UGMA/UTMA), and others.

In addition to saving for college, you have the option of borrowing. There are also many financial aid programs available, in the form of loans, scholarships, and grants. It is important that you start early in your child's life to understand the options and how best to arrange your and your child's financial affairs if you wish to take full advantage of these programs. Again, there are scores of books written on saving and borrowing for college, hundreds of web sites with information, and financial planners specializing in college funding who can help you learn what you need to know.

Finally, we want to emphasize again that you examine any unconscious money scripts around college expenses for your kids. It is not necessarily every parent's obligation to fund all, part, or any of their children's education. Whatever commitments you make to your children regarding their college education, do your best to enter into those consciously, having applied the exterior and interior tools you've learned in the previous chapters.

13

Estate Planning: It's Not "If," It's "When"

Estate planning, perhaps more than any other aspect of money mechanics, is almost impossible to separate into interior and exterior components. We want to emphasize how important it is to do your interior work in this area. The most difficult part of estate planning is getting to it, because there are so many hidden money scripts and difficult emotions attached to even thinking about it. We are afraid to think about death. We don't know how we want to leave our assets. Or we don't think we have any assets to leave. We think wills are for older people. We know we should have one, but we can't decide on the right person to appoint as guardian for our kids. We'll get around to it—one of these days.

If you don't have a will, we urge you to *make one now*. If that means using the tools we have given you in this book to address some of your emotional issues around this responsibility, please do it sooner rather than later. *This is important.*

Who doesn't need a will? Someone who wants to leave behind a legacy of difficulties for those they love. Dying without a will, called dying intestate, means that your heirs will incur the maximum amount of hassle in dealing with your possessions. It also means that you will abdicate to the government and the courts the power to decide how your assets are distributed. That's one form of unconscious behavior around estate planning.

At one time in his financial planning career, Rick thought dying intestate was the worst estate planning mistake anyone could make. Not long ago, he discovered that is not true. Mike and Linda had come to him seeking help with their investments. As a part of his usual process when taking on new clients, Rick asked to see their wills. Mike, who had recently retired from a branch of the military, handed Rick their two-page typewritten wills that had not been revised in 26 years.

As Rick read the wills he became concerned. They didn't mention the couple's three children, because they had been drafted before the first child was born. While the wills left everything to the other spouse in case of either Mike or Linda's death, if they should die at the same time the estate would pass to Mike's brother. That meant the kids would receive nothing. Once this was explained to them, Mike and Linda immediately made an appointment with an attorney. Upon reading the wills, he was so horrified he made them tear the documents up in front of him. He explained they were better off to die intestate than with those wills. According to the intestate laws of South Dakota, at least if both of them died simultaneously, the children would inherit their estate.

Mike and Linda told Rick that had he never asked to see their wills, neither of them would have thought to question them. Over the years several military attorneys had reviewed the wills and told them they were just fine the way they were. Even though Mike and Linda may have made the original wills consciously and to fit their situation at the time, the wills had become so outdated as to be completely contradictory to their current wishes.

*Simply making a will doesn't automatically mean
you are making conscious decisions.*

When estate planning is done unconsciously, you make an appointment with an attorney and say, "I need a will," and the attorney says, "This is how most people do it," and it's done. You just leave everything to your spouse or your kids. While this is certainly better than having no will at all, it isn't exactly planning and it certainly isn't conscious.

Conscious estate planning means thinking about what you have and what you want to do with it. You may want to leave everything to your spouse or your kids. But upon deeper reflection, you may also want to leave money to charities, schools, or other organizations or causes that you support. So do some thinking. What kind of legacy do you want to leave behind? Go back to your list of life aspirations. What kind of estate planning would be congruent with the items on that list?

If you have minor children, you need a will even if your net worth is in negative numbers. The single most important item in it would be naming a guardian for your children. This issue probably stops more estate planning than any other. It's an incredibly tough decision to make, in addition to being one we don't want to think about. But consider the alternative. If you and your spouse were to die in a car accident, the court would appoint a guardian for your kids. Who are the possible choices? Would any of them be the person you would choose? So think about this issue. Discuss it with your spouse. This is a decision that is too important not to make.

Something that might make this choice a little easier is knowing that you can appoint one person as the personal guardian for your kids, but another person or institution as the custodian of any money you leave on their behalf. So if your sister and brother-in-law would be loving guardians, but you don't think they make the wisest money decisions, you could separate those two guardianship functions.

If you expect to have an estate of potentially a million dollars or more, we strongly recommend that you enlist the help of a financial planner or estate planner to discuss your options. You may not think your estate would be anywhere close to that amount, but you may be surprised when you look at the numbers. When you consider savings, retirement plans, life insurance, and physical assets, your estate may be larger than you think.

A skilled financial advisor can potentially save you and your heirs hundreds of thousands of dollars in federal estate taxes.

If you intend to leave your estate to family members, there are many ways to do so—some less desirable than others. If you want a recital of the horror stories that can result from unconscious estate planning, check out *Beyond the Grave: The Right Way and the Wrong Way of Leaving Money to Your Children (and Others)*, by attorneys Gerald Condon and Jeffery Condon. The Condons discuss many examples of family dissension, lasting resentment, and even abuse of elderly parents that may result from ill-advised or poorly drafted wills. Among the issues they address are whether leaving everything equally to one's children is really fair, especially if one child has received more than others during the parent's lifetime or if children's circumstances are different. They also discuss problems that can result if only one sibling is named the executor of the estate, if trusts are not well designed, or if too much power is given to trustees. They advocate careful thought in order to avoid an estate plan that brings out the worst in one's heirs.

If you are part of a stepfamily, your estate planning needs to be particularly conscious. If you leave everything to your spouse, it's possible that on your spouse's death the estate could go to stepchildren and exclude your children from a prior marriage. Or, if you don't have a will, your estate would go to your spouse and children but leave out your stepchildren.

Letters of Instruction

Another item you may want to include with your will is a "letter of instruction." Russ Ketron, CFP®, got the idea of a letter of instruction from his brother, Bruce, an attorney, who has been including these with every will he writes since 1973. These letters may not have legal standing, but they can clearly express your wishes about what you really want to have included in your funeral or what you want your children to do with that family heirloom.

One of Bruce Ketron's clients was dying of cancer and would never see his son grow up. Bruce had the client write a birthday card for each year of the child's life until adulthood. Each card contained whatever wisdom and love he wanted to pass on to his son at that age.

Russ Ketron contends that having a letter of instruction results in more peace of mind and less dissension between family members. He says that over the years the letter of instruction has evolved into many different forms, including guidelines, family mission statements, and audio and video records. He told us, "I still have a tape of my 90-year-old grandfather, made shortly before his death, which followed up on the letter he wrote me on the history and his spirituality of his life's journey. The letter my father wrote on his philosophy of life in which he shared his values, and especially the integrity that guided his life, is one of my cherished possessions."

Rich Colman, an attorney who also uses letters of instruction, points out that, since they are not part of the will, they do not have to be witnessed and notarized. This allows you to change them easily as necessary. A letter of instruction also gives you a way to impart family values, discuss personal assets that may have sentimental meaning, and give guidance on a variety of other issues such as higher education, going into business, and buying a home. All of these important interior aspects would be impractical in a document that had more legal force. Of course, the downside is that the document does not have the effect of law.

Probate

Probate is a public process used by the court system for proving the validity of a will and regulating the process that transfers legal title of property from the estate of the person who has died to the heirs. Passing assets through probate usually takes several months, and it can run into years. Often, this means that assets cannot be liquidated or distributed until the probate process is completed. This is one reason why many people elect to use trusts, property in joint tenancy, IRAs, and annuities to pass assets. None of these methods of ownership result in probate. As long as an IRA, an annuity, or a life insurance policy names a specific person as a beneficiary, that money is transferred outside of probate. In most states, if a husband and wife own their house or other real estate as joint tenants with right of survivorship, that property does not have to go through probate. Provisions such as these are basic ways to ensure that the surviving spouse can continue to manage day-to-day affairs even if it takes quite a long time to probate the estate.

Trusts

An important area to explore when it comes to estate planning is the use of trusts rather than passing one's estate primarily through a will. A trust has three parties to it: the *grantor*, who puts the property into the trust; the *trustee*, whose responsibility is to care for the property and follow the instructions given in the trust document; and the *beneficiary*, who receives income from the trust or eventually receives the property in the trust. Depending upon the state of residence and the specific type of trust involved, one person can be both the grantor and the trustee, or can even have all three roles.

Trusts can be important estate-planning tools because the assets of a trust avoid probate. When a will is put into probate, its provisions are made a matter of public record, so privacy is one reason people choose to avoid probate. The expense of probate is a second reason. A third is that probate, like any court proceeding, takes time—years in some cases. So there may be a period of time when assets are not available, meaning a spouse may not have money available to pay even basic bills. With a trust, on the other hand, the trustee has almost immediate access to the assets. Wills can also be contested while trusts, by their nature, are contracts and are almost never contested.

There are two types of trusts, revocable and irrevocable. Living trusts are revocable trusts. They provide no tax benefits and no liability protection. In some ways a living trust is very similar to a will, in that it contains instructions on how to dispose of your assets upon your death. The difference is that upon your death, the trust doesn't die. The people who die are the trustee and the primary beneficiary, but the trust itself doesn't die, so there is nothing to probate.

Another benefit of a trust is that it will provide for the management of your affairs if you become incapacitated. Again, this can save time, save money, and maintain privacy. Living trusts also provide a layer of privacy and can keep the assets of the estate and how they were distributed from the public eye. If you own real estate, have a closely held business, or have a significant amount of wealth, you should seriously consider establishing a living trust. During your lifetime, you can put everything you own into this living trust. You are typically both the trustee and the beneficiary until your death, when the individuals or institutions to whom you wish to give your assets become the successor beneficiaries.

If you want to leave money to charity, one possibility is to establish a charitable remainder or annuity trust. There are complete books written on the use of these trusts. Very simply, using such trusts can result in tax savings, cash flow for either you or the charity while you are alive, and a bequest at death to the charity or other heirs.

Other possibilities with the use of trusts include dividing your estate into two parts, a *family trust* and a *spousal trust*. The family trust is usually what we call a *credit exemption* trust. This is where the estate places assets that total the dollar amount currently allowed to pass without inheritance taxes. Any assets over the credit exemption amount are placed in the spousal trust. Typically, the income from the assets in the family trust is distributed to the spouse and, upon the spouse's death, to the kids or charity. Doing this keeps the assets of the family trust from being taxed in the spouse's estate. Unlike the assets in the family trust, the assets of the spousal trust can be used or distributed at the will of the spouse. Another popular estate planning tool is a family limited partnership (FLP). An FLP can be a good vehicle for asset protection and estate planning when used by spouses or families.

There are many more fine points of estate planning than we can even touch upon here. This can be fairly complex stuff, so we will not do anything more than mention some of these options. The reason for bringing them up at all is to emphasize that, if you expect you will leave assets to others, you need to talk with a professional and get some estate planning advice. A financial planner or estate attorney will be able to advise you regarding state and federal taxes, types of trusts that may be appropriate, and other issues specific to your situation. Working with such professionals can help you be sure that what happens to your estate is in line with your life aspirations and authentic goals.

Sometimes so many difficult emotions surround the distribution of an estate or passing a family business or foundation to the next generation that executing an acceptable estate plan seems to be the impossible dream. It often just never happens because the family can't get close to discussing the issues. One of the most effective estate planning tools we've seen is a "Family Financial Integration Workshop" where financial advisors and therapists trained in financial integration meet with families for a day or a weekend. It isn't uncommon to see the most impossible estate and succession situations resolved by using such an integrated approach. We talk more about this in Chapter 17.

We also want to say one more time that there is absolutely no excuse for dying intestate. While it may be advisable to have an attorney help you with drafting a will, it is not always necessary. You can buy inexpensive ($25 or less) will kits through office supply stores or find them on the Internet. Nor does your will have to be perfect. Of course, you don't want to end up with a will such as Linda's and Mike's that is so out of date as to be completely contrary to your current wishes. But a will that carries out your wishes less than perfectly is far better than no will at all. And making a will doesn't mean it is in place forever. As your circumstances change, you can easily change your will. The important issue is to get a will in place, NOW!

Kathleen: Because Wayne didn't have a will, his estate was distributed according to our state law. The majority of it came to me, with lesser but significant amounts divided among my three stepchildren. Did this come close to carrying out Wayne's wishes? I can't be sure, because we had not discussed it, but I don't think it did. What I do know about what he would have wanted includes the following: He did not believe in giving large sums to one's children, because he thought it was extremely valuable for people to earn their own way. Had he chosen to leave anything to the kids, he would have included my daughter as well as his three biological children, because he had been part of her life since she was six years old and he loved her. Giving was important to him, so he may well have wanted part of his estate to go to charity.

Had Wayne left money to the kids, he would probably have done so through trusts. Instead, his three children (including an eighteen-year-old) received outright lump sums. Because there are no restrictions or control over that money, I am doing my best to offer guidance and support to the kids, trying at the same time not to interfere or offer unsolicited advice. Because I know Wayne would not have excluded my daughter, I have arranged to give her an amount from my share of his estate that matches the amount the other three kids received. That, of course, has required some planning and organizing.

Because I know giving was important to Wayne, giving is one of my long-term intentions for this inheritance. However, the giving will be done according to my preferences and wishes rather than his, because he left me no instructions. I do know that he trusted my judgment and sense of responsibility when it came to money, and I have tried to use those well. Yet as I have made decisions regarding the estate, I have really had nothing more to guide me than my best guesses as to what he might have done.

Instead of having clear direction from Wayne, based on decisions he made during his lifetime, I am doing "would have" estate planning. I think he "would have" done this, or I think he "would have" wanted that. The truth is that I don't know. I am doing my best, and I don't think I am doing anything he would not have supported. But by not having a will, Wayne not only made things more complicated for his family than they needed to be. He also gave up his right to make decisions about the estate that was built by his hard work and commitment.

ご•ら

14

Protecting What You Have

There is a saying that "It isn't how much money you make that matters; it's how much you get to keep." Managing your finances responsibly and maintaining financial stability require more than just earning money and investing it. A third factor is taking care of what you have. This includes insuring yourself and your property against physical losses and lawsuits, not wasting your money by paying more in taxes than you need to, and protecting your assets from frivolous lawsuits. In this chapter we discuss those aspects of consciously taking care of your resources.

Insurance

Insurance is a significant budget item and a necessity of modern life. Financial planners are usually referring to insurance when they talk about "risk management," which is one of the six major components of a financial plan. There are generally two approaches you can take toward managing financial risk: assume the risk yourself (often called self-insuring) or pay someone else to assume the risk (insurance).

A lot of people have a hidden money script that says insurance is a "necessary evil."

As we discussed in the spending plan section, be aware of any difficult emotions or money scripts that come up as you read about insurance. Like most money scripts, the "Insurance is a necessary evil" script can be true in some circumstances, partially true in others, and false in others.

Yes, insurance can be a necessary evil. This is usually the case when you can't afford to self-insure, but the cost of insurance makes it almost unaffordable. There are cases when insurance is a "necessary good;" it is actually both necessary and affordable. In some cases insurance can be just completely unnecessary, as in the case when a person can self-insure. Probably the worst scenario is when insurance is an "unnecessary evil;" when the cost may or may not be high, but the insurance is simply not needed or the insured is unlikely to collect on a claim.

Necessary Insurance

Let's first take a look at "necessary but evil" insurance, which is when you can't afford to self-insure. For most of us, this description probably best fits two types of insurance: property/casualty liability coverage and health insurance.

Property and Casualty Insurance

Typically, there are two types of property and casualty coverage, the types you generally purchase on automobiles and real estate. One insures the physical or personal property against damage or loss, and the other, which is liability insurance, protects you against a legal action brought against you. While some people can afford to self-insure a total loss to their car, we would argue that very few people can afford to self-insure against a multi-million dollar lawsuit or costly medical expenses.

Until recently, liability insurance was very easy to get and inexpensive. In the past few years, it has become very expensive and difficult or sometimes impossible to obtain. However, until our country adopts some type of tort reform, we recommend carrying as much liability insurance as you can reasonably afford, especially if you have a reasonable net worth.

Another type of liability insurance that professionals carry is errors and omissions insurance, or as it is called in the medical profession, malpractice insurance. You have probably read of cities that are beginning to encounter shortages of physicians because medical liability insurance has become unaffordable. Rick has physician clients who have taken early retirement from their profession because the soaring cost of malpractice insurance made it unprofitable to continue practicing.

Physicians and other professionals aren't the only people suffering from the skyrocketing premiums of the property/casualty industry. We have seen a continual increase in rates and a decrease in the number of companies even offering the insurance. More and more property/casualty companies are pulling out of areas and trimming unprofitable books of business, resulting in increased premiums. We've recently seen premiums for homeowner's insurance jump 25 to 50 percent in one year in some areas. One answer to the rising cost of liability protection is something called *asset protection*. This is owning your assets in such a manner that they are insulated from a frivolous lawsuit. We talk more about that later in this chapter.

Traditionally, folks who are young or have marginal driving records pay very high car insurance premiums. Obtaining liability insurance (required by law) can be astronomically expensive, and often coverage for property damage to the vehicle is simply not available. In cases such as this, where property damage coverage is unobtainable, you have no choice but to self-insure the property. You may want to think twice before investing a lot of money into a vehicle or taking out a large loan on a car that in less than a blink of an eye could be reduced to a pile of rubble, leaving you nothing but a huge debt to a creditor.

Health Insurance

Another "necessary but evil" insurance that very few of us can afford to self-insure is health insurance. You don't need us to tell you that health insurance costs are becoming unaffordable for an increasingly large spectrum of the population. The high cost of coverage is forcing many companies with group health insurance plans to drop certain coverage, like dental care or prescription drugs, or increase deductibles. Individual health policies are almost unobtainable at any cost and, in our town, there are currently only two companies writing medical insurance.

Unfortunately, there is not much on the horizon that indicates any relief. The steady increase of well-meaning government regulations meant to help those who won't help themselves has driven the cost of insurance up to unaffordable levels. It will probably take the near collapse of the entire system for people to realize that insurance is not a

God-given right, but like so many other things, a privilege not to be abused.

In the meantime, your best choice when it comes to health insurance is to get a policy with a high deductible, then put the money you save on premiums into savings so you can afford to pay for your own office visits, prescriptions, and medical prevention plan. This way you are at least protected in case of a major illness or accident. Or, if your employer offers one, take advantage of their cafeteria plan. With this type of plan, you can set aside an amount of pre-tax money that can be used for non-covered medical expenses and fulfilling your policy's deductible. Be careful, however, as these are usually use-it-or-lose-it plans, so you will lose any unused money in your account at the end of the year.

Disability Insurance

Despite that gloomy beginning, there is a brighter side to insurance. There are kinds of insurance you need but probably can afford, and there are kinds you may not even need.

In addition to your autos, houses, and health, you can also insure your income. Many folks are startled to find out that having disability protection is more important than having life insurance. A young person's chances of becoming disabled are actually greater than the chance of an early death.

The function of disability insurance is to provide a monthly income in the event that your earnings cease due to a lengthy injury or sickness. Many large companies offer some type of short-term disability coverage, but very few offer long-term coverage. Therefore, a person must typically purchase long-term coverage personally. Most disability policies will not cover more than 60 percent of your current income. You also have to pay attention to the definition of disability, the length of the coverage, and the length of the waiting period before coverage begins. Since studies we've read suggest that the majority of the disabled either recover or pass on within five years of becoming disabled, policies that insure you for life are often a waste of money. If you have adequate assets or income that you could use in the event of a disability without endangering your retirement plan, you probably don't need this coverage.

Life Insurance

Life insurance is actually another way of insuring income. Its purpose is to replace the earning power of the deceased. Parents with young children and without a lot of financial resources probably have the greatest need for life insurance. We typically find that you can get the highest coverage with the most affordable premiums by purchasing a simple term policy. This is a policy that pays your beneficiary the face amount upon your death. There is no investment component or "savings account" associated with it. The largest risk with a term policy is that you may become uninsurable and therefore unable to renew the policy at the end of the term. This is a legitimate concern and can be minimized by purchasing the longest term policy available. There are companies that will write term policies for up to 30 years. Typically, this is a long enough period to ensure that your children are raised, educated, and making it on their own.

Policies that include an investment feature have much higher premiums. These policies are often called cash value, universal, or variable life policies. In general, we recommend instead purchasing the pure coverage of a term policy. While there may be some cash value type policies that make sense, they are few and far between.

One of those times a cash value policy makes sense is when you want to fund an irrevocable life insurance trust (ILIT), upon the second spouse's death. The reasons for doing this can include providing cash to pay the estate taxes on an illiquid estate (like a family business or a farm) or as a wealth replacement strategy for the heirs. A wealth replacement strategy might apply in a situation such as someone giving a significant portion of his or her estate to charity and purchasing a life insurance policy to replace the amount of the gift. Gerald Butrimovitz, Ph.D., CFP®, says that this strategy works best for young, healthy parents who have significant estate tax problems and want to leave substantial assets to their children.

Butrimovitz adds, "Second to die policies have a lower expense than whole life on two individual single life policies. In fact, you can get an insurance company to convert a couple's individual term policies in part or whole to second to die. This is very useful, if the health of the individuals or insurability has changed since the policy began." Be careful if you transfer existing policies to an ILIT. If the insured dies within three years of the transfer, the transfer to the ILIT will not be recognized by the IRS.

*Don't overlook the fact that a stay-at-home parent
should be insured as well as the wage-earner.*

If you wonder why, take a few minutes and add up all the services the surviving spouse would need to hire to replace the stay-at-home parent. It would cost a considerable amount to replace that person's services. Get enough insurance on the stay-at-home spouse to cover that cost over the number of years the children will remain at home. Another reason to consider insurance on the stay-at-home parent is that the working spouse's productivity will decrease dramatically in the first year of a spouse's death. Replacing the surviving spouse's income for a year or two is a wise decision that will allow time to grieve the loss, and if there are children, be with them more during this difficult time.

Business owners with a lot of debt that they cannot self-insure may also need life insurance. So do partners or shareholders of a small incorporated business who might need income to buy out a deceased owner's shares. We strongly recommend, if you have partners or shareholders in any venture, that you have a buy/sell agreement that sets the terms of a buyout in the case of death, disability, bankruptcy, divorce, retirement, or termination of a partner.

Not everyone needs life insurance.

Take the retired couple with enough liquid assets to provide for a comfortable retirement, the person who does not care about leaving an inheritance, or a single person with no debts and no children. Not much of a case can be made that any of these people would need life insurance. Many financial planners advise clients to drop their term policies when they retire, assuming that they have enough retirement income and assets to last their lifetimes. In the past, many people purchased life insurance in order to pay the federal taxes on their estates. The recent changes in the tax laws lowering, and in some cases eliminating, federal and state estate taxes may have largely eliminated this need for all but the wealthiest taxpayers. We say "may" because tax laws change yearly, one important reason for regular updating of one's financial plan.

Long-Term Care Insurance

Another type of income insurance that is gaining popularity is called long-term care, or LTC. These are policies that pay a set amount per day for a stay in a nursing home, assisted living center, or in-home care. These policies are being aggressively marketed, since LTC insurance is the newest type of coverage available and the pool of potential customers is large.

The rationale for purchasing an LTC policy is twofold: to protect your estate from being significantly reduced because of long-term health costs or to assure that you will have the resources to pay for long-term care, should the need arise.

First, there are two classes of people that probably aren't customers for an LTC policy—the wealthy and the poor. The wealthy don't need it for obvious reasons. The poor don't need the coverage because they have no estate to insure, they can ill afford to spend their precious resources on the premiums, and Title 19 will provide long-term health care for them, anyway.

So, that leaves the middle class with the quandary of whether to purchase an LTC policy. Here are some tips: If your main concern is to be sure that you leave an inheritance, then perhaps life insurance is the best way to indemnify against exhausting your resources through long-term care expenses. Life insurance is typically much cheaper than an LTC policy.

If, on the other hand, your concern is not having the resources to pay for any needed long-term care, perhaps an LTC policy may be a good option. But, as Jim Helba, CFP®, notes, there are options other than laying out a lot of money for a plan that would fully pay for long-term care. "Perhaps partial self-funding of the risk is the middle ground." He suggests that one option for a person in this situation is to purchase an LTC policy with a daily benefit that lasts only one or two years. This gives the family members time to "assimilate the emotional shock of the event and make reasoned decisions as to what assets to systematically liquate to cover the balance of the liability." Also, many nursing home stays don't last more than two years.

Unnecessary Insurance

The final category of insurance is "unnecessary and evil." This is insurance that you have but don't need. An example would be someone who doesn't really need life insurance in the first place but who continues to own a term policy, or continues to carry a "paid-up" policy when the net return is worse than they could receive from a certificate of deposit or equivalent mutual fund. Any coverage that is in excess of what you really need falls into this category. Being over-insured is just plain wasteful, and in some cases the insurance company will not pay you the full coverage if they can prove you are over-insured.

Another example of unneeded insurance is purchasing accident insurance, cancer insurance, or a long-term health care policy when your net worth is more than sufficient to fund a stay in an assisted care facility or nursing home. When you examine the scenarios under which unneeded insurance is purchased, the winners are usually the insurance company and the salesperson, not the consumer.

Having the right insurance is important. It can save you from being financially devastated. But being over-insured can be equally damaging to your financial health. To make sure you have adequate insurance coverage, we would suggest getting an insurance review from someone with no interest in selling you a policy, like a fee-only financial planner. This is not always possible, as some states will not allow a fee-only planner who does not hold an insurance license to give insurance advice, and not every financial planner may feel qualified to do an insurance review.

If this is the case, ask colleagues for referrals of three insurance agents. Make sure at least one is an independent agent who does not represent only one company. Let each of them review your insurance coverage and make recommendations. Select the agent you feel most comfortable with and who offers the most comprehensive and knowledgeable advice. They can help you sort your necessary insurance needs from the unnecessary.

Tax Strategies

In general, the art of government consists
in taking as much money as possible from one class of citizens
to give to the other.

Voltaire (1764)

If you believe you can spend your money more wisely than the government can, then you don't want to give the IRS any more than you have to. We are not tax experts, and tax laws are always changing, so we are not going to go into detail in this section. There are, however, a few strategies for reducing taxes that you might want to keep in mind.

On the other hand, if you have money scripts that say, "Taxes are too complicated for me to figure out," or "The tax system is fair and equitable," or, "Taking advantage of tax 'loopholes' is wrong," and you don't want to modify those scripts, then you can skip this section.

The first strategy is simple and applies to anyone. Pay attention to the basics. Real-estate author Jack Miller is fond of saying, "There is no better paying job in America than being a student of the tax code." Yes, this is left-brained stuff, for sure, and it can be complicated. But realize that there are basically two tax codes in the United States, one for the people who don't want to understand the code and take responsibility for themselves and one for those who do. Guess which group pays the highest taxes? As a class, high wage earners pay far more than their "fair share," and high wage earners who don't take time to understand the tax codes pay the highest taxes of all.

The first step to take is simply to make sure you claim the right number of personal exemptions, figure your taxes at the correct rate, and claim all the deductions to which you are entitled. Some of these might include the child tax credit, home mortgage interest expenses, state taxes, or charitable contributions. Have you contributed the maximum allowed to an IRA or to your employer's 401(k) plan? And, please, don't have too much withheld from your pay so you will get a large refund. This "bonus" is nothing but an interest-free loan to Uncle Sam. Put the same money into an IRA or savings account instead.

For those of you whose financial affairs are more complex, there are additional ways to save on taxes. These include three basic strategies:

- Arrange to have more of your income derived from sources that are taxed at lower rates (like capital gains, dividends, tax-free income, loans, or tax-sheltered income),
- Increase deductions, or
- Reduce FICA taxes.

The first of these involves shifting income so more of it comes as long-term capital gains or dividends. Long-term capital gains (those on property you have owned for at least a year) are currently taxed at a lower rate than ordinary income. So if you need to make changes in your investment portfolio, selling stocks or mutual funds you have owned for a year or longer might be the best way to go. Currently, dividends on stocks are also taxed at a lower rate than ever before and in some cases may be subject to lower taxes than interest income. So you may pay less in federal income taxes on the income from dividend-paying stocks than you will on interest income from bonds. This shouldn't be the only factor in making a buying decision, but is something you should consider as part of the overall return you can expect.

Another way to lower your income taxes is to shift taxable interest income to non-taxable municipal bond income. Be careful here, however. Owning municipal bonds often only makes sense for those taxpayers in the highest income tax brackets. Many people in the lower tax brackets could end up earning less after tax with a municipal bond that with a taxable corporate bond.

Corporations

If you are a small business person, have a serious discussion with a financial planner or an accountant about forming a corporation. First and foremost is that you always form a corporation for business reasons, like limiting your liability. It is inappropriate in the view of the IRS to form a corporation to save taxes. So, our assumption here is that you have already decided to form a corporation for business reasons. That being the case, there are some secondary benefits to incorporating, which are tax incentives that Congress wants small business owners to use.

If you earn more money than you need to live on (you have discretionary income), you need to consider some of the benefits of a C corporation. The federal government taxes the first $50,000 of income retained in a C corporation at 15 percent, and there are no FICA taxes. Plus, there are many benefits available to C corporations that are not available to other entities. You can deduct unlimited job-related education expenses or up to $5,250 a year of non-related education expenses. Many fringe benefits are tax free; these might include using corporate tickets to charitable events, taking home old magazines from work, etc. Also, the first $50,000 in term life insurance policy premiums can be deductible by the corporation without being considered income to the employee-owner.

One of the main disadvantages of a C corporation is the consequences of taking your money out of the company. If you don't end up using retained earnings for expenses or salaries, the most popular method of getting the money out is to pay a dividend. Up until recently, dividends were taxed at ordinary income rates, so you were in effect taxed twice, once at the corporate level and again at the personal level. Today, the corporate tax on dividends is 5% or 15%, depending upon your tax bracket. For high income earners, this could even make it worthwhile to take dividends from a C corporation, rather than pay the higher ordinary income taxes.

There are many other strategies you may be able to employ to lower or defer income taxes, such as taking loans from a company in lieu of income, employing children who are 14 years or older, using various tax credits, and a host of other methods. There are thousands of books written and courses given on utilizing and tailoring such strategies to your situation.

Real Estate and Small Businesses

The second and third tax-saving strategies generally apply more to those of you who own your own real estate or a business, even a small, part-time one. With a business, you want to be sure you are fully deducting anything that is a legitimate business expense—use of your car, an office in your home, or travel expenses, for example. If you have a C corporation, your business might pay non-covered medical expenses, college expenses, or other benefits for its employees, which may only be you. There are many variations of retirement plans that the self-employed can establish which, given specific circumstances, will allow you to stash away your entire salary.

Owners of real estate have the advantage of deducting business expenses and taking depreciation. In the early years of a leveraged real estate investment, depreciation often exceeds the income, which provides you with some additional deductions to offset other income. This usually reverses itself in the later years of the mortgage when the increasing principal reduction on the loan creates a tax liability that is greater than the cash flow. This is called phantom income, because you are paying tax on income (going to debt reduction) that you are not receiving in cash. Phantom income often gives a person another opportunity to experience pain, examine unconscious money scripts, and feel difficult emotions!

FICA Taxes

Another often-overlooked method of saving taxes is to reduce FICA deductions. If you are self-employed, you pay both the employee and employer share of taxes for Social Security and Medicare. That is a deduction of more than 15.3%. However, dividends and rents are not subject to being taxed by FICA. So many owners of small businesses that are S corporations take a portion of the company's earnings as non-FICA taxed dividends, rather than salary.

As an example, suppose you own a small business that earns you $60,000 a year. You file as a sole proprietor, reporting your income and expenses on Schedule C with your tax return, Form 1040. Now, it might be that if you were an employee doing the same job for someone else, you might be paid a much lower salary of $35,000. The difference represents the "profit" the company earns.

One option you have is to incorporate, taking the S corporation election. This means that the corporation files its own tax return, but any net income or loss is "passed through" to the owners on form K-1 and appears on Schedule E of their 1040. In other words, an S corporation doesn't pay taxes. The S corporation will now pay you a salary at the current market rate of $35,000, and pay the shareholder (which is you) the remaining $25,000 as a dividend. What that does is this: On the $35,000 salary, nothing changes. You would pay income tax at whatever bracket you're in, say 15%. Plus the corporation would pay the employer share and you would pay the employee share of the FICA taxes—another 15.3% altogether. But on the dividend there's no FICA tax. So you have just saved 15.3% of $25,000, which is $3825.

Doing this, of course, will lower your Social Security benefits. So you don't want to take that $3825 and go on vacation with it. Instead, save it or use it to fund your retirement plan. Many financial planners will tell you that you will be better off than if you put it into the Social Security system.

Keep in mind that the FICA tax you pay goes directly from your pocket into the pocket of the government. The people currently drawing Social Security are being paid from the taxes currently paid by workers. You do not have a "Social Security account" or savings account that your FICA taxes go into. There is no "strong box." Theoretically, Social Security is a separate trust fund, but that fund has nothing in it except IOUs that must be collected from the salaries of our children.

Again, these are only the outlines of some basic strategies. Some of them might not apply to you. Plus, of course, the tax laws change from year to year. The tax code is complex, unwieldy, and abstract. There is far more gray in the tax code than black and white. *Don't let the complexity of the code stop you from taking responsibility for yourself.* There are books you can read, courses you can attend, and professionals you can hire. So if you think some of these approaches might work for you, we strongly recommend that you consult a tax preparer, preferably a CPA, or a financial planner if your situation is at all complicated. Do-it-yourself is wonderful for many things, but trying to keep up with the federal tax code is not necessarily one of them.

Asset Protection

The term "asset protection" for many people has a connotation of sleaziness or illegality. It implies hiding money in secret bank accounts in Switzerland or the Cayman Islands.

That is not at all the purpose of this section. We do not advocate that you compromise your own integrity by hiding assets, failing to pay taxes you owe, or refusing to take financial responsibility for your mistakes.

Protecting your assets is a defensive strategy, not an offensive one.

In today's world, with the increasing mindset that "somebody must be to blame," anyone who owns a business or has significant net worth is vulnerable to a frivolous lawsuit. All of us are aware of cases where judges and juries have awarded outrageous sums completely out of proportion to an injury someone may have suffered. In addition, there are attorneys so lacking in integrity that they make a living filing lawsuits with little or no merit just because the defendant has "deep pockets." They know that someone is likely to write them a check rather than go through the expense and hassle of defending against the suit. Asset protection is intended to protect you from such lawsuits by making your "deep pockets" less obvious to the general public.

Protecting your assets is a little like protecting your home. You can leave your door unlocked so you can just walk in at any time—but so can anyone else. You can lock the door, which means you have to carry your key and it takes you a little longer to get inside. You can install a security system, which means you have to memorize an access code. The more security you have, the more complicated it is to get in.

At this point, the average person is likely to run into a variety of money scripts. You may find one that says, "I don't want to bother with all that complicated asset protection stuff. Let's just follow the old KISS rule: Keep It Simple, Stupid."

We're sorry, but the old KISS theory doesn't work when you want to protect your assets. This is a situation where Rick's version of the rule applies: Keeping It Simple *Is* Stupid.

Admittedly, the foundation of a good asset protection program is simple:

1. Don't own anything in your name.
2. Use a variety of entities to hold your assets.
3. Place the jurisdiction of the entities in a variety of states.

While the fundamental ideas are simple, designing and implementing an effective plan may require a financial planner who specializes in asset protection specialist, working with your attorney and accountant. And yes, it will demand some additional paperwork.

Most effective asset protection plans involve a tailor-made collection of land trusts, limited liability companies (LLCs), corporations, self-settled trusts, and living trusts. For the best protection, several of these entities should be located outside of your home state. A properly designed plan will put up enough firewalls to protect your assets, but not be so complex as to be "complication for complication's sake."

If you are a sole proprietor, you need to run to your legal and tax advisors and form either a corporation or a LLC. If you own real estate, you need to get those properties out of your name and put them into an LLC, limited partnership, or land trust. If you own personal assets, you need to explore contributing them to a LLC, family limited partnership, or a domestic asset protection trust.

Suppose, for example, you own three real estate properties. If you own all of them directly in your own name, a judgment entered by a court on the behalf of any tenant would jeopardize everything you own, including personal property and investments. You could gain some protection by contributing all three rental properties to a limited liability corporation (LLC). While this would protect your personal property and investments from seizure, all the assets of the LLC (namely the rental properties) would still be at risk.

A better way is to contribute each property to its own LLC. This way a judgment would only attach to the offending property. All the others would remain safe. One of the negatives with this scenario is that you'll have to file three tax returns.

Even better, you could contribute each property to an out-of-state land trust. The beneficiary of the three separate land trusts can be an LLC, formed in another state. This scenario requires only one tax return to be filed, and the use of out-of-state entities will stop most frivolous lawsuits dead in their tracks.

A side benefit of asset protection planning is often a significant income tax reduction. For example, assume your three real properties generated $50,000 a year in net income. Further assume that you did not need this additional income and were in the 31% tax bracket. You would pay $15,500 a year in federal income taxes.

What if you formed a C corporation to hold and manage the real estate? If the net income to the corporation remained the same, the federal income taxes would decrease to $7,500.

Of course, there are nuances a person must know before establishing such a scenario. This is why you need to work with an accountant and an attorney—whose fees you could afford out of your $7,500 tax savings.

A relatively new tool for asset protection is the domestic asset protection trust (DAPT). The same year that Congress passed laws limiting foreign asset protection, someone in the state of Alaska came up with the idea of offering domestic asset protection trusts. The state quickly passed a law allowing people to form a trust in Alaska providing the same protection that had been offered by a foreign asset protection trust.

Following this lead, Nevada, Delaware, Oklahoma, and Missouri also jumped onto the DAPT bandwagon. So far it appears that these trusts offer the best of both worlds. The grantor can be the beneficiary and retain limited control. The grantor or trust protector can amend the trust. These are almost always grantor trusts, which means you don't have to have a separate taxpayer ID and file a return. The key to these trusts is the protection they provide for the assets, particularly in Nevada, which would be our first choice as the situs, or location, of the trust. Once you put an asset into a Nevada asset protection trust, after two and one half years the state will not allow the trustee to distribute those assets under court order or to a creditor.

A law that can protect trust assets from almost any attack brings up the issue of whether this is too good to be true. There has been considerable debate on this in the legal field. The Supreme Court has not ruled on it, and until there's a lawsuit challenging the legality of the asset protection statues in one of these five states, the issue is going to be up in the air. For this reason, most of the legal profession is reluctant to use DAPTs too heavily.

Since almost all asset protection trusts include a method by which you can amend them if the law changes, these trusts can be dissolved. So our position is, why worry about the Supreme Court overturning the state laws governing DAPTs if you can terminate the trust? You are in no worse position for having created the trust and are in a much better position if the law stands up to a Supreme Court challenge. With safeguards such as a trust protector, we think an increasing number of legal advisors and financial planners will use DAPTs, so it is important to know that this option exists.

This discussion is just a small taste of the options available for asset protection. Rick could have written an entire book on this subject; it was only Kathleen's insistence that there is sometimes validity to her script of "Keep It Simple, Stupid" that kept him from it. Obviously, if you are a high profile person with significant assets, you need to learn more. There are not a lot of good books on this subject. Most of the seminars touting asset protection are at best incomplete and at worst complete shams. Your best hope is to find a sage attorney or financial planner who specializes in this area and learn as much as you can.

Part III

Financial Integration

15

Practicing Financial Integration

By now, if you've done the exercises in the previous chapters, you have a good idea of what we mean by financial integration and you have an idea what you need to do in order to begin making your money decisions consciously. Yet you still may be uncertain about what this means for you out there in the "real world." Even though financial integration may seem to be an interesting theory, you might have doubts about how it applies to you on a daily basis.

Is this knowledge something you can use in your day-to-day financial decisions? Will it be helpful if you're sitting in the car salesman's office? Will it do you any good if you're trying to choose new carpet for the living room? Will it help you decide whether you need the help of a financial planner?

The answer to all of those questions is yes. In this chapter, we illustrate the practical application of financial integration with some examples you can apply to your own situation.

CRCK

Rick: Two years ago, when Kathleen and I embarked on this project, I seriously doubted that it would ever come into being, nor did I have an expectation that it would. However, I was very clear that whether a book would really emerge or not, I would learn something valuable. I've written and taught enough to know that I gain as much in my preparation as my readers or students gain from what I produce.

I wasn't disappointed. Indeed, I have learned much. This is not the same book we set out to write two years ago, one year ago, nine months ago, or even four months ago. It has morphed and changed as much as I have over the same time period. In part that has happened because Kathleen and I have little respect for the "don't do as I do, do as I say" approach. As we said in the beginning of this book, we practice what we preach. The operative word here is "practice." We don't claim to be perfect at what we preach.

The fact this book was ever written is a testimony to the principles it espouses. What you hold in your hands is a product of the exercises contained in this book that I applied to my life. Writing is a life aspiration of mine, something I've always loved to do. Writing a book has been on my list of authentic goals for a long time. But the thought of writing a book felt overwhelming; there was certainly a lack of authentic energy behind my desire. I could write a column, or even a longer article, but the thought of a whole book threw my mind into permanent writer's block. I had once started on a book and spent more time staring at a blank computer screen than writing anything meaningful.

Knowing that one of the barriers to authentic energy was a large project, I attempted to break the project down into small tasks, but that didn't seem to work either. My problem was finding the time. I owned five small financial services businesses as well as being a husband to Marcia and the father of two young children. I was writing a weekly financial column and a quarterly newsletter, serving on several volunteer boards, teaching workshops on money and emotions, and developing a housing project. Time was something I didn't have a great surplus of.

This project started as a simple conversation over coffee among friends. Knowing Kathleen was an editor and a writer, I told her I would love to write a book on what I had learned about emotion and money, but whined about the lack of time I had. She started explaining to me some of the ways very busy people write books. She described the various functions an editor could provide. She told me that if I could take the time to be interviewed and to talk into a tape recorder, she could start putting some flesh on the outline of a book. I then could take those very rough drafts and start expounding and refining.

Now that was a moment! You mean, there was help available, that I didn't have to do it all myself? Talking about what I knew to someone with a tape recorder sounded light and effortless. I could do that. And looking at a rough draft rather than a blank page was something I could do, too. We began to talk about this project as a real possibility, and we discussed our respective contributions. The more we talked, the more we realized that, even though the topic of uniting the interior and exterior of money was unique in itself, we could add a deeper dimension by uniting our respective points of view and expertise. Kathleen is in many ways the typical consumer of financial products and advice, representing the person to whom this book is written. And I, of course, represent the financial planning profession. We determined that this project would be more powerful if we worked as co-authors. We talked about our financial arrangement and worked out a win-win agreement. And gradually, this book began to take shape.

అ∾ఓ

Strategies for Healing and Change

Your money scripts, and the unconscious behavior and decisions that have resulted from them, may have caused a great deal of pain in your life. The process we have described thus far is intended to help you heal that pain and learn to make healthier, more conscious decisions. If you do the work we have suggested, you will begin a significant process of change and growth.

Living your life with financial integrity is an ongoing journey, rather than a destination.

We would love it if reading this book could help you transform overnight and begin living your life in complete financial integrity, but we know that isn't the way this kind of change takes place. You will continue to cycle from unconsciousness to consciousness, discovering new money scripts and undergoing the sometimes tedious process of modifying your behaviors. Often, about the time we've convinced ourselves we've modified a money script forever, a deeper, even more unconscious version appears when life's circumstances change. Living in financial integrity will mean learning to become comfortable with the process of transition.

The good news, however, is that your quality of life will continue to improve to the degree that you become more conscious around your money decisions. As you are learning to do things differently, you may find some of the following strategies and reminders useful.

1. *When you feel stuck in the process of change, it's often useful to go back to the basics.* Don't underestimate the importance of identifying your money scripts. Remind yourself as often as necessary

to pay attention to your body sensations and take time to feel your difficult emotions.

2. *As you use the tools of financial integration, you will come to understand for yourself how important it is to become at ease with difficult feelings.* A significant shift comes when you start to learn that you won't die from experiencing the pain. Accepting difficult feelings is also like paying attention to a whining child—once that need for attention is met, the child can stop pestering you. Difficult emotions are dissipated and their underlying money scripts modified when you accept and feel them. Until you develop the courage to accept your emotions, they will linger in the background, refusing to allow you to let go of your most entrenched money scripts.

3. *You can use journaling or other techniques of interior awareness to consciously and deliberately modify your rigid money scripts.* For example, if you have a script of, "I can't spend money on myself until everyone else's needs are met," you might write, "Others' needs are important and deserving, and so are mine."

4. *Even if you feel silly or awkward, it is valuable and important to consciously practice doing whatever is the healthy counterpoint to your money script.* Practice this regularly in small ways, and you will build the emotional muscles necessary to do it when the larger decisions come up.

5. *You can consciously choose to counter money scripts when they're repeated in your current life—aloud or in your head, whichever seems appropriate.* Your mother may fuss, "You'd better hang onto your job, because you might not find another one." But you aren't a child any more; you don't have to follow that script if your job isn't the right place for you. Depending on your circumstances and your mother, you can tell her so, or you can let her words go right on by. Her fussing almost certainly means she cares about you and wants you to be secure; you can choose to appreciate that positive intention, yet quietly let go of the money script because it doesn't fit.

6. *Don't discount the importance of complete and accurate external knowledge.* It is an important component of healing past pain as well as a resource for wiser decisions in the future.

7. *As you are growing and healing, nurture and support yourself.* When you're struggling with a painful money script that brings up difficult feelings such as shame, guilt, or fear, consider asking yourself the question, "What would a child with these feelings need?" Go back mentally to the innocent child you were when you learned that money script. Because it's that child who learned the money script, it is that

child who feels the pain associated with it. No matter what your chronological age may be, that child is still a part of who you are. What knowledge, reassurance, or support would you give that child if you could? If you were five or six years old, what would you need? What did you need in the past that you did not receive? Whatever that may be, you can use tools such as journaling, feelings meditation, and psychotherapy to provide it in the here and now.

Practicing Financial Integration In Your Everyday Decisions

The following is a summarized or shorthand version of the financial integration process you've learned throughout this book. This isn't necessarily presented as a step-by-step process, because the sequence in which you apply the elements may vary in different circumstances. Think of these as reminders you can use to stay clear and conscious when you're faced with a specific financial decision. Also, please don't think this brief summary can serve as a shortcut you can use instead of going through the processes we've described earlier. This will only work if you have first done the real interior work of beginning to identify your money scripts, recognize and be at ease with your difficult emotions, and understand your life aspirations and authentic goals.

With that in mind, when you have a "real-world" financial decision to make and you want to make it consciously, what do you need to do?

Be Aware of Body Sensations

If you are talking to a salesperson or discussing a financial need with your spouse, and you become aware that your stomach hurts or your shoulders are tense, pay attention to those sensations and the emotions they are likely to represent. Learn to develop awareness of what your body is feeling and any resulting pain. Pain is the first indication that there is an unconscious money script lurking about. These are valuable clues that you may be encountering one of your own money scripts or that you are not ready to make a decision.

Use the Pause

Giving yourself a time-out in order to reach clarity can be one of the most valuable tools you can use in the middle of a financial transaction. The classic tacky sales technique of "this deal is only good right now" is used because it works. If you are encountering pressure—either exterior or interior—for an instant decision, chances are that decision won't be a conscious one. If you aren't ready internally to make a decision, step back from it. Yes, you may miss some opportunities, but you almost certainly will miss some mistakes, too. Another opportunity will always be there. And the more consciously you begin to make your decisions, the more opportunities you will find.

A time-out doesn't have to mean a week or a day, either. Sometimes all you need is ten minutes to go think something through and pay close attention to how you feel. There's absolutely nothing wrong with saying, "I make it a rule never to decide on a major purchase without taking some time to think it over." You can always excuse yourself for some reason or another to get away by yourself for a few minutes.

Be Aware of Your Money Scripts

Even a basic awareness of your most habitual money scripts can be highly valuable. Suppose, for example, that you have a script that says, "Always buy the cheapest thing you can find." When you're faced with a need such as buying a new washer and dryer, you can remind yourself not to blindly follow this script and buy the cheapest model you can find, but instead to look consciously at features, warranties, and quality.

Apply the Tools of Interior Awareness

Sometimes this can be done instantly, and other times it is going to require some time. It is possible that in the process of buying something as simple as a washer and a dryer you may become aware of a firmly entrenched and unconscious money script for the first time. You could experience what seems like a completely irrational flood of difficult emotions and know that this is not going to resolve itself with a few moments of feelings meditation. This is when getting some additional help will be necessary.

Get the Exterior Knowledge You Need

Doing some research before you make a decision is almost always useful. In some cases, that may mean simply checking to see whether another store has the same item at a lower price. At other times, it may involve taking a class, reading a book, or asking others for recommendations.

Practice Integrity in Small Ways

We have talked a great deal about becoming clear about your life aspirations and authentic goals. That applies to smaller decisions as well as major life choices. A part of making conscious money choices is knowing what you want—and you won't know what you want if you don't develop the habit of asking yourself the question. Do you really want to buy this or do that? How will it feel if you make that particular decision? Does it fit with your life aspirations? If you're making a major purchase, ask yourself these questions ahead of time. Write out a list of exactly what you're looking for—before you go shopping.

One part of integrity is knowing what matters to you. Another aspect, which is often more difficult, is being able to communicate what you want or what you believe to be important. Fostering integrity may require some practice in saying what you think and feel. For some of us, who may have money scripts that we don't deserve anything, that may be incredibly hard. Sometimes it's important to practice this with small decisions, such as the restaurant you'd prefer for dinner or whether you really want to go see that movie. Don't just say, "Oh, whatever you want, it doesn't matter." Stop and think about what you do want, and then state your preference. Expressing your opinion, like any other behavior, takes practice if you are to do it regularly and competently. Taking what may appear to be tiny or trivial steps such as these can be a necessary and effective way to begin acting consciously and with integrity.

Ask for Help

In some situations, asking for help may be part of getting the exterior knowledge you need. At times it may mean brainstorming with a friend to expand your range of choices, or discussing a decision with a financial advisor. For deeper and more painful money scripts, it may require calling a counselor or even participating in a program like the Financial Integration Workshop. Just remember, you don't have to do this all by yourself.

A Practical Application

As an example, let's apply these elements to a fairly common financial decision: buying a car. How might you go about making that particular choice in a conscious way?

1. Get the exterior knowledge. Compare models for reliability, fuel economy, resale value, and all the other factors that might be important to you. Look at your budget and decide how much you will choose to spend. Narrow the choices down to a small range of models within your price range. You can read ads, do research on the Internet, and ask knowledgeable friends, but make sure you do your research before you set foot on a car lot. If you start out "just looking" before you know what you're looking for, you may end up buying a vehicle that isn't what you really want.

2. Take time to figure out what you genuinely want. Within the appropriate price range and the way you will use this vehicle, what is it that you really want to have? Pay attention to your feelings as you imagine yourself in certain vehicles. What do you really want from a car? Spend enough time and check out enough possibilities to be clear what kind of car will fit you.

3. Remind yourself to be alert for any of your money scripts that might influence your decision. You might even consider writing down and carrying with you a list of positive statements that are the opposite of your core scripts. If you have a script that tells you, "Only losers buy used cars," but your car-buying budget is small, you might need a reframed script such as, "Winners are smart enough to buy what they can afford."

4. As you're looking at cars and talking with salespeople, pay attention to your body and your emotions. Continually monitor what sensations are happening in your body as you interact with the salesperson.

5. Remind yourself to use the pause. You can take whatever time you need to make up your mind or process a body sensation or emotion. For example, if your stomach knots up when the contract is put before you to sign, pay attention to that. Rather than plowing on with the deal and signing the document, take a moment. Go to the bathroom, take a short walk, or tell them you have to "think about this overnight." Check out whether what you are feeling is simply tied to inappropriate money scripts or is a warning that you are out of financial integrity. If that means you miss out on buying a particular car, that's okay. There are literally lots and lots of cars out there for sale.

6. Ask for help. This may mean getting advice and information from a friend who is a car expert. You might take someone with you when you go car-shopping to remind you to think before you sign. If you're getting a used car, have an independent mechanic check it out before you buy it.

CRCK

Rick: Don't get the impression that Kathleen is the only one of this team who makes unconscious financial decisions. During the process of writing this book, my 1991 Infiniti threw its timing chain and was pronounced economically dead on arrival by the attending mechanic. I had always wanted an SUV that would give us more options for hauling things like kids and the stuff they accumulate. Now that we are living on a hill with a view, owning at least one four-wheel drive vehicle could come in handy. So I researched all the options, narrowed my list to two or three makes and models, and set out shopping.

Two weeks later I was the proud owner of a 2000 Honda Accord EX with just 10,000 miles on it for $11,000 less than a 2004 model. Confused? My friends certainly were, and so was I.

I bought this vehicle because it was such a good buy and I was in a hurry, even though it wasn't four-wheel drive and didn't meet my other criteria. I didn't pause to ask, "Is this the right car for me?" I failed to do the interior work to determine what I really wanted in a new car. So right now I'm driving a vehicle that, despite its quality and reliability, just doesn't completely appeal to me. I haven't had to walk up our hill in a snowstorm yet, but if I do, I will really regret my unconscious decision to go for the bargain instead of getting the four-wheel-drive I really wanted.

≈≈≈

CKf

Kathleen: As another example, let's suppose I had used these reminders before I bought my house. How might my experience have been different?

Pay attention to your body and your emotions. As I signed the offer and wrote out a check for the earnest money deposit, my shoulders were tensed up to my ears and my stomach was beginning to hurt. I had plenty of signals telling me I didn't want to do what I was doing. I ignored them all.

Pay attention to your money scripts. Had I stopped and listened to my body's signals and the emotions of fear and sadness behind them, I would have been more conscious of my money script about needing to settle for whatever I could get. I could have kept reminding myself that there were plenty of houses for sale, that I didn't have to buy anything, and that I had plenty of time to find the right one.

Use the pause. This one alone might have kept me from making the decision I made. I could have said, "I need another day to think this through." I didn't. Because the house was a good buy, someone else would probably have bought it had I waited. I could have asked myself, "How will I feel if I wait and someone else buys the house?" Since the answer would have been "Relieved," I would have been clear that I didn't want the house.

Apply the Tools of Interior Awareness. Had I paused, I could have gone home and done a feelings meditation, journaled, talked to a friend, or processed the situation with my counselor. Unfortunately, I never got to this point.

Get the Exterior Knowledge You Need. Ironically, I had done exactly that, to a point of writing down a list of things that were "must-haves" for any house I might buy. The trouble was that I discounted myself by ignoring my own list. I could have discussed that list with David before we looked at a single house. I could have carried it with me and compared it with any house I looked at. Instead, I left it at home in my computer, where it didn't do me any good at all.

Ask for help. Again, this is something I did. I just didn't ask for the right kind of help. After I had looked at the house once, I asked my friend Patty to look at it with me the second time. She did, and she liked it. Knowing that she did only added weight to the message, "This house is such a good buy, you'll be stupid of you don't take it." I didn't really need her opinion of the house, which had nothing to do with whether it was the right house for me. What I needed was someone to listen while I talked my way through the question of whether I really wanted this house. Because I didn't know that clearly, I wasn't able to ask the right questions.

Practice integrity in small ways. Expressing my opinion clearly was not a behavior I was used to practicing; I had made a habit of exactly the opposite for too many years. As a result, it was not easy for me to state what I wanted or needed in a house. In recent months, I have been consciously practicing speaking up. Do I prefer a morning or afternoon appointment at the eye doctor? I'll decide which works better for me, and then say so. Did I like that book or movie? I'll tell you what I really think. What restaurant would I like better for dinner? I think about what I want, and then say so.

Sometimes I feel silly doing this over things that don't matter much, sometimes I worry that I'm going to be too bossy, and sometimes I think I'm becoming mouthy and obnoxious. But I'm also finding that it can save a lot of time and trouble when I say what I want. This is true even if that's only the first step in negotiating a plan that turns out to be something different from what I would have chosen. And the more that I practice speaking up, the easier it gets—on larger decisions as well as small ones.

࿇

Transition and Discomfort

Did you ever get a new bicycle as a child? There it was, bright and shiny and wonderful. You could see yourself pedaling off down the street, riding to school or the playground to show your friends, zipping along with delightful freedom and ease. Then you took it outside, started down the sidewalk, wobbled and tipped over, and skinned your knee.

Learning new skills is like that. You may have deep, sudden shifts in your perceptions and feelings, but there will still be a period of messiness and chaos as you learn to do things differently. Financial integration isn't something that happens overnight and leaves you miraculously "cured." You will make mistakes. You will fall back into old habits.

Any time you're unlearning an established pattern of behavior and replacing it with a new one, you're going to experience a period of discomfort and disruption. Not only will you have times of slipping back into old behaviors, but you may find that it takes some experimentation to discover better ones. Knowing that you don't want to continue doing what you've done in the past is only one aspect of change; another is figuring out what you want to do instead. You may have to try out several alternatives to the money scripts that you want to change before you find something that fits for you.

You may experience pendulum swings from your previous unconscious behavior to the opposite extreme. Suppose you have always operated according to a money script that says, "Don't spend anything; money should be kept in the bank." As you begin to see other possibilities, you may find yourself impulsively buying frivolous things, wanting to splurge on gifts, or considering extravagant vacations. This is normal. If you are concerned that you're going too far in the opposite direction, you can always ask someone—perhaps your spouse, a friend, or your financial planner—to help you set some boundaries for your new behavior. However, if you are genuinely working toward consciousness in your money choices, chances are that you'll work your way back to a more sensible middle ground before you make any significant mistakes.

Please, treat yourself with gentleness and compassion
as you learn to make conscious money decisions.

You won't do this perfectly the first time, or the second or the third. You don't learn to ski or ride a bicycle without falling down a good many times, and you don't learn to cook without burning something at least once. Give yourself the time you need to make mistakes as you practice your new conscious behavior.

Keep in mind, as well, that practicing consciousness around money is an ongoing process. You learn gradually, you slip backward, you experiment and make mistakes. You also deepen your conscious awareness as you continue to grow, and you will encounter new situations that will generate new money scripts or trigger existing ones you aren't yet aware of.

One thing we strongly recommend is that you go through the life aspirations and authentic goals exercises annually. As life happens, as your circumstances and your needs change, your life aspirations may change and certainly your authentic goals and tasks will change. Some will decline in importance, some will increase, and others will be accomplished. In addition, going back to those exercises periodically can help you keep your aspirations clearly in mind, help you identify the things that may have crept into your life that don't fit your aspirations, and help you maintain the energy to keep moving toward them.

Practicing financial integrity is not so much about knowing the answers in every financial situation, but about knowing enough to ask the right questions. As you deal with financial decisions and the day-to-day mechanics of money, you can use the clarity and knowledge you gain from the financial integration process to help you stay on the path that will lead you steadily closer to fulfillment of your life aspirations.

16

Balance and Integrity: Others In Your Life

Much of the financial integration process is focused on you as an individual—what your hidden money beliefs are, what you need, and what you want for your life. That doesn't mean you do this in isolation, unless of course you choose to live as a hermit. At some point, you are going to involve others in your journey to financial integration. Some of those other people will be spouses, family, and friends who are part of your life. Some will be professionals you employ to assist you. In either case, you will need some tools to apply what you've learned so that your financial healing becomes a part of building and maintaining healthy relationships.

We focused previously on identifying your own life aspirations and authentic goals, and we emphasized the importance of honoring and following your dreams. That is a wonderful and necessary aspect of living a full and satisfying life. It is, however, only one side of the coin when it comes to living with authenticity and integrity. The other side is that you often must integrate your aspirations with those of others.

We are not advocating that you follow your own dreams with such single-minded focus that you ignore or run over the other people in your life. Doing so may be honoring your aspirations, but it's hardly honoring yourself as a member of the human community, and it's certainly not honoring those around you. An important component of living with integrity is according due respect to the aspirations and needs of others in your life. Another is acknowledging those who teach, help, and support you along the way.

None of us achieve our aspirations by ourselves. Artists, who may or even must create their works in solitude, nevertheless learn from mentors and teachers, and often they are given the opportunity to practice their craft through the help and even financial support of others. Great explorers have always had financial backers and those who accompanied them—Lewis and Clark were the ones to get their names into the history books, but the expedition's enlisted men paddled the canoes, put up the tents, and butchered the antelope for supper. Successful businesses are not made solely by their founders or owners—Bill Gates may be the head of Microsoft, but he isn't the one who writes the software or answers the phone in the technical support division.

How, then, do you move toward fulfilling your life aspirations and at the same time encourage others in your life to do the same? Doing this is not necessarily easy. It requires compromise, communication, balance, respect, and honesty.

Mutual Support Between Spouses

Suppose you have identified a life aspiration to be an explorer and risk-taker. At the same time, you are a husband and the father of two young children. It is probably not realistic for you to head out on a six-month expedition to explore the South Pole or the headwaters of the Amazon. So a part of balance for you may be to recognize that, for the present, you aren't going to satisfy this particular aspiration on any grand scale. Instead, another of your life aspirations, that of being a responsible father, takes precedence in your life right now.

That doesn't necessarily mean you have to put your adventuring aspiration completely on hold for 20 years. You can look for other ways to honor your need to explore. Those may take the form of recreation such as rock climbing or skydiving, of finding ways to stretch yourself and innovate in your work, or even of involving the family in appropriately adventurous vacations such as camping in the mountains or crewing a sailing ship.

What if, to turn this example around, you have a life aspiration of providing a secure future for your family, but your spouse is the one with the life aspiration of being an adventurer? Your role, then, might be to ask for your spouse's help in making wise long-term financial decisions, while in exchange you support your partner's adventurous side. That might mean encouraging an activity such as skydiving that you personally would never be so insane as to attempt.

Or suppose one of you has an aspiration to be a world traveler, while the other's aspiration is to be a community leader and public servant. You want to spend the summer in China; your spouse wants to run for mayor. How do you both get what you want and need?

We can't tell you a specific solution for this or any other situation, but we can tell you one way to find a solution. Use the three Cs: communication, creativity, and compromise. You talk about what you both want and need, you brainstorm creative options, and you compromise and adjust to one another so you both get some of what matters to you.

The important part of using the three Cs is to be sure one spouse isn't doing all the compromising. Temporarily postponing or adjusting your life aspirations in order to accommodate those of your partner is being respectful and mutually supportive. Giving them up or postponing them indefinitely is being co-dependent. The flexibility and support has to go in both directions.

Marriage has been described as a "base camp," where one spouse creates a supportive place from which the other can go out and explore or face the world. That's an excellent description as long as you take turns running the base camp for each other. Nobody wants to always be the one left behind to collect the firewood, cook the meals, and wash the explorer's dirty socks.

Again, we aren't saying you are selfish or wrong to feel strongly about your life aspirations or work hard to discover and nurture them. That is a crucial part of becoming who you are meant to be. It is also a crucial part of successful compromise. You can't negotiate respectfully and creatively unless you first know clearly what you want and what you believe. Rick's house-purchase story is one example of successful compromise. It worked well in part because both he and Marcia knew what was important to them—both individually and as a couple.

Working toward your life aspirations isn't necessarily an all-or-nothing proposition. It can be a part-time, intermittent journey. The important things are that you are aware of your aspirations in the first place, that you start on the trip, and that you keep making progress. There is a saying from Alcoholics Anonymous that fits here: "Progress, not perfection." The journey isn't much fun if you concentrate on the destination so obsessively that you wind up alone by the time you get there.

Teaching Your Children

If you are a parent, one aspect of becoming conscious about financial choices is purposefully trying to teach your children more balanced money scripts than you may have learned yourself.

*One way to teach your children is to break the barrier of silence
that makes money a taboo subject in most families.*

You can begin to discuss money matters with your kids in ways that
are appropriate for their ages. You can show them the family budget,
you can talk about how you set priorities for spending and how you
make financial decisions. You can teach them about giving, encourage
or even require them to save a portion of their allowances or earnings,
and involve them in planning family vacations or activities within a
given budget. You can answer their questions honestly and directly.
You can even talk about money scripts that may have been handed
down in the family and how those have affected family members'
behavior.

There are various ways to teach kids about financial responsibility.
As parents, you may choose to give allowances or not, to pay kids for
chores around the house or not, to require kids to save or let them make
that decision themselves, to encourage or to limit summer jobs. You
may wish to take advantage of any programs your community may
offer, such as Junior Achievement, meant to help kids learn about
taxes, the economy, and business. You might want to investigate
financial classes or other resources for yourself or for your children.

We don't have a set of rules that are the "right way" to teach kids
about money. There is, however, one thing we would emphasize. If you
teach them nothing else, allow your kids to learn that when a budgeted
amount of money is gone, it's gone.

*One of the most important things you can do for your children
is to keep from enabling them financially.*

It is extremely hard for almost any parents to say "no" to a child in
need, whether the need is an extension on this week's allowance for a
ten-year-old or helping out a twenty-year-old who has overspent on a
credit card. But taking away the painful consequences of irresponsible
financial decisions is rarely doing your child a favor. Be clear ahead of
time about the boundaries and limits with your children when it comes
to money, but be firm as well about maintaining those limits. Letting
your kids experience their own pain and their own struggles around

money choices is not being mean or hard-hearted; it is giving them the gift of responsibility while the consequences are minor.

CR CK

Rick: One of the things my wife and I do with our children is have a rule that toys cannot be left upstairs at the end of the day, but are to be taken downstairs to their rooms. This rule is primarily for me, because I can hardly exist in a space of chaos and clutter. I can handle the toys being all over the place downstairs, but when the mess starts to creep upstairs, that's encroaching on the "adult" space in our house. So any toys that London and Davin forget to take downstairs go into my "collection." Then periodically the kids can buy them back from me, or they may become gift wrapped for a special occasion.

London came to me the other day and said, "Dad, I really need the pig and the donkey you put in your collection last week for the story we're going to act out. Could we get them out of your collection just to use for the story, and we'll put them right back?"

I thought about it, but I said, "No, honey, our agreement was that toys left upstairs go into my collection and they don't come out until I have a sale or a special occasion." Since I knew that London was currently broke, having spent all her money on other animal toys, even having an impromptu sale was not an option.

"Please, Dad. We could put them right back, I promise."

I told her, "Well, I'm sorry, my collection isn't for loaning."

Looking into her pleading little face and saying "no" was not easy. It made me feel like the most hard-hearted and unreasonable parent imaginable. It would have so easy instead to say, "Okay, just this once." But this was the consequence of her decisions not to pick up her toys and to spend her money on other things. To give in to her at this moment would rob her of a wonderful learning opportunity while she was young and the cost low. Financial lessons not learned at a young age just end up becoming more expensive as we grow older and the consequences are more severe. I had to concentrate on answering her request consciously, trying to be firm and consistent with the lesson about consequences and responsibility that we are trying to teach her.

≈∽

As parents, we have a responsibility to teach our children and help them grow. It would be so easy if we could just tip them sideways, pour everything we know into one ear, and have them get it. Unfortunately—or perhaps fortunately—it doesn't work that way. Our kids will never "get it" from listening to what we say. They will learn part of what they need to know from watching what we do. The rest of what they need to learn can only happen from their personal experience, from the struggle that is so essential for their growth and so hard for us to let them do.

It is natural for us as parents to want life to be easier for our kids than perhaps it has been for us. On the other hand, almost all of us know that if we make their lives too easy, they will be denied the satisfaction and self-confidence that come with overcoming challenges. How to balance that—how to be supportive but not to take away the struggle—is the critical question.

It's a question for which we don't have a definitive answer. We do know it's essential that we as parents constantly ask ourselves the question. That is one way to keep ourselves behaving consciously when it comes to kids and money. Another suggestion we have is to reframe what you wish for your children. Instead of thinking, "I want my kids to have it easier than I did," you might think instead, "I want my kids to be happy and successful and fulfilled. In this situation, what is the best thing I can do to help them become that?" In many circumstances, the best thing to do might be nothing. Stepping back and letting them struggle with their own difficulties may be the best gift you can offer them.

The real challenge with this comes when parents have plenty of money. How do you create challenges, or allow your kids to meet their own challenges and to go through their own struggle, when you and they both know that you could easily afford to help them? How do wealthy parents teach their children responsibility and consciousness around money?

Again, we don't have the answer. We can only offer a few suggestions. Communication is all-important. You can talk with your kids about money as an asset that needs to be managed responsibly. As they grow older, you can involve them in family foundations or other vehicles for managing and perhaps giving from the family's wealth. Chores and responsibilities can still be part of their lives. Your task as parents is to find ways to allow your kids the struggle that is so necessary. If there is no need for financial struggle, perhaps you need to expand your thinking and find other ways to provide that opportunity. One thing all parents can do in various ways is to allow kids to make their own age-appropriate decisions and let them experience the consequences without stepping in.

Regardless of your economic circumstances, perhaps the most important thing you can do in order to teach your children is to become as conscious as you can about your own decisions around money. The strongest way of helping your children learn conscious money behavior is to model it in your own life.

Children learn from what you do much more than from what you say.

17

Finding and Working with Advisors

During your journey, there is a high probability that in some manner you will have the need to hire a financial planning professional or a counselor. In this section we want to give you some suggestions to help you select the right professionals to support you in your financial integration journey.

Financial Advisors

How do you find a financial professional who will support you in doing your interior work and becoming conscious about your money choices? How do you find financial advisors who operate with integrity? A few of you may be fortunate enough to find a financial planner who practices the principals of this book. Most of you, however, are going to need to do a bit more work and "train" a traditional financial planner to work with you.

First, let's cover some definitions. In this chapter we are using the term "financial advisor" quite broadly to encompass financial planners, attorneys, accountants, bankers, insurance salespeople, stock brokers, mutual fund salespeople, administrators of retirement plans, trust officers, and anyone else whose profession includes helping people make financial decisions. When we refer specifically to a "financial planner," we will be talking about someone who is a Certified Financial Planner® and therefore trained as a "generalist" to help clients in the following six areas: estate planning, retirement planning, cash flow management, risk management, tax planning, and investments.

Please note that the financial industry uses these terms and many others interchangeably. Financial planning is an embryonic profession. There is no government certification or license required to call oneself a "financial planner." Anyone can put the words "financial planner" on a business card. There are even more terms advisors and planners use to describe themselves, such as "wealth counselors," "wealth managers," or "comprehensive wealth advisors." Even more confusing, some CFPs®, though they have the degree and the training, choose not to do financial planning at all, but may specialize in a certain area such as life insurance or mutual funds.

It is up to you to be sure someone advertising as a financial planner is actually a Certified Financial Planner® and is actually engaged in doing financial planning.

There are a lot of product salespeople out there masquerading as "financial planners." So finding a "true" financial planner, as opposed to a product salesperson, takes some knowledge and searching.

The Three Tiers of Financial Advisors

The first tier are those who are just out to take your money with no regard whatsoever for your welfare. To put it delicately, the crooks. These are the ones with the "double your money" deals and the "invest right now because this offer is only good today" sales pitches. Never, ever invest with someone who calls you up out of the blue with a "special one-time opportunity." Stay away from anyone who promises you exclusive inside information or is selling a specific "pick of the day" stock. Into this category fall those who boldly hold themselves out as financial planners solely as a guise to sell you their product. The product they are pushing is unimportant, as it could be anything from legitimate investments like a mutual fund to something more questionable like an abusive tax shelter dealing in jackalopes. (A jackalope is an animal native to South Dakota and Wyoming with the body of a jackrabbit and the antlers of a deer or antelope. Some people claim they are mythical creatures.)

Stay away from "advisors" whose only intention is to separate you from your money.

The second tier of advisor includes those who are not really out to do harm, but who are operating unconsciously themselves. These are typically advisors who are selling a specific product or service—which may be a perfectly good product that could be a legitimate part of a diversified portfolio. However, in their zealousness, they often advise customers to put inordinate amounts of their portfolios into this product or service. These typically are "product salespeople," but this category can include any unconscious advisor or planner who offers a service with a strong bias. They don't intend to give anyone bad advice, but the overriding reason for their recommendation is the sales commission or fee they receive from their products or advice.

This category represents the largest number of financial advisors, who are usually licensed to sell a variety of products such as life insurance, annuities, mutual funds, managed accounts, limited partnerships, or real estate. It can also include CPAs, attorneys, and trust officers who "push" a specific strategy, a one-size-fits-all philosophy, or a particular bias. When you deal with these individuals, it is highly important that you have acquired a fair amount of exterior knowledge. You will need to be in the intellectual position of telling them what you need, not vice versa.

The third tier is the advisor who operates with conscious integrity. That might mean someone who has done some personal interior work. It also might include someone who deals strictly with the exterior functions of financial advising or planning, but who does so with great care and attention to clients' overall well-being. They could be compensated totally or in part by commissions, but most will charge a fee for their services, unrelated to any product sale. Those planners who receive no commissions are typically called fee-only.

Regardless of how they charge, you will be best served by Certified Financial Planners® who are on their own interior journeys and are doing their own interior work.

Remember, financial planners can only take you, their client, as far as they have traveled themselves. Gayle Colman, CFP®, of Carlisle, MA, is well known for admonishing financial planners, "You can only take your clients as far in their interior journey as you've traveled yourself." This attitude, which may seem intuitive to some, is rare. To find financial planners who have done their own interior work, which includes traveling the road to the past, is an extreme exception. It will be very difficult to employ a financial planner who will support your interior journey, unless that person is also on his or her own interior journey. Such a financial planner has the best chances of actively assisting you in your effort to make conscious financial decisions.

There is a growing body of financial planners who are doing exactly that. At the time of this writing, however, their numbers are still few. There is also a growing number of workshops for financial planners that teach them how to assist their clients in establishing the equivalent of life aspirations and authentic goals. We've referred to this as the "looking forward" part of the interior work. The current buzzword for this function among financial planners is "Life Planning" or "Financial Life Planning." A financial planner who has completed courses offered by The Institute For Financial Life Planning, Money Quotient, or The Kinder Institute can help you in this regard. You can find links to these and similar courses at our website.

Of course, by now you can recognize the weakness of only looking forward, and you have learned that we can only look forward as far as we are willing to look backward. *Looking backward is not currently something that is embraced by many financial planners, even those who are on the cutting edge of the interior finance movement.* Financial planners are as scared as anyone else of looking at the past. When the concept of "financial therapy" is mentioned in the same sentence as financial planning, they tend to run screaming out of the room. Therapy is something that is okay for their clients and others, but not something that they see as having any relationship to financial planning, their practices, or to them personally.

Finding financial planners who have done and are continuing to do their own financial therapy is an altogether different matter from finding a "Life Planner." We know of only one financial therapy program currently offered, and that is the Financial Integration Workshop created by Rick and Ted Klontz which is offered by Onsite Workshops (www.onsiteworkshops.com). More such offerings are sure to be created in the future as demand for this important work increases. A list of financial planners who practice financial integration and who have taken this workshop is available at www.consciousfinance.com.

By now you can see that finding financial planners who have done their own financial therapy is a tough assignment. There are not a great many of them at this point, so one may not be available in your area. And if you do find one, it may be that working with that person may not be a realistic option if your finances do not justify or allow you to afford their services.

In that case, your best option is to do your own interior work well enough so that you can wisely and effectively use the exterior services of a more traditional financial planner or advisor. This means that you become conscious enough so you know what your money scripts are, have done the interior work necessary to identify and feel your emotions and find clarity, know what your life aspirations and authentic goals are, and can communicate with integrity about what you need and want.

In the same way you need to be careful in hiring a contractor to rebuild your deck or in choosing an auto mechanic, you need to use common sense in hiring someone to help you with your financial planning. In this case, you will be your own financial general contractor. You will need to articulate your needs and expectations very clearly. You may even want to encourage the planner to read this book or take some of the courses currently offered by Financial Awakenings, Onsite Workshops, The Institute For Financial Life Planning, Money Quotient, or the Kinder Institute.

How To Interview A Financial Planner

First, let us clarify that the process described on the following pages is not the definitive manner or the only way to interview a financial planner. Take from it as much or as little as you wish, depending on what works and is comfortable for you.

The first place we would start is to ask for references from attorneys, accountants who do not have a financial planning division, or friends who have financial planners. Internet sources in addition to our website include the National Association of Personal Financial Advisors, www.napfa.org, and the Financial Planning Association, www.fpanet.org. You can also look on the Internet or in the yellow pages for financial planners in your area.

If you do enough research, you will start to hear several names mentioned repeatedly. Try to narrow your field down to two or three financial planners to interview. A good way to do this is to access the financial planner's website. This "electronic brochure" will give you even more information about the planners, their firms, and their practices. You can also call the planners and ask them to send you information on their services and practices.

Once you have selected two or three planners to interview, call each one's office and ask for an appointment. Most planners will grant a free initial consultation that will give you each a chance to experience one another and assess whether there is a foundation for a business relationship. Conscious planners will be interviewing you as diligently as you are interviewing them.

The planner may send you a copy of an engagement agreement or a short questionnaire for you to fill out and bring to the meeting. It is at this meeting that you will have a chance to find out about the planner's personality and practice.

Here is a list of questions that you may want to ask the planner. This is not an all-inclusive list, nor are the questions in any particular order.

1. *What are the characteristics of your typical client?* If the planner serves a very narrow niche, such as specializing in employees of Microsoft, and you are a small independent business owner, you may not have a good match. Ask them what type of client they do their best work with.

2. *What is your education?* You want to know what colleges prospective planners attended, whether they have master's degrees or doctorates, and especially whether they have earned the CFP® designation. Find out if they have attended any courses on coaching or counseling or hold any certifications in these fields.

3. *What is the process you use? How long does it take? What should I expect?* All planners work differently, even those with interior skills. Don't be afraid to ask questions as planners explain their processes. Make sure you leave with a good understanding of what to expect.

4. *What kind of interior finance work have you done yourself? What is your own relationship with money? What money scripts or unconscious beliefs about money do you have?* If the planner gives you a blank look in response to these questions, that doesn't necessarily mean you should head for the door. Remember, many planners will not have much of an idea what you are talking about. Instead, explain what you mean by interior finance work, and explore whether the planners seem open to learning more and to supporting you to continue your own interior work.

Rick, thinking that all planners would recognize they are mortals around money issues, once suggested jokingly that the way to determine whether planners were on their own interior money journeys was to ask whether they had any money issues. If a planner said "no," the questioner should run out of the office immediately. The person he was talking with actually did ask that question in an interview with a planner, and the planner replied, "No."

5. *What are the terms of your engagement agreement?* Most planners will have an engagement agreement, and all fee-only planners are required to give you full disclosure documents. If you haven't received these ahead of time, ask for them. Ask the planners what their procedures are when clients leave them. Find out what the planners consider to be their responsibilities and what they consider to be yours. Ask about conditions under which they would refer you to another planner, an accountant, an attorney, or a therapist. Make sure each planner goes over the agreement thoroughly and that you understand all the terms and conditions. As always, ask questions.

6. *What is the average size of your clients' accounts?* This information is often obtainable, even for planners who do not participate in the annual survey in *Bloomberg's Wealth Manager* that lists several hundred planners and their average account sizes. Why would you ask this? Because if the planner's average client has an account size of $10,000,000, and your account is $200,000, you may not have the best fit. The same is true if you have an account size of $10,000,000 and the planner's average account is $200,000. Certainly, you will want to consciously explore the issue with the planner.

7. *Can you give me the names of three clients I can call as references?* In order to protect clients' privacy, planners do not routinely give out clients' names without permission. Still, be a little leery of planners who will not give you any names as references. Most planners do have several clients who have authorized the release of their names and phone numbers to prospective clients. Even if it is their mothers, their sisters, and (on good days) their spouses, all planners should be able to come up with three people who can tell you something about their character.

8. *How will information be delivered and meetings be conducted if we can't meet in person?* Because of modern technology, you don't necessarily have to be in the same geographical location as the planner. Many planners have websites where data can be uploaded and viewed easily by clients during phone conferences.

9. *Will you describe what you consider to be a fully diversified portfolio?* Go back to our explanation of asset class diversification and find out whether the planner's definition of a diversified portfolio matches it. This is an important factor in successful long-term investing, and you deserve a planner who both understands and practices it.

10. *How do you charge for your services?* When it comes to financial planners, there are those who are commission-only, which

means they do not charge fees to clients but earn their money solely through commissions on products they sell. Others are fee-based, which means they operate on a combination of commissions and fees. Others are fee-only, meaning they sell no products for commission but charge clients directly for the services they provide.

Our bias is toward fee-only advisors. There are two reasons for this. One is that commission-only planners, no matter how pure their intentions, require you to buy something from them to be compensated for their time.

Commission-only planners are essentially salespeople.

No matter how honorable and full of integrity they might be, they still do not get paid except through what they sell. That fact cannot help but influence their judgment. This is a bit too much like asking for advice from a doctor who isn't going to get paid unless you have surgery or from a mechanic who doesn't charge for labor but who only makes money through selling you parts. The second reason is that very few commission-only planners will be doing any extensive interior work with clients, because there is no provision for the planner to be compensated for that work. While there are some planners of impeccable integrity who operate in this fashion, they are few and far between.

If you do choose to work with a commission-only advisor, be sure that person represents a wide enough range of products to be able to provide you a genuinely diversified portfolio. Be sure also that you have done your homework and made a conscious decision that you can work effectively with this planner.

Fee-based financial planners represent the broadest group of financial planners today. They earn their money through a combination of commissions on products they sell and fees they charge for advice or financial plans. There are a number of excellent interior planners in this group. Again, the most important item is that you know exactly how the fees and commissions are earned and how they are charged. Insist on knowing exact details of how the planner is compensated, and how much. One thing to remember is that *the law does not require commission-only or most fee-based planners to disclose any conflicts of interest they, or their companies, may have in their advice or products they sell you.* Their fiduciary allegiance is to their employers rather than to you.

The greatest majority of financially integrated planners fall into the fee-only category. One of the biggest benefits of using fee-only planners is that, unlike commission-only or most fee-based planners, *they must disclose to you all conflicts of interest they or their companies may have regarding any of their recommendations to you.*

If you are at all in doubt about choosing a planner, we suggest you stick with a fee-only planner.

Fee-only planners have various ways of setting their fees. Some have minimum annual retainers, others charge based on a percentage of your account, or assets under management (AUM), and others use some combination of the two.

If it is just exterior knowledge that you need, there are also some fee-only financial planners who will work with clients for an hourly fee. This can be a valuable resource for someone who does not have a large enough portfolio to justify paying annual fees to a planner, but who still could benefit from some financial planning advice. You might be able to go in for a two-hour appointment, which may cost you $100 to $300 an hour, but which would be a tremendous value. What you can learn in those two hours about planning for your future can save you the amount of that fee many times over. One place to find planners in your area who provide hourly services is through the Garrett Planning Network, Inc. (garrettplanningnetwork.com).

Another option for primarily exterior assistance is an on-line fee-for-service provider. As with anything on the Internet, you need to be sure the people operating the service are real advisors with integrity. Currently, we know of one such site we can recommend called www.myfinancialadvice.com. The mission of MyFinancialAdvice is to bridge the gap between competent, ethical financial advisors who would like to provide their expertise on an as-needed, pay-per-use basis and consumers who want affordable, unbiased financial advice but don't have easy access to it. You can register on the site and choose from a number of advisors' profiles and their areas of expertise. Most charge by the minute for advice.

Finally, whatever questions you ask, do your research. You may want to come back for a second interview with the planner before making your final selection. Make sure you feel safe and comfortable with this person and that the planner will support you fully in your interior journey with money.

And always remember that anything that sounds "too good to be true" probably is. If a planner starts to "sell" you on any product or strategy at these initial interviews, you probably want to run, not walk, out of the office. Remember, you're the customer. This is your money. While it is ill-advised to reject or ignore the advice you're paying someone for, it is just plain stupid to blindly follow someone's advice just because they're the expert. No one will care more about your money and your financial affairs than you.

Therapists

We've written earlier about the value of working with a therapist, so we won't repeat ourselves here as to why the guidance and help of a good counselor is so essential to working through our most entrenched money scripts. What we will do is offer some suggestions for finding the right therapist to help you in your interior journey.

Just as when hiring a financial planner, the best choice is to find a therapist who is actively addressing money issues on his or her own interior journey.

This is not always easy, as not all therapists have done their own personal healing. Finding therapists who are on that interior journey and who also understand money is even harder. There may well be fewer therapists who have addressed their money issues than there are financial planners who have gone through financial therapy. Talking about money is the unspoken taboo of the mental health industry.

You may think it is ironic that money is seldom, if ever, explored in the therapist's office. Many counselors feel very comfortable and justified in helping clients examine relationships with work, partners, families, sexuality, family of origin, nicotine, alcohol and other drugs, food, spirituality, chronic illness, and so on. Why not money?

One reason is that many members of the therapeutic professions take unconscious vows of poverty. Olivia Mellon (1994) uses the term "Money Monk" to refer to those who look to what they perceive as the higher meaning of life, feeling that it is to some degree degrading and debasing to be concerned about something as mundane as money. Therapist Ted Klontz maintains, "The counseling profession is over-represented by money monks." To back up his claim, Ted says, "Try talking to the average counselor about raising their fees, even to just match the cost of inflation and increased costs of doing business. There is an unspoken professional bias against counselors who might seem interested in the money side of things."

It is not uncommon in graduate school for counselors to get a very clear message that it is not acceptable to go into the counseling profession looking at a business model. We are not aware of any course work in any university that teaches prospective counselors how to implement a business plan. According to Brad Klontz, Psy.D., a clinical psychologist who recently graduated from a prominent school of social work, the unspoken message was, "If you came into the counseling profession to make money, you are in the wrong profession!"

It is not our intent in telling you this to frighten you away from therapists. We do, however, want to emphasize that it is unlikely that a therapist will suggest any work with you about your money issues. You will need to take the initiative to bring up those issues and make clear that you wish to work with them.

How To Interview A Therapist

Just as we suggested in finding a financial planner, the first place we would start is to ask for references from any friends who have seen therapists. If you are fortunate enough to have friends familiar with therapy (No, that isn't a joke; some of the most emotionally healthy and balanced people we know have been through therapy.), ask them about the therapist's style and what a typical session might be like. Ask them how long they've been going to the therapist and what type of progress they've made. Another good source of referrals for therapists is www.onsiteworkshops.com. While they do not list recommendations on their website, they can tell you if there is an approved Onsite group leader in your area. You can also find at www.conciousfinance.com a list of therapists who have gone through the Financial Integration Workshop and who are on their own interior journeys.

While it's generally harder to find referrals for therapists than it is for financial planners, eventually you will probably find one or two therapists mentioned repeatedly. Most therapists don't have websites and don't grant a free initial consultation, so you will probably invest some money in determining whether you have a good fit. It may be possible to have a phone conversation with the therapist in advance to help determine if this is a good choice for you.

Here is a list of questions that you may want to ask the therapist. Some of these are similar to the ones you would ask a planner. Again, this is not an all-inclusive list, nor are the questions in any special order.

1. *What are the characteristics of your typical client?* If the therapist specializes in ex-convicts, sexual abuse survivors, or drug addicts, you may not have a fit. Find out the type of client he or she works best with. If therapists start working with you and determine they cannot effectively give you the help you need, find out when, where, and to whom they might refer you.

2. *What is your education?* You want to know what colleges prospective therapists attended and their level of education. While we have known excellent therapists who didn't even have bachelor's degrees, your chances of getting a good therapist are slightly better with one who has at least a master's degree, and better yet if he or she has obtained specific training in co-dependency and experiential therapy.

3. *What is the process you use? What might a typical session be like? Do you offer an experiential therapy group?* You'll want to find out whether therapists are more cognitive or experiential in approach, whether they offer group therapy, and something about how they work. Every therapist has a little different style, and some styles are wildly different.

4. *What type of interior work have you done yourself?* Therapists don't have to give you their life histories, but it's reasonable to ask whether they work with or have worked with a therapist themselves, whether they have participated in group therapy, whether they attend workshops for their own personal benefit as well as professional training, and whether they encourage their clients to participate in 12-step programs. Do the therapists have access to a full range of feelings? It will be hard for them to encourage you to feel your feelings if they don't do it themselves. It is also important to ask about their view of feelings meditation and how it fits, or doesn't fit, with their view of therapy. Some therapists don't support any type of meditation as an effective tool, just as some meditation teachers don't feel therapy has any benefits. Finally, it is important for you to know that they don't

view themselves as "having arrived," but have an ongoing commitment to practicing what they preach.

5. *What kind of interior work have you done around money issues? What is your own relationship with money? What money scripts or unconscious beliefs about money do you have?* Again, you may get a blank look in response to such questions, but it is important to have a discussion around money issues and find out whether therapists have ever addressed their own issues in this area. Chances are that therapists you interview will not have done any work on financial issues, so your focus may need to be on the therapists' willingness to explore in this direction and to work with your money concerns. Any therapists who are not willing to at least read this book or listen to your explanation of money scripts are probably not going to be the best guides for your journey toward financial integration.

5. *Do you have an engagement agreement or treatment plan?* Some therapists will have engagement agreements you can review. Make sure, whether they have such an agreement or not, that they set clear boundaries about time, missed appointments, fees, and your responsibilities. Also, find out what their standard is for knowing when you are finished with their services.

6. *How do you charge for your services?* Again, therapists' answers to this question may give you some clues to their own level of consciousness when it comes to money. Those who are businesslike about explaining fees, possible insurance reimbursement, and the like are probably better choices than those who seem uncomfortable discussing such matters.

Finally, whatever questions you ask, do your research and trust your own feelings. It is important that you feel comfortable and safe with them and that you feel respected. And, yes, it is okay (and even important) to be able to laugh with your therapist. If you feel uncomfortable after several sessions, it may not be because of your own fears or nervousness about therapy. Perhaps you and the therapist are simply not a good fit. It is not unusual to try out several therapists before you find a good match.

One note of caution, however. If you have fired your third or fourth therapist for the same reason, (such as all of them giving you similar feedback, which does not match your version of reality), you might want to begin considering the fact that all of them just may be right. Part of what competent therapists will do is gently confront clients' denial or refusal to accept their own share of responsibility. Nor is therapy necessarily going to be fun or easy. Working through painful issues is just that—painful. In order to help you, the therapist needs to help you face your pain, not allow you to keep avoiding it. Competent ones do so in ways that are not abusive or shaming, but are supportive and encouraging.

The bottom line, of course, is that you are the client. This is your life, your interior journey, and your money. Just as with a financial planner, while it is ill-advised to reject or ignore the advice you're paying someone for, it is just as detrimental to blindly follow their advice because they're the expert.

The Ultimate Financial Integration Experience

If we could wave a magic wand and create it, what would be the ultimate financial integration experience? We suggest it would include having your therapist and your financial planner work collaboratively. Ideally, every meeting concerned with the financial aspects of your life would be with both a financial planner and a therapist present in the session.

RK

Rick: Let me give you a glimpse into the future. The best financial planners of the future will be those who are not only on conscious interior journeys around their relationships with money, but those who will have received some degree of training in counseling. It may be as little as a course in coaching or as much as a degree in psychology, but at some point in the future, the best financial planners will have such training.

Until it becomes standard practice for a financial planner to have both exterior and interior training and skills, a collaborative approach is going to be the most effective way to help people achieve the greatest degree of financial integration.

Even the best financial planners know there are areas that cross the boundary from "financial life planning" or coaching to therapy. As long as planners have no training in counseling, they can only support clients so far. But how far is too far? *It would seem to me that even those planners who are currently doing financial life planning must at some point back away from clients' interior work—often at precisely the wrong time—because they don't have the skills to help their clients go further.*

What if, when you are in your financial planner's office, you hit a moment when an entrenched money script raises its head? Perhaps the planner has addressed some budget issues you cannot resolve: overspending, underspending, or not following a savings plan. Maybe you are stuck on the design of an estate plan, on succession planning for a family business, or on taking too many or too few risks with investments. Whatever the reason, you start to experience a rush of emotion, your eyes glaze over, and you can no longer hear what the planner is saying. Your painful emotions are blocking your ability to take in or deal with cognitive information. The planner may continue to talk and explain the topic, but *you are no longer mentally or emotionally present.* Your planner may not recognize it, but for all intents and purposes, the session is over.

How would the outcome of this scenario be different if a counselor, trained in financial integration, was sitting beside your planner? The counselor, recognizing that you had left the conversation, could step in and take over. The counselor would have been privy to all the financial information and your reactions up to that point. He or she could seize the opportunity to lead you to a deeper awareness and transformation. That moment would be lost if the counselor wasn't present. It is likely that getting you to the same place again might require the time and expense of several therapy sessions over a much longer period of time.

A financial planner and counselor working together are exponentially more capable of facilitating a transformational experience around their client's relationship with money than either one is individually.

This is not theoretical. I do this type of facilitation with therapists trained in financial integration therapy. Typically the clients (individuals, couples and even families) are referred to me by a financial advisor or family therapist. I work in conjunction with the referring advisor in gathering the financial data and then set aside a time that a trained therapist and I will work with the client. This could be as short as an afternoon or as long as a week, depending on the depth and breadth of the problem. After our work is done with the clients, we send them back to the referring advisor with a clear understanding of their issues and a plan of action.

Using this process, I have witnessed some of the most impossible financial situations and issues turned around or resolved. I have seen the life-changing outcome it can create for clients, which surpasses anything that either the counselor or I could do independently. One business management firm is so sold on this process that they have told clients who are having trouble modifying destructive financial behaviors they must go through this process or the firm will no longer work with them.

One key to these successful results has been the fact that both a financial planner and a therapist were in the same room, at the same time, with the clients. This allowed us to apply information, observations, and skills that would never have been available if only one of us was working with the client. It was the combination that was so powerful.

Now, in this setting, it is important that everyone in the room understands the financial planner is the planner and the counselor is the counselor. Both professionals need to understand their respective roles and observe appropriate boundaries. In order to do so, both need to have done their own work in the other's professional field. The counselor needs to have addressed his or her money issues, and the financial planner needs to have done his or her own financial therapy.

I really want to stress this. *To produce the best possible transformative results for the client, the financial planner and counselor must both have addressed their interior and exterior money issues. Anything short of that standard will produce inferior, if not disastrous, results.*

For some financial planners, such collaboration may raise questions of appropriateness or integrity. Does a financial planner belong in the room while a counselor is helping a client work through deep, painful issues? If those issues affect the client's relationship with money, absolutely. That, however, assumes that both counselor and financial planner are ethical and competent; that both have done and continue to do their own interior financial work; that no agenda is forced on a client; that clients go only where they want and are willing to go; and that clients can pass, stop, leave, or confront at any time without judgment, shaming, or manipulation from either the planner or the counselor.

∂∽∾

While you and your financial planner may see the theoretical value of being able to offer a combination of financial planning and therapeutic skills, there may be difficulties in its practical application. It may be difficult to find a planner and a therapist willing or capable to do this work. Or the added cost of this combination of services may be out of reach. Not everyone would need or could afford such services, but those who did would experience superior results. If, however, you have the means and the need to engage both separately, it makes a lot of sense to ask them to work together periodically. Almost any therapists or planners who have done their own interior work around money will be open to exploring this idea with you.

Just as more financial planners are coming to understand the value of interior work with clients, so is the mental health profession beginning to realize the need to address financial issues, for both themselves and their clients. Among those we have talked with recently are a master's degree counselor who now offers financial therapy around budget issues, a recent college graduate who completed her major in financial planning and is now working on a master's degree in family therapy, and a Ph.D. psychologist who is earning his CFP® designation.

This overlap of the two professions is in its embryonic stage, but it is beginning to happen. Whether it grows to fulfill Rick's vision of the future of financial planning will ultimately depend on the demand from clients of both financial planners and therapists. People are becoming increasingly aware of the importance of balance and self-fulfillment in all aspects of their lives, including their relationship with money. As awareness of the value of financial integration spreads, those who want help in reaching this level of financial consciousness will begin to ask for it. The result can be an exciting collaboration among professionals to help clients heal money issues at deeper levels than they ever dreamed possible.

18

Conscious Giving

It's easy to assume that giving is always a good and beneficial thing. It is something that seems right to do, whether it takes the form of tithing ten percent to your church, donating to local charities, or bringing home gifts for your kids every time you travel. Certainly, giving is often a positive experience. Yet it also can be tainted by power struggles and manipulation, accompanied by guilt or resentment, or done in ways that promote destructive dependency. Like many other financial choices, deciding whether and how to give is rarely as straightforward as it may seem.

Kathleen: I've had an experience of giving that started out with joy and pleasure, but ended up in frustration, anger, and resentment. Wayne knew a couple—we'll call them the Martins—who were struggling both financially and emotionally because one of their children had a life-threatening illness. The mother had to quit her job in order to take care of the child, and as a result the family had no health insurance. In addition to ordinary living expenses and local medical expenses, they needed to travel periodically to a treatment center in another state. Friends had organized some fund-raisers for the family, but they still needed additional help.

Wayne suggested that we give $1000 in cash to them anonymously. We enlisted the help of my daughter, who wasn't known to the Martin family. I dropped her off around the corner from their house and kept my motor running while she ran over and knocked on their door, handed the father the money (sealed inside two envelopes so it would take longer to open), dashed back to the van, and we made our getaway like Bonnie and Clyde. It was great fun. That is one of the most purely satisfying and joyous experiences of giving I have ever had.

A few months later, the Martins were facing eviction from their rental house because they had been unable to pay their rent. The landlord had given them as much time as he could, but finally couldn't carry them any longer. Wayne told them to find a cheaper place to live and we would pay their rent until they were able to get county housing assistance. This should have taken three or four months.

They found a place, we paid the deposit and first month's rent, and they moved in, expressing their relief and gratitude for our help. They were to have an appointment the following week to complete the paperwork for the housing assistance. At the end of the month we paid the rent again; no problem, everything seemed to be going fine.

A few days later, Wayne was killed. One of the financial matters I was left to take care of was the assistance to the Martins. Because it was a commitment Wayne had made, and because I thought it was a good thing to do, I continued making their rent payments.

By the end of the third month, however, the problems began to surface. I expected that by this time the Martins would have been nearing the top of the waiting list for housing assistance. I found out, however, that they weren't even on the waiting list yet because they hadn't completed the necessary paperwork. I asked them about it. Oh, yes, they assured me, it was almost finished. They expected to be on the list by the next month.

I hesitated to press the issue. After all, their daughter was about to have major surgery out of state, the family's need was still great, and I had enough money to keep paying their rent for a time. But by now, because the Martins were failing to take the necessary steps to qualify for the housing assistance, I was beginning to feel taken advantage of and used. The clean sense of pleasure that had accompanied our original $1000 gift was turning to frustration and resentment.

The daughter's surgery was successful and her once-bleak prognosis was reversed. This was a time for genuine rejoicing, but of course it didn't mean that the family's financial situation was automatically improved. It did, however, make it easier for me to come to a decision to end my financial support. At the end of the fourth month, I told the Martins that I would be able to pay their rent for two more months and then I would have to stop.

By the time I wrote my last rent check for the Martins, my emotions about this particular piece of giving were a scrambled mess. I was relieved to be done with it. I felt guilty for ending my support. I wasn't sure I was doing what Wayne would have wanted me to do. Most of all, I was angry and resentful because I felt I had been taken advantage of.

This project of helping a family in need that had begun with such pleasure had become a source of pain and frustration.

Looking back on this incident, the question I can ask now is whether our well-intentioned giving was helpful or harmful to the Martin family. The first $1000 gift was clearly helpful. So was the initial rent assistance. Things began to get messy later, though, because the Martin's response to the help was not what either Wayne or I expected. In our minds, we had an agreement to help the Martins for about three months. Our expectation was that they would complete their side of the bargain by doing everything necessary to qualify for housing assistance.

The first problem with this, of course, was that this "contract" existed only in our minds. It was never stated clearly as an agreement between us and the Martins. The second problem was that they had a strong incentive to postpone their eligibility for assistance. After all, we were paying their full rent. Replacing our help with support from housing assistance would have cut their rent in half, but then they would have been responsible for making the reduced payment.

In the long run, our help may have done as much harm as good. I don't know. What I do see now is that we could have done this in a way to lessen the chances that it would turn sour. The initial cash gift was no problem; it was a wonderful form of giving that I would do again. It would have been better, however, for us to have offered the rent payments with a clear ending date. Had we said, "We can pay your rent for three months," the unspoken contract that existed only on our end would instead have been a reality for both parties to the transaction.

What our giving did was somehow to take away the Martin's authentic energy around helping themselves. This, of course, was exactly the opposite of what we intended to do.

૎૏

"Buddy, Can You Spare a Dime?"

Just as giving to people you know presents a problem, so can giving to people unknown to you. If people who appear to be homeless ask you for money, do you give it to them? If you do, does it feel like the right thing to do? If you don't, do you feel guilty? In either case, do you assume the money they collect will probably be used for drugs or alcohol rather than food?

$\mathcal{R}\mathcal{K}$

Rick: Several years ago, I cut out a story from the *London Times* about a man whose profession was begging. I remind myself of it every time I need the courage to walk by someone asking for money on the street, because the focus of the article was on the good living this man made begging. He said, "I probably shouldn't be talking to you; this could hurt the business." I feel guilty if I ignore a panhandler, but I don't know who's genuine and who's "in the profession."

I have a friend who responds to requests from panhandlers with, "Sure, bud, let's go to the nearest restaurant." He either has a very big heart or is a great enabler; I'm not sure which. I do know that he has bought very few meals in his life, as his offer of a meal is consistently turned down.

❧

We don't have the answer to the problems of panhandling or homelessness. What we do agree on is that we both feel comfortable saying no to most beggars, as long as we are supporting homeless shelters or other places that provide help for them. We give to our local food bank. We both donate to a local mission that not only provides shelter for homeless people, but also works toward helping them find jobs, overcome addictions, and get back on their feet whenever possible. Because we know these local agencies are legitimate and well run, we believe giving to them provides more effective help than giving five dollars to someone on the street.

Writing a check to a food bank or mission doesn't necessarily provide a warm and fuzzy feeling of satisfaction. You don't see your money being deposited and buying groceries for the 50 people that it may have fed. You don't see their faces or hear their stories. Yet that is no reason to discount the value of this type of giving. Whether you dish up the meal personally or help pay for it, you are still providing valuable help.

We aren't saying you shouldn't give to people on the street. What we are saying is that such giving needs to be done consciously. Our way of doing so is to give to charities whose purpose is helping such people, making sure those agencies use our donations wisely and have goals that we support. That isn't necessarily the only right way to do this kind of giving. One of our friends does usually give cash to those who ask him for a handout. He knows that the money may be spent at the closest liquor store; he also knows that it may be used for food or shelter. His reasoning is that he can afford five or ten dollars, that he is not being taken advantage of as long as he freely chooses to give, and that this kind of giving is one way of showing his gratitude for his own good fortune. He doesn't spend time worrying about whether the money he gives will be used wisely; he gives without judgment or resentment; and as a result he is comfortable with his conscious and deliberate choice.

Giving in Non-Monetary Ways

Giving does not necessarily mean writing out a check. There are many other ways you can give—of your time, your skills, and your experience.

ℛℵ

Rick: I recently had an eye-opening conversation with a retired couple who are my clients. They retired a few years ago, just at a time when the stock market was down in the early 2000s, which meant they had been consuming some of their principal in order to meet their day-to-day needs. As a result, they cut back their spending from the level they had originally hoped to maintain. They should be all right in the long term, but they don't have any excess. When I had my last quarterly update with them, what they wanted to know wasn't how well their portfolio was going to meet their needs or whether they could increase their spending. Instead, they asked, "What do retired people like us typically give? How much should we be giving?"

These are people who have given all their lives. They've given to their church. They've given to charities. He, as a practicing physician, gave through providing free or discounted medical care. Giving has been and still is something they expect of themselves.

I fully support this attitude with my clients. Yet here I was, faced with this generous and warmhearted couple, needing to tell them, "No, you can't afford to be giving." I told them instead, "You have given all your lives, and you have also given in ways that weren't monetary. So maybe it's your turn—time to take care of yourselves. Or maybe it's time you gave yourselves permission not to give financially."

We discussed ways that they could reframe their giving. Maybe their days of giving money are over, but they can give in other ways— of their time, their expertise, and their wisdom. A resource they don't have much of right now is money, but they do have the resources of time and experience. There are many ways, such as volunteer work or mentoring, they can share those valuable resources.

≈≪

This kind of giving can be seen as part of a natural progression. As a child and a young adult, you give by learning from people; you offer them the opportunity to give you something, which is valuable for both giver and receiver. In your prime, when you have health and energy and money, you give of those resources. And when you're retired, you may not have the financial resources, but you have the time and you have the wisdom. You can volunteer, you can run for local office, you can take a leadership role in community organizations. All of these are ways you can give back to your community in the latter part of your life.

Reciprocity

A barber moved to a new town and opened a shop. On the first day, the local florist came in for a haircut. When he went to pay for it, the barber said, "No, this one is free. It's my way of introducing myself to the community."

The florist thanked him and went away. The next morning, when the barber came to work, outside his door was a beautiful flower arrangement as a gift in return from the florist.

That day, the owner of the bakery came in for a haircut. Again, the barber told him, "This is my gift to you as a way of introducing myself."

The baker expressed his thanks and went out. The next morning, when the barber came to work, outside his door was a box containing a dozen pastries and a loaf of fresh bread.

Later that day, an author came in. As before, the barber explained that the first haircut was free. The author thanked him and left.

The next morning, when the barber came to work, outside his door were six other authors, all waiting to take advantage of their free haircuts.

At the heart of healthy and conscious giving is the idea of reciprocity. Reciprocal giving is seen as an exchange or a cycle rather than a system in which one person or entity always does the giving and another always does the receiving. Inherent in the concept of reciprocity is accepting your place and your responsibility to both give and take as part of your community. This is true whether you define "community" as your neighborhood, your city, your state, your country, or the planet.

Reciprocal giving can build authentic energy and self-respect for both the giver and the recipient. Giving that does not include any reciprocity, on the other hand, has crossed the line to become enabling. Enabling, which we have already described, destroys authentic energy and erodes self-respect.

Kathleen: In the rural area where I grew up, giving was seen as something that went both directions. If someone were injured or ill, for example, the neighbors would automatically pitch in to help with field work or chores. That mutual exchange of help was part of being a member of the community, something that everyone did. Taking charity would have been seen as degrading or humiliating. But accepting the gift of help from neighbor to neighbor was fine, because along with it came the self-respect of knowing you had given and would give back to them in your turn.

This is the kind of giving that builds connections between people and creates a sense of community. It supports and builds the recipients' authentic energy because it assumes that they are both willing to give and capable of giving something back. If I happen to be the one who is in a position to be able to give right now, and you happen to be in a position of needing to receive right now, and I give to you, it is part of an ongoing flow, because we both know that next time our positions might be reversed. We also know that when you have a chance, you will give in your turn.

An opposite kind of giving is charity, which is giving from the "haves" to the "have-nots." There is no reciprocity. Instead, there is an unspoken assumption that the "haves" are obligated to give to the "have-nots," who are further assumed to be incapable of providing for themselves. It doesn't occur to anybody that they might have anything to give in return. This form of giving is damaging to the recipients' pride and sense of self-respect, in part because it takes away from them the opportunity and responsibility to give in their turn. It labels them as "less than."

One of the difficulties with institutionalized or governmental giving is that it can take away the sense of reciprocity.

It interrupts the cycle of giving from person to person. Instead of one neighbor helping out another, we have a "welfare system"— whether that may mean a check for a low-income family, an educational grant, or a corporate tax break. The flow is one way. There is no particular sense that this is a helping hand from one human being to another. Instead, the source is that vague entity, "the government." It is not easy to recognize that this is in reality a gift from one's neighbors through taxes they have paid, because "the system" stands between the recipient and the giver (whose giving in this case is involuntary). Because there is little or no awareness of the source of the support, it is too easy to create in the recipients a sense of being entitled to whatever benefit they have received.

To illustrate this in a different way, suppose it's Sunday night, you don't have any money, and you don't get paid until Tuesday. You don't have much in the kitchen: just some macaroni and cheese, some peanut butter, a bag of frozen peas, half a gallon of milk, and a rather dry loaf of bread. You're not going to starve, but you don't exactly have the makings for a gourmet meal. What you'd really like to have is pizza, but you don't have any money for pizza. Are you going to go knock on your neighbors' doors and say, "Will you give me some money so I can order a pizza?"

Of course you wouldn't. Maybe you might ask that of a close friend, especially if you gave them rides to work several times last week when their car wasn't working. That would be reciprocity. But if you don't have that kind of give-and-take relationship with your neighbors, you aren't going to ask them to give you money for pizza. Instead, you'll make do with bread and peanut butter.

But what if in your neighborhood there was a restaurant called The System that would give you a pizza if you went in and asked for it? You'd have to fill out a bunch of paperwork and tell them all kinds of personal information, but the pizza would be free. You might well decide it was worth filling out some forms to take advantage of this windfall. You probably wouldn't have any sense of obligation to pay anyone back for the pizza. Nor would it occur to you to wonder who was really paying for it. You'd be surprised if someone told you that all your neighbors had been required to contribute some money to The System's free-pizza fund. Getting a pizza this way would be essentially the same as asking your neighbors to give you money for it. The difference is that you wouldn't be aware they had paid for the pizza, because you wouldn't have received it from them directly. You would have dealt only with The System.

Certainly there are many people who use welfare as the temporary safety net or helping hand that it was intended to be. One of the people we interviewed for this book was a woman who at age 22, with a baby and a two-year-old, was abandoned by her husband. She was on welfare for a time, living with almost no furniture in a barely adequate apartment. She also worked hard, sometimes holding two jobs at once. She went to college one or two classes at a time, eventually getting a degree that qualified her for a well-paying, professional career. This woman, who had incredible energy and drive, never fell into the "poor me, I'm entitled, I'm a victim" trap. It was clear to her that getting out of poverty was up to her, and she did it.

When we interviewed her, she talked with anger about the illogical restrictions and frustrating bureaucracy of the welfare system. In her opinion, it served to keep recipients dependent rather than to help them become independent. She also talked with gratitude about the intermittent help she had received from her family and about the network of friends she had at that time in her life. This group of mostly poor, mostly single mothers passed around kids' outgrown clothes, looked after one another's children, and helped one another out. The giving from the welfare system was charity, tainted with messages saying, "you are incapable, you are a victim." The giving among friends and family was reciprocal; together, they made up a mutually supportive community

Giving Anonymously or Publicly

Many people prefer to do their giving anonymously, whether it is a small individual gift or a huge donation. When Grand Forks, North Dakota, suffered severe flooding in 1997, an anonymous "Angel" donated 15 million dollars for flood relief. There was widespread criticism of the reporters who revealed the donor to be Joan Kroc, the widow of McDonald's founder Ray Kroc, who gave much of her fortune to charity. They had violated her wish to keep this particular gift private.

At the opposite end of the spectrum is giving on a grand scale and having your name on it. This is why we have the "Mary Alumna Scholarship" for a university, the "Bob Browser Room" in the library, or the "John P. Swimmer" pool at the YMCA. Some agencies and charities use this form of recognition quite consciously in their fund-raising efforts. For example, a summer theatre in our area had a fundraiser to update their building, asking people to buy a new seat that would then have their name on it.

Kathleen: Wayne once told me with delight about a secret gift he had given. A woman who went to his 12-step meeting was talking one week about her fear and worry because her car was in the shop for an essential repair, and she didn't know how she was going to afford to pay the bill. She happened to mention the name of the repair shop. The next day Wayne went down there and paid her bill, anonymously and in cash. At the meeting the next week, this woman told them with gratitude and relief about the bill being paid. She had been praying about it, she said, and God had taken care of it. Well, it's a wonderful feeling to know you've been part of the answer to somebody's prayers. Wayne could have given her the money directly, but he had much more fun making the gift in secret. He talked with glee about how careful he had been to control his expression while she was talking so she wouldn't suspect him. The satisfaction of not getting caught was a big part of the pleasure he took in helping someone in need.

Giving publicly can be a way of trying to control the way your gift is used, a form of bragging to the world about how well you've done or what a wonderful person you are, a way to be recognized, or a way to encourage giving by others. There's certainly nothing wrong with getting credit for your giving. In some cases, publicizing the donation of a well-known person can be a way to promote a cause or encourage giving by others.

Giving anonymously might be done in order to protect your privacy, to keep your relationship with others from changing, or to protect yourself from being overwhelmed with additional requests for money. It also may come from a reluctance to be seen as rich, a fear that giving will set you apart from others, or uncertainty about whether you are giving wisely.

We aren't going to say whether you "should" give anonymously or publicly. Neither one is necessarily right or wrong; either can do a significant amount of good and provide you a great deal of satisfaction. What we will ask you to do is think about your motivation. There may be unconscious money scripts behind either choice. Use the financial integration process to help you uncover those scripts and to make your giving choices more conscious ones.

Giving to Children

We have talked in the previous chapter about giving to one's children. Again, we don't have a set of rules about what, when, or how much you should or should not give to your kids. While we may not have answers, what we can do is raise a few of the questions relating to this issue. Our goal is to encourage you to do your own interior work so you can make more conscious decisions in this area.

When children are small, you have an opportunity to teach them about giving in small but significant ways. They will learn both directly from what you teach them and indirectly from the example you set. Here are some of the things you might think about if your children are young:

Do you have them make out a Christmas list for Santa Claus? Some parents do this, while others avoid it because they think it encourages greed and a sense of entitlement. Do you help them pick out birthday or holiday gifts for other family members? Do you expect them to pay for such gifts or give them the money? Do you expect and enforce the writing of thank-you notes? Do you let them know about the charitable giving you do? Do you automatically bring home gifts when you travel?

𝒞𝒦

Rick: For a while when I was coming back from trips, I would bring London and Davin something, until they got to the point of expecting it. Some of my trips are literally a matter of "get off the plane, go to meetings all day, get on the next plane." So there isn't always an opportunity for shopping, and I didn't come back with a gift one trip. London was in tears. I explained to her that if presents were always expected, they wouldn't really be gifts; they wouldn't be surprises, would they? Several times after that I didn't come back with a gift. There were still tears.

On one of my last trips, I didn't come back with anything. London got up early the next morning and came running in to see me, and her first question was, "Wow, Dad, you're home! Did you bring me anything?" And I said, "No, honey, I just didn't have time." During the week I had sent her some balloons from the flower shop at the hotel, so I told her, "I sent you the balloons, but that was all." She said, "Well, Dad, that was enough." So she's learning. It was the first time we didn't have any tears or a scene around, "Oh, you didn't bring me anything."

This hasn't necessarily been easy for me. But it has been good in two ways. For one thing, it was freeing to give myself permission when I'm hurried to not feel obligated that I have to get a gift if I want to avoid a big scene. We did have the big scene, several times. I had to keep reminding myself that the big scene is necessary right now. As the Love and Logic (www.loveandlogic.com) parenting materials say, it's a lot less costly to have these smaller scenes now than to have expensive ones when you're an adult. And the second and more important reason this has been a good thing to do is that London is starting to internalize it. She's learning that a gift isn't something she's entitled to or automatically going to get.

෨ఄ

As children get older, new questions come up about giving. Do you buy them a car or require them to save their own money for at least part of the purchase? Do you require them to give away part of their allowances or earnings? How much do you give them when they are young adults and making those first steps out into the world?

𝒦𝒻

Kathleen: My stepson just graduated from high school and has a physically demanding construction job for the summer. He had previously worked with his dad for two summers, but he had not had a job this past year because his mom was receiving Social Security benefits for him after Wayne's death. He told me this week that he had become much more aware about his spending. "When I think about buying that meal or something, I ask myself if it's really worth an hour of work that I'll have to do to pay for it. It was too easy before, when the money was just there."

It is clear to him, in his current stage of young adulthood, that there is a big difference between money he is given and money that he earns. It is equally clear to me that he is proud of his ability to earn his own way. Giving him too much at this point in his life would take away that sense of pride and achievement.

෴

The last and perhaps the biggest question about giving and children is whether or how much you want to give to them as part of your estate. This is a particularly tough issue for those who are wealthy. If you could leave your kids enough so they wouldn't ever have to work, would you? Should you? Would that be a blessing to them or a burden?

One man who thinks it would be a burden is Warren Buffett, whose investments have made him one of the wealthiest people in America. He has made it clear that he has no intention of leaving the bulk of his huge fortune to his three children. According to an article in the October 2003 issue of *Advisor Today,* he has described the perfect inheritance as "enough money so that they [family] feel they could do anything, but not so much that they could do nothing."

Inherited wealth is a classic destroyer of authentic energy. If you want to leave a significant inheritance to your children, it is essential that you also consider how you can leave them the knowledge and perspective they will need in order to manage that wealth. One possible way to do that might be to set up a charitable family foundation during your lifetime, involving your children in its management and decisions.

If the money comes from a family business, it would be valuable for adult children to learn the realities and responsibilities that come with managing a business. Even if they are not interested in a career in that field, they can be taught to see the business as far more than a source of money that they have done nothing to earn.

Perhaps the crucial issue here is to incorporate the idea of stewardship. It is important for inheritors to understand the concept that wealth can be a tool and a resource, and as such, it is important to use it wisely.

R&K

Rick: It is amazing how few parents prepare or talk to their children in any manner about inheritances. One of my clients recently inherited 18 million dollars from her mother. Up until just a few months before her mother's death, they had never discussed what would happen upon her death, nor did the daughter have any idea of the value of her estate. Prior to receiving this inheritance, the daughter and her husband had lived month to month. Since his career was in the military, they had moved frequently and never even owned their own home, something they had always wanted.

When we discussed the potential changes in their lives because of the inheritance from her mother, the room was filled with gloom. In addition to their grief over her mother's recent death, they could not even accept the fact that they were actually going to receive the money. They would talk about "if" the inheritance happened, not "when." When I told them it would be okay for them to start shopping for the home they had always wanted, my words fell to the floor with a thud.

The couple told me, "We should be happy, so why do we feel so guilty? Why does this feel depressing?" We explored their money scripts, two of which were, "If you don't work for money, you don't deserve it," and "Money that you don't work for is not yours to keep." With those underlying beliefs, there was no doubt why this was such a heavy, fearful time for them. Had mom sat down with them and described how much she was worth and what her intentions were, they could have processed this while she was alive. She could have let them know how happy she was to give this to them. Or, as a result of those conversations, she might have even decided to give some of her estate in other ways, such as to charity.

Giving Can Bring People Together
or Create Barriers Between Them

Kathleen: Wayne and I owned a rental house that the same tenants had lived in for over 15 years. A few years ago the husband was killed in an accident. Because we didn't know what he might have had for life insurance or what the widow's immediate financial situation would be, I suggested it might be very helpful if we gave her a month's free rent. Wayne's immediate response was that we shouldn't be cheap about such a gift, that he would be willing to let her live in the house rent-free for a year if necessary.

I wasn't able to articulate it at the time, but I knew that a gift of that magnitude would be a mistake. A month's worth of free rent was a generous and helpful gift that she could (and did) accept gratefully and appreciate. A year's worth would have been a burden; it would have crossed the line from helping to charity. It would have created an obligation, thereby separating us instead of bringing us closer.

That is in part what happened with the Martin family we described at the beginning of this chapter. My giving to them put up a barrier made up in part of my resentment. It may also have been made up of a feeling of obligation on the part of the Martins. I did not ever build a genuine friendship with the family; the money got in the way.

Conscious Giving Checklist

As a guide toward making conscious choices when it comes to giving, we have developed the following list of questions to ask yourself. They aren't necessarily the "complete guide to conscious giving," but they may provide a starting point.

1.   How will I feel if I make this gift? Satisfied? Resentful? Taken advantage of? Joyful? Powerful?
2.   Will this gift help someone solve a problem, or will it take responsibility for solving the problem away from them?
3.   Will this gift encourage the recipient's independence or foster dependence?

4. Is this a "should" that I would do out of guilt or obligation?
5. Am I giving this gift freely and willingly?
6. What might be the consequences if I don't make this gift?
7. What might be the consequences if I do make this gift?
8. Am I giving this gift in order to help someone else or to get attention and recognition for myself?
9. Are there ways that I could help this person other than through a monetary gift? Perhaps there are other creative solutions to the problem that we could find together.
10. Is there any exterior knowledge I need to obtain before I make this gift?
11. By making this gift, would I be usurping someone else's responsibility to take care of their own affairs?
12. Do I need to pause before I say yes or no to this gift? Being surprised or rushed into giving is very likely to lead to an unconscious decision and some resentment or regret. Whether a request comes from a charity or your child, you can always say, "I need to think about this, and I'll get back to you."
13. Will this gift create energy or deplete energy for me? For the recipient?
14. Will this gift create a barrier or a bond between us?

Conscious Receiving

If a family member asks you what you'd like for your birthday, does your mind immediately go blank? If you get a gift certificate to a store, do you have trouble using it up? Chances are that you have at least one person in your extended family whose invariable response to a gift is, "Oh, you shouldn't have." Or a person who seems to accept gifts gracefully enough, but then puts them away at the back of a dresser drawer. There they languish unused until they go out of style or become obsolete, forgotten for years until someone decides they might be worth fifty cents at the spring rummage sale.

At the other extreme, you probably know people who "borrow" clothes or money or tools that they never seem to remember to return. They're great at coming up with ideas for projects, but then never seem to get around to doing their share. When it's time to pick up the check, they never seem to have their wallets handy.

Having trouble accepting a gift on one hand, and feeling entitled to take everything you can get on the other, are the opposite faces of unconscious receiving. Both are the result of blindly following money scripts. The person uncomfortable with taking might have scripts such as, "I can't have anything until everyone else has everything they need," or, "It's better to give than to receive." The common bottom line of such scripts is a belief that "I don't deserve it."

The person who takes without giving back in like measure is more apt to be following scripts based on fear or resentment. "I'd better take everything I can because there might not be enough to go around," or, "I shouldn't have to pay my share because I haven't been treated fairly."

Conscious receiving includes being able to ask for help when you need it and accept that help with gratitude, because you know you are doing your part to take care of yourself and you are comfortable that you can and will help someone else when it's your turn. It means avoiding the trap of entitlement and victimhood as well as the equally unconscious false pride that says you shouldn't need any help.

Conscious receiving means accepting a gift with gratitude and pleasure rather than suspicion, resentment or guilt.

It means that if you're offered a gift that feels like an attempt to manipulate you, you can either say no or ask the giver directly what is expected in return. It means feeling comfortable that you don't automatically have to "match" a gift with something in return. It means understanding that it's important for all of us to be able to give, so accepting a gift graciously is in itself a gift back to the giver. It means being able to say "thank you" rather than "you shouldn't have." It means acting with integrity when it comes time to do your share in a group effort or pay your share of a group expense.

How can you know if you are receiving a gift consciously? By using the tools of financial integration, particularly paying attention to your emotions. If you accept this gift, what will you feel? Gratitude? Resentment? Guilt? Does it feel as if the gift has strings attached or is being used to manipulate you? You might use the "conscious giving checklist" from the perspective of the recipient to help you figure out what's going on, especially if an offered gift doesn't quite feel right.

We've already discussed the idea of reciprocity when it comes to giving. The same principle is at work if you are the recipient rather than the giver. Conscious giving and conscious receiving are the two necessary components of a healthy exchange, a transaction that builds bonds instead of barriers.

Healthy giving and receiving are not about money, power, or manipulation. Conscious and joyful giving builds energy for both the giver and the recipient. It feels like an exchange between equals rather than an act of condescension from someone higher to someone lower. Conscious receiving is accepting a gift in that same spirit of equality, with gratitude that is untainted by resentment or obligation. Conscious giving and receiving are, always and fundamentally, acts of grace offered freely from one person to another while maintaining respect and dignity on either side.

19

Lasting Change

As a way of summing up financial integration, let's look at how one famous literary character applied the principals of this book and transformed his life. His name is Ebenezer Scrooge.

You probably need no introduction to Charles Dickens's *A Christmas Carol* and the infamous Mr. Scrooge. Scrooge was a successful businessman who certainly had the exterior knowledge of money down pat. He had learned how to make money and how to save money. By the world's standards, he was financially successful. By Conscious Finance standards, however, he lacked financial integrity. Scrooge lived his life unconsciously.

First, he was a slave to his money scripts. Some of the more obvious scripts were, "You must work hard for money," "Don't spend money, save money," "The money will run out," and, "More is better."

Second, Scrooge was in constant pain. There was no capacity in his life to feel joy or peace, as he was filled to capacity with the difficult emotions of fear, sadness, and anger. Of course, he was completely unaware of any of this.

We have said that we can only look forward as far as we are willing to look backward. While the Ghost of Jacob Marley alerted Scrooge to his money scripts, he had no hope of modifying or changing those scripts until he became willing to look at his past, how it was affecting the present, and how it would continue to affect his future.

Indeed, his money scripts had cost him dearly, as shown by a look into his past. He had been abused by his father, which certainly established a foundation of low self-esteem. That sense of not being valued was only deepened when he was sent off to a third-rate boarding school where he was badly treated. It was there that young Scrooge learned to hide his pain by focusing outwardly on his studies, which later in life became focus on his work.

As a result of his work addiction, he lost the love of his life. Rather than feel this pain, he turned to his core money scripts and worked harder to accumulate money. Working harder just guaranteed him more loneliness. And the lonelier he became, the sadder he became and the more he reacted with anger to those around him. To many people, Scrooge is the embodiment of selfishness because he would not give a nickel to the poor. This might be true if Scrooge spent lavishly on himself, but that was not the case. He treated himself just as he did others. It was his low self-worth that fostered his inability to spend money on himself or anyone else. This behavior, as illogical as it seems, makes perfect sense when we remember his money scripts, "Don't spend money, save money," and "The money will run out."

The Ghosts of Christmas Past, Present, and Future who visited Scrooge showed him the bitter cost of his money scripts. As a result, he became willing to come out of his unconsciousness and do the hard work of changing his behavior. His transformation was similar to the process of financial integration. His visit to the past with the first ghost helped him identify and feel the childhood pain that was the source of his money scripts. It also allowed him to regain his awareness of his life aspirations. The Ghost of Christmas Present opened his eyes to the reality of what he had become and what people thought of him, which impelled him to take responsibility for his actions and discard his resentments and blame. The third ghost gave him the opportunity to change his behavior in order to align it with his rediscovered core values.

Because of this intervention, Scrooge opened both his pocket book and his heart to others. He began to give, both of his wealth and of himself. As a result, lives were blessed and changed—including, above all, his own. This story as a metaphor for financial integration is explored more fully in a book by Rick, Ted Klontz, and Brad Klontz (*The Financial Wisdom of Ebenezer Scrooge,* Health Communications, Inc., 2005).

Scrooge, of course, is fictional, and so is his miraculous overnight transformation. In real life, we are forced to operate without helpful ghosts or the gifted imagination of Charles Dickens. One reason *A Christmas Carol* has remained so popular, however, is the essential truth of its optimistic message. People can change. They do change.

Without the convenient devices available to novelists, the transformation just takes a bit more time and effort. Indeed, both of us would have liked an overnight transformation to financial integration.

In truth, though, overnight transformations are neither realistic nor desirable.

Financial integration is not about reaching a destination of financial and emotional bliss where we will forever live our lives.
It is about following a conscious way of life that will make our journey all the more rich, rewarding, and enjoyable.

Both of us have found the benefits of working toward financial integration more than worth the time and effort it has taken. That work continues to help us become more aware of our life aspirations and much more comfortable using money as a powerful tool to help us achieve them.

ℋℱ

Kathleen: One of my acquaintances likes to joke that he "got my money the old-fashioned way: I inherited it." A common reaction to the idea of inheriting wealth is envy. "What a stroke of good fortune." "Gee, are they ever lucky." "Just imagine having all that money, and they didn't even have to do anything for it."

Well, I've done more than just imagine that scenario. Having inherited, not wealth exactly, but a substantial sum nevertheless, I can tell you that inheriting money is a lousy way to get it.

At the time Rick and I agreed to write this book, I knew who I was and where I belonged. I was married to a husband I loved. Together we were trying to figure out how to support our children as they took their first steps into adulthood. We were also taking some first steps of our own, into financial prosperity. Because Wayne had done well with his business in the previous few years, our net worth had rather quickly grown into a number that was impressive to both of us. We had decided it was time to consult with Rick and get started on a good financial plan. There was no particular sense of urgency about talking with him, though. We had plenty of time, we thought; the future seemed both bright and secure.

That comfortable illusion was destroyed a few weeks later when Wayne was killed. As I've already shared in earlier chapters, the pain that followed his death included some difficult financial consequences and decisions.

By now, as we finish this book, I have made my way through many of the toughest of those decisions. The estate has been settled, leaving me rather ironically with a net worth that is almost the same as the net worth we shared at the time of his death. I am still not completely comfortable with that number, but I am beginning to see some of the benefits associated with it. I have the security of knowing my children aren't going to have to take care of me financially in my old age. I have the freedom to choose the work I want to do. I have the ability to give generously. I have been able to help my kids, both with some of their young-adult struggles and in working toward their career goals.

Perhaps the chief benefit of being financially independent is a sense of confidence. I am not dependent on anyone else for my monetary well-being. I do not have to compromise in my opinions or my choices because someone else is paying the bills. That new confidence and assertiveness is working its way into the non-financial aspects of my life in many positive ways. The knowledge that I genuinely have enough to take care of myself is freeing and empowering.

Because of the financial integration work I have been able to do with Rick, I can appreciate and value the financial security I have. Though using my inheritance wisely continues to be important to me, and though I still think of myself as the steward of that money rather than its owner, I am not consumed by guilt or fear over having it. I am still not completely comfortable with my new position and my new life, but I keep moving closer to that comfort point. The tools and strategies for achieving financial integration have been essential for me in this challenging journey.

จจจจจ

CRCR

Rick: As I continue to apply the principles contained in this book, I continue to reap their benefit. Just this last week I was reflecting on changes that I've made in my professional life. Within the last year I've stopped almost all my day-to-day involvement with one of my businesses that, financially speaking, was my most successful endeavor. It was the business that made my house payment and paid the bills. The problem was, it didn't feed my soul. I got up in the morning dreading the day. I didn't like the business and hadn't liked it for 20 years. But for most of my adult life it defined me and fed me, so I felt obligated to give it the bulk of my energy and time.

When I started doing my own interior and exterior financial work, I became painfully aware of my dislike for this business. Once in a workshop I was asked to respond to the following question: "If the doctor told you that you had five to seven years to live, how would you live your life?" Of the many things I wrote down, one of them was that I would sell this business. That was my first conscious hint that maybe I needed an occupational shift in my activities. But even the thought of quitting this business evoked deep emotions of fear.

It has taken five years of conscious work to be in a place to let my involvement in that business go. I've had to uncover many money scripts and feel the difficult emotions that held them in place. I've felt so many difficult feelings around this issue that I wondered if I would ever get through them. I have removed barriers that were sapping me of my authentic energy. I became able to consider other options that would allow me to give up my direct involvement in that business without sacrificing my family's financial well-being. Today, I no longer work on a daily basis in that business. I still own it, and I check in with my capable managers, but my energy is going where my passion is, which is integrated financial planning.

As a result, I am making less money than I have in a long time. That, of course, was a core of my fear. You may remember that one of my major money scripts is fear that "the money will run out." So now I find myself in transition from the old toward the new. I am not even fully sure of what I am transitioning to or what my professional life will look like a year from now. I have encountered more change and financial challenges in the past few months than at any time in my life. Yet, to my own amazement and that of those close to me, I have never been more energized or happier professionally. In the midst of this financial chaos and change, I have never been more conscious or more at peace.

$\approx \sim$

The word "encourage," looked at literally, means "provide with courage." Our hope is that this book will encourage you to overcome the hidden beliefs that have been standing in the way of your financial consciousness and comfort. It takes a courageous person to embark on and continue the journey of financial integration. It takes courage to journey to the interior. It takes courage to emotionally examine your past. It takes courage to hear the truth of the present and to look at it clearly and objectively. It takes courage to look toward the future, accepting the things you cannot change and beginning to change the things you can.

Our wish for you is that your financial journey into the future will be a conscious one. May you learn to use money wisely as the valuable tool and servant it is, rather than making it your master. May you gain the peace and confidence that come with the ability to give money its proper place in your life. Above all, we wish you the fulfillment and satisfaction of achieving your life aspirations.

And, as you make progress toward those aspirations, may you enjoy the journey.

Resources

Instead of providing here a list of resources that will quickly become outdated, we have chosen to put that information on our website in order to keep it current. For an updated list of books, websites, financial planners, therapists, and other resources you may find helpful, go to our website, www.consciousfinance.com.

Order Form

For additional copies of *Conscious Finance,* send a copy of this form and a check or money order for $18.95 per book ($16.95 plus $2.00 shipping and handling) to:

Conscious Finance, LLC
PO Box 9101
Rapid City, SD 57709

Name _____

Address _____

City/State/Zip _____

Number of copies: _____ Amount enclosed: _____

For information on quantity discounts, or to place a credit card order through a secure server, go to our website, www.consciousfinance.com.

WE ALL KNOW SOMEONE WHO COULD BENEFIT FROM THE GIFT OF CONSCIOUS FINANCE

It's the perfect gift for anyone searching for financial clarity and self-awareness. It is a powerful tool for helping someone move from making unconscious and destructive financial decisions to making more conscious and functional choices.

ORDER FORM

For additional copies of *Conscious Finance,* send a copy of this form and a check or money order for $18.95 per book ($16.95 plus $2.00 shipping and handling) to:

Conscious Finance, LLC
PO Box 9101
Rapid City, SD 57709

Name _____

Address _____

City/State/Zip _____

Number of copies: _____ **Amount enclosed:** _____

If You Want Book Autographed, Print Name of Recipient

_____

For information on quantity discounts, or to place a credit card order through a secure server, go to our website, www.consciousfinance.com.